Black Bodies, Black Rights

[ELIZABETH FARFÁN-SANTOS]

Black Bodies, Black Rights

THE POLITICS OF QUILOMBOLISMO
IN CONTEMPORARY BRAZIL

University of Texas Press AUSTIN

Requests for permission to reproduce material from this work should be sent to:
Permissions
University of Texas Press
P.O. Box 7819
Austin, TX 78713-7819
http://utpress.utexas.edu/index.php/rp-form

♾ The paper used in this book meets the minimum requirements of
ANSI/NISO Z39.48-1992 (R1997) (Permanence of Paper).

Material from chapters 2 and 3 was published previously in "'Fraudulent'
Identities: The Politics of Defining Quilombo Descendants in Brazil," in *Journal
of Latin American and Caribbean Anthropology* 20 no. 1 (2015): 110–132. Other
material informed the previously published article "*Quilombolismo*: Fighting
and Dying for Rights," in *Trans-Scripts* 1 (2011): 131–153.

LIBRARY OF CONGRESS CATALOGING-IN-PUBLICATION DATA
Farfán-Santos, Elizabeth, author.
Black bodies, black rights : the politics of quilombolismo in contemporary
Brazil / Elizabeth Farfán-Santos. — First edition.
pages   cm
Includes bibliographical references and index.
ISBN 978-1-4773-0922-3 (cloth : alk. paper)
ISBN 978-1-4773-0942-1 (pbk. : alk. paper)
ISBN 978-1-4773-0923-0 (library e-book)
ISBN 978-1-4773-0924-7 (non-library e-book)
1. Blacks—Brazil. 2. Blacks—Political activity—Brazil. 3. Blacks—Race
identity—Brazil. 4. Blacks—Brazil—Social conditions. 5. Blacks—Civil
rights—Brazil. 6. Quilombos—Brazil. I. Title.
F2659.N4.F375   2016
305.896′081—dc23   · 2015033635

doi:10.7560/309223

For my family, who has waited so long.

Contents

Preface

LA NEGRA TOMASA

My aunt dressed me in a bright red dress. I was only three, and everyone in my family thought I looked funny because the red exaggerated my dark-brown skin. "Parecias la negra Tomasa, mija [You looked like the black Tomasa, sweetie]," my aunt would say, laughing as she remembered the image. For my family, the reference to the negra Tomasa came from a 1980s Caifanes song called "La negra Tomasa." The Caifanes are a Mexican rock group, and at the time "La negra Tomasa" could be heard in every dance hall and taxicab in Mexico. Even as I write, the chorus runs through my head: "Estoy tan enamorado, de mi negra Tomasa. Que cuando se va de casa, triste me pongo" (I'm so in love with my black Tomasa that when she leaves the house, I get sad.) The "negra Tomasa" is also a mammy reference. She represents the caricatured black-faced, red-lipped mammy that could be seen all over the Americas in the twentieth century. She is a symbol of a deeply embedded racial discrimination and denigration of the black body and identity that makes up the foundation of the mestizo narrative throughout Latin America.

When I was growing up, my father, my sister, and I were the darkest people in our family. My mom is a Chicana from Chicago, and even though her parents were born in Monterrey, Mexico, they looked East Asian. My mom told me that her father used to be called Chino Latino (Chinese Latino) when he was growing up because of how "Asian" his Mexican friends thought he looked. My mom inherited his distinct look. Nobody outside of our family ever believed that my sister and I belonged to my mother. I remember many occasions when my mom had to explain to people why we were so dark and she was so light. That is why when my aunt dressed me in a red dress, I became the negra Tomasa, a name and story that would follow me for the rest of my life. When I was in middle school, my dark skin was also a red flag for some of my Chicano friends who nicknamed me "Blackie." It sounds painful now as I am writing it down, but I don't remember it being that traumatic. I had grown accustomed to being different, even among the people closest to me.

I remember these stories about my dark skin—my "blackness" and negra Tomasa—because they are continuously recounted as jokes during family reunions. When I was a teenager, I hated my skin color. I never wore bright clothing—especially red. It wasn't that I was ashamed of being characterized as black; as a teen, I didn't want to stand out, much less be the constant butt of everyone's jokes. My sister, who is ten years younger than I, grew up to have the same concerns. She was never called "negra Tomasa"—I guess she can thank me for that—but she also hated feeling like she stood out. It took both of us a lot of work to see the beauty of our skin color. It took me years of study to understand the long history that has made Mexicans and Chicanos re-create a discourse of disdain for blackness.

As a Mexicana and Chicana, I am shaped by identity politics and by my capacity, as a woman of color, to navigate among different forms of representation and belonging. The color of my skin, a dark incommensurability within a mestizo ideology that privileges whiteness, represents a major part of my embodied sense of being and the racial politics that inform my perspectives. I experienced my "Chicana awakening" in college; it was the moment I would understand that I am permanently marked by difference—a difference that is overburdened with dualities, paradoxes, and contradictions, a difference that belongs neither here nor there and that is under constant scrutiny. Like most Chicanas, I had my awakening through the poetry and prose of Gloria Anzaldúa, who taught me to live at the borderlands of my identities and to embrace all of my dualities.

> Nosotros los Chicanos straddle the borderlands. On one side of us, we are constantly exposed to the Spanish of the Mexicans, on the other side we hear the Anglos' incessant clamoring so that we forget our language. Among ourselves we don't say *nosotros los americanos, o nosotros los españoles, o nosotros los hispanos*. We say *nosotros los mexicanos* (by *mexicanos* we do not mean citizens of Mexico; we do not mean a national identity, but a racial one). . . . Deep in our hearts we believe that being Mexican has nothing to do with which country one lives in. Being Mexican is a state of soul—not one of mind, not one of citizenship. Neither eagle nor serpent, but both. And like the ocean, neither animal respects borders. (Anzaldúa 1999, 84)

I came to this study of *quilombolas* in Brazil through a strong sense of the lived experience of identity formation and racial exclusion. Thus, I write from the position and sentiment of object of study as much as one of researcher. I engaged this project because I saw in the Bahian town of Grande Paraguaçu the struggle to make sense of all of the contradictions and conflicts that surfaced in trying to fit an everyday life, an embodied sense of being black in Brazil, within a plethora of authoritative and pre-determined categories of ethnic authenticity. The pain and desperation that was caused when the quilombolas of Grande Paraguaçu were accused of fraud—of misrepresenting a cultural identity—led me to want to further investigate the power structures of identification and recognition and the pain caused by misrecognition. The narratives that I present in this book offer a look into the everyday lives of quilombolas as they fight in anger and frustration against a system that still does not value their lives and forms of embodied knowing. For the quilombolas who were driven to paint the words "I know what it is, that is why I AM a quilombola" on the wall of their home in bright-blue letters, I hope this book will represent a document of solidarity so that *quilombo* justice can speak against entrenched social ideologies of antiblack discrimination and racial exclusion.

Acknowledgments

This book would not exist without the time, dedication, and sacrifice of many people in different parts of the world. There are so many people to whom I am grateful, and I fear that these few pages will not do them justice. Nevertheless, I will try.

I am especially grateful to the women and men of Grande Paraguaçu for allowing me to enter their homes and participate in their lives. With all of the conflict and violence these quilombolas have faced since they began the recognition process, I am privileged to have been able to get to know them. I am thankful for their patience with my clumsiness and ignorance of a lot of things and for believing in my sincere intentions. Their hard work, resilience, and bravery touched my heart and pushed me to think harder, past easy assumptions and quick resolutions.

This topic also gave me an intimate appreciation of how anthropologists, both now and in the future, can contribute to public policy and public conversation. For her help in making sure I remembered that "anthropologists are people too," I thank Anita Souza of INCRA, the Institute of Colonization and Agrarian Reform. It took trust and bravery for Anita to confide such an intimate and emotional story to a perfect stranger. In addition to Anita, I would like to thank Aline Motta of the Palmares Cultural Foundation for making her entire office available to me and for spending long hours making sure I understood how everything worked. I am thankful to the researchers of GeografAR at the Federal University of Bahia for introducing me to their cutting-edge research and for sharing their views on the importance of space and land. Finally, I thank my historian friend and colleague in Cachoeira, Luiz Cláudio "Cacau" Dias do Nascimento, for pushing me to think beyond easy ideologies and to ask difficult questions. I am thankful to him as well for making sure I had access to all of the resources I needed in the field. Without the direction and guidance of these people, I would have been lost in Bahia.

I would like to express a special appreciation to the historian João José Reis at the Federal University of Bahia for his mentorship and support throughout many research trips to Salvador. João has supported my research in Bahia since I first met him in 2005. Moreover, João's critical research on the history of quilombos has guided my research questions and provided much of the ideological foundation of my work.

This project would never have been conducted without the financial support of the National Science Foundation, which provided the funding necessary for me to live in Brazil throughout the duration of the research. The resources and time for quiet contemplation provided by a Mellon Post-doctoral Fellowship in the Humanities Research Center at Rice University were essential in the completion of this book project. At Rice, I benefited from supportive conversations with colleagues and friends in numerous areas. I was fortunate enough to have arrived at the same time as Robert Slenes, a prominent historian from Brazil. Dr. Slenes was a visiting scholar at Rice for one year. In that year, he was patient enough to engage numerous conversations with me about my work and ideas. He read my work and helped me navigate quilombo historiography. As part of a dual-degree initiative between Rice and the University of Campinas in São Paulo, that same year, Rice invited two graduate students from the history department: Joice Oliveira and Ludmilla Souza. These incredible women became my close friends and allies as I worked to write my book. I want to especially thank Joice for her encouragement. I would never have met any of these people had it not been for the dedicated work and passionate conviction of the Rice historian Alida Metcalf. Alida has supported me throughout various stages in my life. She has become a dear friend and adviser. She is someone I will always look up to for her kindness, compassion, and grounded humanity.

Finally, during my postdoctoral fellowship, I organized a conference on affirmative action in Brazil for which I invited top race scholars including Ed Telles, Juliet Hooker, and Lilia Moritz Schwartz. Conversations with these scholars were invaluable in my understanding the broader importance and connections of my work. At Rice, I also benefited from conversations with Linda Driskill, an English professor and advocate of all things Brazilian who bravely entered my world at the final leg of this writing project. She helped me perfect my prose and assert my literary voice as a writer and new scholar.

I have always felt I made the right choice in choosing anthropology as my discipline, but in the years I studied this topic, my conviction deepened. I am particularly thankful to my graduate school professors at UC Berkeley for molding me into a tough and always critically engaged scholar. Each one of them had a critical voice in this document, and without them it would not be as great. I thank my adviser, Nancy Scheper-Hughes, for sticking by me even during the most difficult times. My respect and admiration for her commitment to activism and public engagement have given me the conviction and strength to find my own voice in anthropology. I am thankful for Nancy's support, patience, and guidance, without which I would not have made it. I am also thankful to Charles Briggs for his attention to my ideas and for pushing me to do *exceptional* work. I thank Sharon Kauffman for her unending support and encouragement. Without her honest critiques this work would be something else. I thank all of these remarkable professors for their patient and committed efforts. Also at Berkeley, I am thankful to Liu Xin, James Holston, Donald Moore, Jeffrey Skoller, and Clara Mantini-Briggs for our many conversations that led to the formation of my strongest convictions as an anthropologist.

For their unending support, I am thankful to my mentors and friends Dr. David Spener, Dr. Meredith McGuire, Dr. Richard Reed, Dr. John Donahue, Dr. Arturo Madrid, and Dr. Antonia Castañeda. These scholars have invested many hours of supportive conversations, coffees, and lunches to motivate me to finish this book amid all of the stresses of everyday life.

I am especially indebted to my dear friend and mentor Dr. Susan Lieberman. There are simply not enough words to thank Susan for everything she has done for me. She read every chapter of my manuscript, giving me honest feedback and encouragement. Susan has been the perfect friend for pushing me to work harder and achieve more. Always honest and firm but also caring and kind, Susan has helped me build my own ground without fear or doubt.

I am thankful for the supportive reviews and critical perspectives of Charles Hale at UT Austin and of an anonymous reviewer of my manuscript. I am also most grateful to my editor, Casey Kittrell, and to the copyeditors Tana Silva and Victoria Davis at UT Press for their guidance and hard work in seeing this book through to the end.

This book is dedicated to my family, especially my parents, my grandparents, my husband, and my son. I am eternally grateful to my parents for committing to my education and future even when limited resources made it difficult. My mother I thank for making a lifetime of sacrifices for me, many of which I will never know. I thank her, especially, for enduring several years in a difficult job to help pay for my undergraduate education. During the last month of my writing marathon, my mother took the steering wheel of parts of my life that became impossible to balance. Once a week, my tired mother, after cleaning two houses, would still drive to my small apartment to cook meals for my family. She calls me every day just to see if I'm OK, and it has been her voice and encouragement that have helped me make it through this project. My father I thank for teaching me to work hard and for reminding me that I could change the world. A quiet man who never stops working, my father has been a model of embodied passion and resistance in my life. I am also thankful for the many sacrifices he has made for me, especially the sacrifice of leaving his native Mexico to find a better life for his family in the United States. I have heard in fragmented, painful stories of the many hardships my father endured when he first came to this country. I carry these stories with me in everything I do—in my passion, *ganas*, and conviction to work harder and achieve more despite obstacles.

My grandmother is one of my best friends, and my grandfather was my biggest fan. I am so fortunate to have grown up with them. I still remember that my grandfather would ask me almost every day what I would be when I grew up. One day, when I told him I wanted to be an anthropologist, he sighed deeply and simply said, "Aye, Layita. Bueno." It felt like we had the same talk every day. My grandfather passed away in 2005, and I still miss him deeply. My grandmother, who helped raise me, has cried tears of joy every time I've achieved something new. She always reminds me to stay focused and to be strong. She encourages every aspect of my life, even my stubbornness, and for that I am grateful. Without the love and constant encouragement of my parents and grandparents I would never have made it this far.

My husband, Ibraim do Nascimento Santos, has been my most important companion over the years. The process of writing this book meant that he often had to take the reins of our life with a tight grip. Ibraim's patience and unending support provided a foundation for our marriage even in the most difficult moments. He has truly been my partner and has continually helped me visualize this finished project—even when I doubted I could finish. I have rewritten this acknowledgment for my husband more than a dozen times, and I still cannot seem to get the right words down. Ibraim has been an honest ear and patient heart. Without his love and care I would not have survived this process.

My beautiful son, Oliver, was born at the beginning of this project and has grown throughout it. I am thankful to him for making the process more human and for his unconditional love. It was his funny new expressions, smile, big brown eyes, and wild, uncontrollable curls waiting for me at the door every day after a long day of writing that gave me the energy to keep going. I am so thankful to have him in my life.

This book has touched and been touched by many people. It would not exist if these people and many others did not believe in me and make real sacrifices for my success. I am thankful to all of them for helping me complete such an important phase in my life.

Acronyms

GOVERNMENT AGENCIES

FCP, Fundação Cultural Palmares (Palmares Cultural Foundation)

GeografAR, Geografia dos Assentamentos na Área Rural (Geography of Settlements in the Rural Area). The project is based at the Federal University of Bahia (UFBA, Universidade Federal da Bahia). The research group formed in 1996 to work on mapping different living situations and communities in rural areas of Bahia, including *assentamentos* (settlements), quilombos, and land occupations. http://www.geografar .ufba.br/site/default.php.

IBAMA, Instituto Brasileiro do Meio Ambiente e dos Recursos Naturais Renováveis (Institute of Environment and Renewable Natural Resources)

IBGE, Instituto Brasileiro de Geografia e Estatística (Brazilian Institute of Geography and Statistics)

INCRA, Instituto Nacional de Colonização e Reforma Agraria (National Institute of Colonization and Agrarian Reform)

SEPPIR, Secretaria Especial de Políticas de Promoção da Igualdade Racial (Special Office for the Promotion of Racial Equality)

Sepromi, Secretaria de Promoção da Igualdade do Estado da Bahia (Office for the Promotion of Equality of the State of Bahia)

NONGOVERNMENTAL ORGANIZATIONS

AATR, Associação de Advogados de Trabalhadores Rurais (Association of Lawyers for Rural Workers). This is a group of community lawyers who represent rural workers in land disputes with private landowners and the state. The AATR holds workshops in Bahia to promote awareness of and knowledge about legal processes and constitutional rights for rural communities.

ABA, Associação Brasileira de Antropologia (Brazilian Anthropological Association)

CONAQ, Coordinação Nacional de Articulação das Comunidades Negras Rurais Quilombolas (National Coordination for the Articulation of Rural Black Quilombo Communities)

CPP, Comissão Pastoral de Pescadores (Pastoral Commission of Fishermen and Women in Bahia). This NGO helps fishing communities sustain their artisan fishing practices by organizing community workshops and fund-raising initiatives. In Grande Paraguaçu, the CPP helped the quilombolas obtain two new canoes so they could fish more efficiently. The CPP also held a workshop on sustainable fishing to make sure everyone understood how to fish sustainably, what it meant, and why it was important for their own survival.

Introduction

A "PROBLEMATIC" FIELD

As the taxi drove into the quilombo along a narrow dirt road, the only road into Grande Paraguaçu at that time, we swerved into the fields to let cargo trucks by and to avoid hitting loose cattle that blocked the road. It was the middle of the harvest season. Several patches of sugarcane fields were on fire and the sky above them darkened by black smoke. I asked the taxi driver why we had such a hard time finding a ride into the quilombo. "Honestly, most people don't want to ruin their cars on this road. Plus, people don't want to be involved with this problem." "What problem?" I asked, pretending I didn't know that he was referring to the *quilombola* fight for land rights in Grande Paraguaçu. "I don't really know a lot about it, but you hear rumors, you know. The people out here are trying to steal the lands of Ivo Santana." "O povo aqui é problemático [The people here are problematic]; they are being ungrateful to a landowner who has given them so much, someone who has been a *padrinho* (godfather) to all of them." I listened quietly, looking out the window as we drove more slowly around men on horses carrying bundles of plants from the forest and women with their hair bundled in fabric, skillfully balancing sacks of manioc on their heads. I was not surprised by the taxi driver's words. In just a few years, Grande Paraguaçu went from being a quiet, rural community to becoming known as one of the most conflictive quilombo-descendant communities in Bahia.

Grande Paraguaçu is a municipal district of Cachoeira, a historical city of Bahia about two hours inland from Salvador, the state capital.[1] My husband was born and raised in Cachoeira. Most of his family still lives there, and since we arrived in Brazil just a couple of weeks after Christmas we spent a month visiting them before moving to Salvador. While we were in Cachoeira, I described my research project to curious family members and friends. I even made a preliminary visit to Grande Paraguaçu. I learned very quickly that many people in Cachoeira did not agree with the quilombola fight for land. Residents expressed fear of visiting the community and repeated rumors that the people in Grande Paraguaçu were dangerous, belligerent, problematic. I was frequently warned to stay away from *esse povo* (those people), especially by women who were horrified that I would even consider living there alone. The separation of Grande Paraguaçu and Cachoeira was made more poignant and even symbolic by the dirt road and limited transportation. Still, the residents of Grande Paraguaçu moved in and out of Cachoeira daily as a part of their routine. While the residents of Cachoeira feared the supposedly belligerent quilombolas "out there," they all intermingled daily without regard or notice. Quilombolas do not look different from the residents of Cachoeira or Bahia. There is no physical mark of difference to distinguish them or make them stand out. Still, the imaginary of fear and disdain surrounding the quilombola fight for land was loud and clear.

Thousands of black communities in Brazil are currently petitioning for legal recognition and land rights as the modern descendants of quilombos (historically known as runaway slave communities) under a provision in the Brazilian constitution. In 1988 the Brazilian government enacted the nation's seventh constitution. Following two decades of military dictatorship (1964–1985), the 1988 constitution's fundamental objectives, outlined in its Title I, included the "promotion of well-being for all without prejudice as to origin, race, sex, color, age, and any other forms of discrimination." Most ground-breaking, however, was the constitution's transitory Article 68, which conceded land rights to the descendants of quilombos, or *comunidades remanescentes de quilombos*. In one brief statement, the article declared:

> The definitive property rights are recognized for the descendants of quilombo communities who are still occupying their lands, and the state should grant them land titles.[2]

Article 68 was included as a temporary form of reparations for the exclusion of blacks from the legal right to own land before and after abolition, but it was only the bare bones of what would follow. A series of subsequent laws and processes were created in 2003 to complete what the constitution had begun—to define "quilombo descendant" and put the law into political and social practice. The authors of the 1988 constitution would probably never have imagined that more than two decades later, nearly two thousand quilombo descendant communities would have been culturally recognized and certified by the Palmares Cultural Foundation (Fundação Cultural Palmares) (Bennett 2008). Article 68 has been hailed as a success for black rights, particularly the right to cultural difference and access to landownership for rural black quilombo communities.

Still, it is important to ask what the stakes are of becoming a quilombo descendant for the residents of a community. Quilombola recognition follows a trend since the end of the twentieth century for the cultural recognition of different ethnic groups and their access to cultural rights under multicultural statutes and policies. Quilombola rights were founded on a spirit of liberalism and multiculturalism. While this has, on the surface, a progressive appeal for those opposed to racism, in fact, the focus on cultural rights for ethnically distinct quilombo-descendant groups still overlooks the problem of racial discrimination and unequal access to land for most black Brazilians.

Conflict over quilombola rights is widespread, increasing as more communities obtain recognition without rights, and carries important consequences for race relations and the political representation of blackness in twenty-first-century Brazil. In this book, using a year of field research (2009–2010) in the quilombola community of Grande Paraguaçu and Salvador, Bahia, I explore why a seemingly well-intentioned constitutional clause gave way to violent disagreement. Moreover, I illustrate, through the enraged pleas and mobilized action of one quilombola community, how the bureaucratic structure that was built to support Article 68 has underscored, and paradoxically, reinforced a persistent historical, political, and social structure of exclusion and violence in the right to landownership for poor, black Brazilians.

Grande Paraguaçu presents a primary example of how the quilombola process of recognition has come up short when it comes to the protection and distribution of actual rights for black communities. The quilombolas of Grande Paraguaçu were accused of fraud, and the community spiraled into a violent land conflict shortly after it obtained cultural certification from the Palmares Cultural Foundation in 2005. Although the people of Grande Paraguaçu are politically recognized as the descendants of a quilombo, this recognition has been disputed by private landowners and Brazilian courts, leaving the community in the difficult yet increasingly common position of having to prove their authenticity and fight for rights that are guaranteed by the constitution. This situation of what quilombolas call "disrespect" within an unjust system that does not defend the "rights of poor, black communities" has led the quilombolas of Grande Paraguaçu to unite with a growing national quilombola movement—a movement that is reimagining the quilombo-descendant identity so that it speaks to modern forms of racial inequality and exclusion.

This book is organized into five chapters that reflect the broader argument of this research, that there are multiple layers of understanding that become a part of the quilombo-descendent identity and lived experience. I highlight the fact that the quilombo-descendant identity is constructed in multiple ways and grounded in different frameworks of knowledge production that imagine blackness within different intellectual, political, social, and individual commitments.

BLACK IDENTITIES AND CULTURAL RECOGNITION AS A POLITICAL AND INTELLECTUAL PROBLEM

The problem of "authenticity" has been increasingly documented for Afro-descendants throughout Latin America (French 2009; Hale 2005; Hooker 2005; Mintz and Price 1976; Sansone 2003; Wade 1995). Since the end of the twentieth century, scholars have pointed to an impasse in the recognition of racial and ethnic identity and subsequently rights for Afro-descendants (Mintz and Price 1976). These discussions came at a time when Latin American multiculturalism began to shift from a sole promotion of mestizo identity (Appelbaum, Macpherson, and Rosemblatt 2003; Stepan 1991) to a recognition of cultural difference and multicultural citizenship for indigenous and Afro-descendant communities (Hale 2005; Hooker 2005). In order to obtain cultural recognition and rights, Afro-descendants have had to navigate between the history of Africa and slavery that is written into their national identity and the blackness they live and embody (Gilroy 1993; Wade 1995).

One of the problems in the recognition of cultural rights for Afro-descendants is the ideological division between "race" and "ethnicity" in Latin America. Here the category of "ethnicity" has long been reserved for discussing "indigeneity," while black Latin Americans or Afro-descendants have been largely reduced to a phenotype and category of "race" (Wade 1997).[3] This division in ethnic and racial categories not only has separated research into two artificial camps but has also determined government policies for each group. The problem here is that black communities in Latin America exist in a paradox of inclusion and exclusion; while they might be included as culturally assimilated citizens and potential mestizos, they are also racially excluded in economic and political life.

The politics of cultural recognition, however, requires that blacks assert an ethnic or culturally distinct group identity in order to obtain similar collective rights as indigenous groups, such as, land—this means that most Afro-descendants and some indigenous groups who also see themselves as part of the national identity—integral members of society and not isolated groups—have a difficult time making "valid" or "authentic" claims to collective rights (Hooker 2005, 306).

Thus, scholars recently studying blackness in Latin America have found that in order for a black identity to be authentic in the eyes of the state, it must be ethnically constructed in the broad language of African ancestry or cultural tradition. Local narratives of blackness as they relate to the embodied experience of being black in a particular region or space often get lost in the attempts to connect an African diaspora to one source (M. Anderson 2009; Golash-Boza 2011; González 2011; Pinho 2010; Sue 2013). What gets lost in the discourse of cultural recognition and the labor of defining a legitimate black (ethnic) identity are everyday narratives and embodied experiences of racial exclusion and inequality (Caldwell 2007; Hanchard 1994a; Perry 2013; Twine 1998; Vargas 2011). I join these scholars in further complicating the concepts of "race" and "ethnicity" by merging them within a reimagined category of blackness. Here I demonstrate how blackness in Brazil operates through the body—a body that is marked as black and that must constantly mediate various social, cultural, historical, and political narratives of personhood and belonging. This mediation, in turn, represents a physical and emotional labor and struggle that are part of the experience of blackness in Brazil, an experience that links the quilombola fight for land rights with broader demands for racial justice in twenty-first-century Brazil.

The quilombola issue is steeped in the problem of authenticity and what determines a legitimate black identity deserving of collective rights. Lawyer and anthropologist Jan Hoffman French argues that the quilombo-descendant identity is a legal identity that has itself created a new cultural formation, primarily through the political process. French compares the quilombo community of Mocambo in the Sergipe-Alagoas region with an indigenous community called Xocó in the same region. She demonstrates that even though both communities share kin relations and a common cultural history, each chose a distinctive ethnoracial identity; one chose to identify as quilombola and the other as indigenous. French argues that as Latin American governments move toward cultural recognition as a way of redistributing rights, communities are learning to strategically perform essentialized identities as a tactic for obtaining certain rights. In her research in Mocambo, French argues (2009), residents were reconstructing their cultural lives in an effort to perform their quilombola identity, particularly by transforming certain cultural practices and even a family story to fit the dominant historical narrative of the colonial quilombo.

As a lawyer, French focuses on law making to come up with a new framework she calls "legalizing identities" that can be applied more broadly to understand how black and indigenous identities are transformed with the help of the government and then performed for the purpose of obtaining rights and resources. While French points to an important interplay between policy and identity formation, I disagree with her performance analysis and conclusion that communities are "strategically performing identities" as a "tactic" for obtaining rights. A performance analysis makes it too easy to assign valuation regarding the authenticity or "truth" claims of quilombolas; it puts the question of authenticity at center stage without complicating its presence—a disturbing elephant in the room blocking a real truth that we cannot see but also cannot ignore.

My research in Grande Paraguaçu has led me to a different conclusion. In fact, I highlight Grande Paraguaçu's accusation of fraud by the media and landowners to show how easily the lived experiences of quilombolas and poor black communities more broadly are dismissed and made fraudulent when it comes to obtaining rights that would potentially shift power relations. Although I discuss the quilombola legal process of recognition, my focus is primarily on the resulting impact of the overall process. I demonstrate that many black communities are becoming consumed by conflict and in fact are not winning rights, in part because their claims to cultural and racial difference are under attack by influential actors and society more broadly.

This attack emerges out of several factors having to do, on one hand, with the particular ways blacks have been incorporated into (and subsequently excluded from) the written history of the Brazilian nation. On the other hand, the conflict over quilombola rights boils down to a social and intellectual debate about whether black Brazilians warrant special rights from the government, a bitter debate that has taken several forms. In education, the debate is fueled by an anti–affirmative-action group of intellectuals and media outlets that are committed to upholding the old myth of racial democracy and vehemently oppose the use of race as a factor for public policy (Bailey and Peria 2010, 592; Vargas 2011). In the land issue, a political action group called the Banca Ruralista, made up of wealthy landowners, has challenged quilombola rights, especially the right to self-identification, as unconstitutional in the Brazilian Supreme Court. Thus,

I contend that quilombola rights are not just about the performance of identity but rather about the legitimation of racial inequality as a valid focus of public policy.

The Comissão Pró-Índio of São Paulo recently documented the situation of quilombola rights in 2013,[4] noting that while thousands of communities have achieved cultural recognition, only a handful (less than 10 percent) have actually been granted land rights, with most (nearly 87 percent) still stalled in the beginning of the process (CPI-SP 2013). Here I highlight the work of Charles Hale (2005), who anticipated that Latin American governments would use identity politics and cultural recognition as part of a new series of "neoliberal multiculturalist" policies that promise rights to marginalized groups on paper without any real structural change. The premise here is that if the ideological and political structures of racism, which have historically led to the marginalization and invisibility of black lives while upholding the authority of the white elite, are not directly addressed, then cultural recognition alone will not reverse hundreds of years of exclusion.

The quilombolas of Grande Paraguaçu demonstrate how poor black communities are promised rights without legitimacy or support. For example, quilombolas have the right to self-identify, but in order to obtain land rights they have to go through a long process of documentation and authentication as landowners contest their rights every step of the way. The winner in this situation is the subject with access to documentation and proof, legal support, and financial power. Furthermore, rural black communities are promised land rights within a contradictory social structure in which few blacks own their land—where the majority of blacks in urban areas live on the margins in favelas and in the impoverished *subúrbios* (suburbs) of major cities (Nascimento 1980, 149–150; Perry 2013).[5]

Therefore, rather than focus on the performance of identity, I am interested in the individual, social, and political experience of becoming a quilombo-descendant community without winning land rights. I document the long bureaucratic process of authentication and the narratives of suffering and conflict that take place as one community fights for rights. Cultural recognition without rights has led rural black communities into struggles for quilombola justice as a call for black justice and land rights as affirmative action. Here quilombolas want the state and society to see quilombola rights as exactly what they are, reparations for hundreds of years of exclusion from the right of black Brazilians to own land as well as a recovered cultural ancestry and past—a legitimate claim to space and a cultural and racial identity.

A major part of the process of becoming a quilombola has to do with the political and intellectual framing of the terms *quilombo* and *quilombola*. Here, I examine the intellectual labor of anthropologists in their role as "culture experts" within the government. While the term *quilombo* has existed for nearly five hundred years, the term *quilombo descendant* was created by the constitution and subsequently defined with the help of the Brazilian Anthropological Association (ABA, Associação Brasileira de Antropologia). Brazilian anthropologists helped the government specify the cultural boundaries that established quilombo descendants as separate groups or communities deserving of collective rights. Anthropologists worked to reimagine quilombo descendants as ethnic groups, as opposed to racial ones, as a way of fitting Afro-Brazilians within the politics of multicultural rights. Moreover, anthropologists helped make the new political category of quilombo descendant translatable to modern, rural, black communities by emphasizing their particular cultural and labor practices. Anthropologists were not the only people influential in defining the quilombo-descendant identity; black-movement activists also played a central role. Still, I give anthropologists special attention due to their historical role as agents of the state and particularly as the official social scientists appointed by the government to work in the cultural recognition process of these communities.

In redefining quilombo descendants as ethnic communities, anthropologists have worked to disconnect modern quilombolas from a dominant historical memory of colonial quilombos. Brazilian anthropologist Mauricio Arruti argues (2008) that it is impossible to even speak of *quilombos* without adjectives, such as *remanescente* (descendant), "contemporary," "urban," and "rural." These adjectives are used to distinguish quilombo descendants from the historical and colonial quilombos that have been used to disqualify their contemporary reality. After finding the right adjective, Arruti contends, "it is still necessary to define the content of each adjective, since we are talking about a contested category" (315). Some Brazilian anthropologists have even argued that when it comes to the political work of documenting quilombola cultural practices and land use, the government should hire trained anthropologists with specific experience working in rural, black communities (O'Dwyer 2010). O'Dwyer contends that anthropologists are especially positioned to make sense of the historical, cultural, and social narratives of black communities identifying as quilombo descendants.

We cannot fully understand the conflict surrounding quilombo recognition without first understanding the anthropological changes made to the very definitions of "quilombo" and "quilombo descendant." The political authority given to anthropology in the recognition of quilombo rights raises important issues about the history of anthropology in the production of the Brazilian national identity and, more broadly, anthropology's own problematic and conflictive engagement with race and racism as legitimate categories of social experience.

I place anthropologists directly in conversation with historians by exploring the ways historians have written about past quilombos and subsequently how anthropologists have applied this historiography in the field. The concept of the "quilombo" dominated twentieth-century Brazilian historiography as historians sought to imagine slave resistance through the great slave revolts. The quilombo of Palmares became the most important example of African resistance in the history of Brazil despite there being very limited historical documents on it. For nearly a hundred years, Brazilian historiography reproduced the image of Palmares and quilombos as isolated war camps politically and socially separated from society. Quilombo history was what Marshall Sahlins called "heroic history" (1985), a history of battles, heroes, and villains. Although the historiography is now clear that quilombos were not isolated camps hidden in the middle of the forest, the image and sociopolitical importance of Palmares as a symbol of African and black resistance continues to dominate the social imaginary surrounding quilombos and as a result quilombo descendants. This has created a difficult model of comparison for rural black communities. This book reminds us that the way in which quilombos were written into Brazilian history has also had an important impact on the social, cultural, and political representation of quilombo descendants and Afro-Brazilians more broadly.

POLITICALLY ALIGNED FIELDWORK

The taxi charged us one hundred dollars for the forty-five-minute trip into Grande Paraguaçu. When we complained to the driver about the high fare, he told us no taxi driver would risk driving us into these areas for any less. "I'm actually giving you a good price," he boasted. "Most taxis in Cachoeira will charge you one hundred and fifty dollars." It was just a preliminary visit to Grande Paraguaçu, and we were not exactly sure where we were going, so we didn't complain too much. When we arrived in the town, among the first things we saw were white, paper signs posted on the walls of a dozen homes that read, "We are not quilombolas!" Taking these signs as a clue to not assume that everyone in the town was a quilombola, we walked over to a bar and asked some people where we could find the quilombolas. They told us that they were all in a meeting at the local elementary school. A little nervous and unsure of how I would introduce myself, we left the taxi driver, who had no interest in joining a quilombola meeting anyway.

When we walked in, a young woman in her mid-twenties immediately welcomed us and asked us to introduce ourselves to the group. We stood there in the middle of a circle of about fifty quilombolas of all ages, men, women, and children. They were silent as they waited to hear who we were and why we were there. In what felt like a whisper, Ibraim and I introduced ourselves to them.[6] I spoke briefly and honestly. I told the group that I was a North American anthropologist, that I had heard a lot about them in the news and around the city, and that I was interested in learning more about their experiences in the quilombo process. Sandra, the organizer, turned to the circle and said, "Will you allow them to sit in on your meeting?" She asked in a firm voice, assuring the community members that they could choose to say no if they felt uncomfortable or unsafe. One man spoke up first, saying that this meeting and their fight were very serious and that we should not stay unless we believed in the movement and were there to support it. He added that if we were only there to steal information to use against them, we should leave. Another man immediately responded in our defense. He explained that we were students and that we were obviously interested in learning about them and their cause. "Se eles estão aqui, é por que eles acreditam em nós e apoiam os quilombolas!" (If they are here, it is because they believe in us and because they support the quilombolas!) Others spoke up too, and pretty soon everyone was speaking at once. When the noise calmed down, Sandra asked the group to take a vote and to raise their hands if they agreed to allow us to participate in the meeting. It was unanimous; we were allowed to stay.

Before we could thank everyone and sit down, the man who spoke in our favor announced that he and everyone there was sorry for being so mistrusting and suspicious:

> A lot of people come into our town, especially reporters and researchers, claiming to want to learn about our movement when really they are just gathering information for the landowners. Or they turn around and write news reports calling us frauds and liars. That is why we have become so suspicious of outsiders. But don't worry, we trust you now, and we know you are here to support our cause.

Although I was grateful for the community members' acceptance, their strong statement of trust made me nervous. My fieldwork had just begun, and I was still trying to understand the actors and the stakes involved in the quilombola conflict. I was not there to betray the community, to spy on them for landowners, or to publish slanderous reports, but I also was not yet sure how I would support their cause.

I envision my role in anthropology as one of advocacy and political engagement. I was immediately empathetic to the quilombola cause, but there was still a lot I needed to learn. This introduction to Grande Paraguaçu was an important wake-up call. It gave me a sense of the stakes involved in the quilombola fight—a fight that encompassed real lives and real futures. It was clear that these community members had serious expectations for me. They wouldn't have allowed me to stay unless I proved my support. This wasn't just some ideological exploration. And I knew that I would have to align myself if I wanted to document the real and serious conflicts involved in the quilombola land process.

But more than just resolve my own moral and political positioning, I also understood that as an anthropologist and ethnographer in Brazil, I automatically became part of a tradition of anthropologists who worked closely with communities and the government as mediators, representing a bureaucratic structure and public needs. Anthropologists in Brazil are politically aligned, and their research is expected to be applied (Ramos 2003, 111). Quilombolas understood that I did not actually work for the government, but they still believed my presence would help their struggle. This perception made sense because the only other anthropologists who had visited the community worked for the National Institute of Colonization and Agrarian Reform (INCRA, Instituto Nacional de Colonização e Reforma Agrária). Not only did I have to reconcile my theoretical purpose in the field with the political engagement demanded of me by the community, but I also had to constantly carve out my research position as separate from the government.

Activism and Anthropology "from the Gut"

My anthropological introduction to Grande Paraguaçu came as a warning to avoid any activist or politically motivated ideas in my research. The ethnographic research report for Grande Paraguaçu was assigned to Anita Souza. Anita was twenty-six years old then and was born and raised in Brasília, the capital of Brazil. She moved to Bahia when she was awarded the anthropologist position in the Quilombos Sector of INCRA. When I first met Anita, in a hallway of the INCRA office, she seemed tired and perhaps untrusting of my intentions. She asked me many questions about my work and my project before I could begin the interview with her. It wasn't until our second meeting that I was able to get to know Anita. Our second interview was during a visit to the quilombo-descendant community of Olho d'Água do Basílio in the mining city of Seabra, in northern Bahia. As we sat in the cold reception area of a small motel waiting to see if any of my interviews would actually take place, Anita told me the story of why she was leaving INCRA and Grande Paraguaçu. In a serious and melancholic tone, she lamented that her job had gone in a violent direction:

> Grande Paraguaçu was my first job at INCRA. The state opened a slot
> for an anthropologist in Bahia. I took the exam and passed. Like anyone
> who passes in a state competition for a federal job, I was very excited to
> have secure employment. All I knew was that I would be working with
> land regularization for quilombos; I did not have any expectations or
> militant ideals going into the job. I had never worked officially as an
> anthropologist, so I was new to everything.

Before working at INCRA, Anita had supported the Movimento Sem Terra (Landless Workers Movement) and what she described as "militant movements like the Zapatistas." However, she emphasized that she had not gone into her INCRA job with activist motivations. "It was just a job. A good job," she said. In 2007, when Anita had finished collecting all of her data in Grande Paraguaçu, she went to Brasilia to visit her family and to write up her report for INCRA. "While I was in *Brasilia*, I saw a news broadcast by the *Jornal Nacional* calling Grande Paraguaçu a fraud. You heard about it?" Anita asked, pausing. "Yes, I saw the video online just before coming to Brazil," I responded. The reporter from the *Jornal Nacional* interviewed people in Grande Paraguaçu about their quilombola identity and history. The footage revealed a series of vaguely identified people denying slave ancestry and unable to explain any of the quilombo history that the reporter claimed was documented in the community's petition for cultural recognition.

The report also accused quilombolas of deforestation in the attempt to take over the entire area. "It was absurd!" Anita exclaimed. "I was so angry because I knew the report had been paid for by a landowner and because I knew that the ones deforesting were the landowners and not the quilombolas." Anita began to get agitated as she continued the story:

The next day I received a phone call from my supervisor saying that the president of INCRA in Brasilia was being interviewed by the media and needed me to send him a statement of my work on the community. This was my first job, so I was writing from my own gut and nothing I had prior experience with. I stayed up all night writing a six-page letter that explained to the president of INCRA the situation of Grande Paraguaçu. I denounced the landowners as the real deforesters and land violators. I stated that the landowners were intimidating the residents and using the media as a way of criminalizing the population. I really put a lot into the letter because I was so angry at the news report.

Anita was so incensed by the *Jornal Nacional*'s accusation that she decided to also forward the letter to her colleagues involved with the social justice of quilombolas in Bahia. One of the colleagues she included was a lawyer and member of the Association of Lawyers for Rural Workers (AATR, Associação de Advogados de Trabalhadores Rurais). This lawyer had deep connections in Grande Paraguaçu and had worked to resolve these types of disputes in the past. Without informing Anita, he sent her letter to a listserve he had created from dozens of public email addresses subscribed to the AATR. It turned out that the particular landowner Anita was accusing was on that listserve and also received her letter. "The next thing I knew, I was being sued for libel!" she said. "I found myself in the frightening situation of being sued by a powerful landowner and with no idea what to do." According to Anita, INCRA immediately disassociated itself from her. The organization gave an official statement that because Anita sent the email from her personal account, she acted independently and without their consent. Anita had to find and pay for her own lawyer.

I was so paranoid during that time because the landowner's wife would call me and make a ticking sound on the phone, insinuating that my time was running out. I was so scared of everyone around me! I thought I was being followed and that my phones and Internet were tapped. It took me a long time to calm down and live normally.

It was such an awful time. I remember that a friend of mine told me to make a list of all the people that I thought could help me. At the very top of the list I put the anthropologist of the Ministério Público [Federal Public Ministry]; she worked with us a lot, and I admired her greatly. Ironically, she was the first to betray me. She wrote a letter to the president of INCRA saying that my report on Grande Paraguaçu was too politicized and thus not properly executed. It was incredible! Here I was being sued, and there was the community being wrongly accused of fraud and at risk of losing their claims to their lands, and this top anthropologist writes this letter that just makes all of our lives that much more fragile. I was heartbroken. The worst part is that this landowner is not just suing me for a fine. No. He wants to put me in jail!

At this point Anita stopped because she was so upset she could barely continue speaking. I didn't ask her any more questions because I could see that the situation was still affecting her deeply. The case had not ended yet and would remain open for four years unless the landowner took more aggressive action, in which case Anita risked imprisonment. Even without the organization's support, Anita did not quit her job at INCRA. It was a stable federal job that allowed her to support herself on a comfortable income. Those types of jobs were not easy to come by in Brazil.

It was a horrible period of my life that made me rethink a lot of things, especially my work as an anthropologist in quilombola communities. I have asked to be transferred from Salvador to an INCRA office in another place. If I do not get transferred, I will surely quit. I need to move on with my life. I am not a militant person, and I just do not think it is worth it to keep working in an area that is so problematic. I want to do film. That is what I am more passionate about. I want to go back to school and get my master's degree. I just want to move on with my life.

Although Anita was shaken by the landowner's threats to put her in jail, she also expressed concern about the quilombolas. She did not want to lose her job, but she also did not want to just abandon the community's case. She knew that if she left, the case would lose even more credibility and might even be thrown out altogether. Shortly after my fieldwork ended, Anita did leave the community to pursue a film degree in Europe. Although Anita's case raised serious questions about the people the government hired to fill one of the most important positions in the quilombola land process, I was also interested in Anita's repeated assertion that she was not an activist. Obviously the word "activist" was tainted by the Public Ministry's accusation that Anita's report was politicized and thus inappropriate. But it didn't make any sense. What did the Public Ministry's anthropologist mean by "too politicized"? It seemed to me a contradiction of INCRA's role in the quilombo process.

During our first interview, INCRA research analyst Amélia Quiroz told me that INCRA's primary responsibility was to represent, support, and protect the interests of the quilombola community—the institute's funds were limited, and it rarely had the means to provide substantial support such as legal representation. Nonetheless, Anita's report and letter seemed appropriate to the requirements of her position.

It was clear to me that Anita's crime had been her choice to defend the community against slanderous media by writing "from the gut." That is, Anita's letter wasn't about anthropology and a narrative of cultural authenticity; it was an impassioned and necessarily urgent denunciation of injustice. Anita watched as the lives and rights of hundreds of quilombolas were threatened on prime-time television in carefully manipulated "facts" and intellectually positioned lies. Anita understood the malicious motivations behind the *Jornal Nacional*'s report and the repercussions it would have on Grande Paraguaçu and all quilombolas if it went uncontested. Just as I soon would, Anita had heard countless narratives of landowner threats and violent intimidations targeted at quilombola leaders. Like the quilombolas, Anita spoke and wrote feverishly out of anger—an anger that boiled at the callous way in which racism, violent misrecognition, and power were flaunted in plain sight. In her famous and brilliantly inspiring speech on "the uses of anger" in response to racism, Audre Lorde affirmed,

> Anger expressed and translated into action in the service of our vision and our future is a liberating and strengthening act of clarification, for it is in the painful process of this translation that we identify who are our allies with whom we have grave differences, and who are our genuine enemies. (1997, 280)

Anita is a white woman of considerable economic and social privilege, and still she was shocked and angered by what she knew was a gross and violent misrepresentation of the quilombolas of Grande Paraguaçu. Rather than remain silent, Anita acted and used her voice and (perceived) authority to defend the community. Although she didn't feel any fear in her initial expression, once she faced the wrath of oppression and violence targeted at her own person and freedom, she recoiled in fear and silence, repeatedly denying any activist leanings and ultimately severing her alliance (if it ever existed) to the quilombolas. Lorde recalls, "I have seen situations where white women hear a racist remark, resent what has been said, become filled with fury, and remain silent because they are afraid" (280). Anita's experience in Grande Paraguaçu demonstrates a great deal about race, privilege, and power in Brazil. Later I will show a different form of anger—that of other targeted bodies, the black bodies of quilombolas in their demands for justice. Quilombolas face much worse accusations and forms of oppression than Anita could ever even imagine because unlike Anita's protected white subjectivity, black bodies are systemically denied and written out of the political and social structures of justice. Unlike Anita, the quilombolas of Grande Paraguaçu couldn't afford to ignore their oppressors and move to another country or even another city out of fear. I will demonstrate how quilombolas use anger as a motivating force to confront injustice without fear and for the protection of their very livelihoods.

Indeed Brazil, like the United States, exhibits political contradictions when it comes to the inclusion of blacks in all aspects of society. Although the state, thanks to years of pressure from black-movement activists, has implemented affirmative action polices that recognize racial exclusion, "longstanding institutional and ideological practices further the imposed marginalization of black communities" (Vargas 2011, 248). Even with the promise of race-based policies, entrenched institutional racism continues to inhibit access to rights and any real change in the racial power structure. In the quilombola case, Decree 4.887, signed in 2003, grants quilombolas the right to self-identification while simultaneously centralizing and complicating the anthropologist's position in the land distribution process; moreover, the entire bureaucratic process for quilombolas allows uninhibited legal power to landowners to rebuke quilombola claims at all levels of the process. Anita's story was a reminder of the power relations involved in the quilombola land struggle. Rather than frighten me out of political motivations, however, it further highlighted the stakes involved and made my position in the field irrefutable. It allowed me to see just how heavily the odds were stacked against the quilombolas. If a white, federal employee, hired to protect the interests of a community, could be sued and threatened for doing her job, then where did that leave the men and women of Grande Paraguaçu? Watching silently as Anita sobbed, her face red and swollen, my mind wandered as I thought more about my own responsibilities and rights as an anthropologist and woman of color in the field.

Speaking frankly about everything she had seen so far as the INCRA analyst, Amélia confided in me during our first interview that what was happening to the quilombolas of Grande Paraguaçu was "unjust," and after meeting the community and watching Anita fall apart out of fear, I could see that clearly. I was certain then that my research would not be complete without a combination of scholarship and political engagement, as others have suggested (Hale 2006; Manz 2004). As a Chicana, race scholar, and public anthropologist, I understand race as both an embodied social and cultural reality and as a shifting category dependent on history, recovered memories, and political transitions. What I saw in my first encounters with the quilombola issue was an intellectual debate about authenticity, led by the government as it devised various standards for recognizing and granting rights to eligible quilombolas. On the other hand, there was a cry for justice and due process from quilombolas who felt disrespected and intimidated by landowners and a slow bureaucratic process. Like Anita, I too am writing from the gut and, necessarily, from anger. In the words of Audre Lorde, "My response to racism is anger" (278), as I too have lived with that anger. Thus my alignment with the quilombola movement and the quilombolas of Grande Paraguaçu is also grounded in my own embodied experience of exclusion and marginalization as I have lived them. I recognize, with utmost seriousness, that I too, like Anita, enjoy certain privileges, mostly that my livelihood is not at stake in the quilombola fight and that I would eventually return to my own, unthreatened home.

Still, if scholars of color have taught us anything, it is that solidarity against global racial oppressions and across racial boundaries is necessary for creating a new social order and for exposing the everyday violence and many faces of racism (Hooker 2005; Mohanty 2003; Perry 2013; Vargas 2011). Thus I could use my voice and privilege, even if limited, to support and defend the quilombolas in their fight to reclaim their authenticity. For that reason, I see my work and moral choices within a politically aligned anthropology as part of a conversation on what Perry calls "a diasporic continuum" of racialized, black experiences within global structures of racism (2013, xiv).

I believe that what is missing from anthropological literature on the quilombola issue are the narratives of conflict and suffering that have become an all-too-common part of the long process of waiting for land rights. I argue that in order to understand the lived experience of becoming a quilombola in twenty-first-century Brazil, we must witness quilombola narratives in all of their complexity, be they angry proclamations, passionate pleas, silent stares, or sorrowful reflections. These narratives, I argue, are part of a contemporary, embodied experience of blackness in a contradictory political moment in which black Brazilians continue to experience exclusion and marginalization even as the government recognizes racial inequality (Caldwell 2007, 12).

My introduction to the quilombola community of Grande Paraguaçu was important in helping me understand that there is no position of neutrality when it comes to the quilombola issue—or even to issues of racial discrimination and social justice. I had to choose a side if I was going to have a project at all. I learned quickly that I could not stand on the sidelines as a quiet observer. By necessity my methodology came to reflect conflictive terrains, which I had to learn to maneuver and integrate. The bureaucratic apparatus and the quilombola community each demanded rapport and made their needs clear up front. Ultimately, the direction and results of my investigation highlight as much my commitments to racial justice as they do the limits of anthropology in quilombola research.

The Stakes of Politically Aligned Fieldwork

The problem of who is and is not a quilombo descendant and who deserves land based on that category involves hundreds of people in different places and with varying commitments: quilombolas, nonquilombolas,[7] private landowners, government officials, non-governmental organization leaders, activists, and anthropologists. While some of these people work together, they also often criticize each other. The quilombola issue is an intellectual, political, social, and intimate one, and I wanted to be involved in all of those discussions. From the very beginning, however, it was challenging for me to gain rapport with two essential groups, the nonquilombolas and the key private landowners in Grande Paraguaçu. Whether I knew it or not, my "side" was chosen the moment I decided to attend a quilombola meeting in Grande Paraguaçu as my introduction to the town. Afterward, my ability to interview people on other sides—namely, private landowners and those residents who dismissed the quilombola identity— was significantly limited. If I was caught visiting the home of a nonquilombola or a landowner, I could have lost my rapport with the quilombolas and even have been asked to leave the community.

In the middle of my fieldwork, I witnessed the quilombola leaders remove a Brazilian researcher and filmmaker from an important community event. The young researcher was a film student from Cachoeira who was known for doing video projects for the very landowners who were opposing the land process in Grande Paraguaçu. Although he professed his innocence and academic neutrality in the issue, the quilombolas were upset that he had not approached them first. He was pegged as an opponent, and his camera made him a spy. Similarly, after living with the quilombolas for several months and making my presence known throughout the town, I was labeled a quilombola supporter. I discovered this while filming a counterprotest organized by nonquilombolas. As I was filming, two women ran toward me and nearly tore the camera out of my hands, yelling at me to get out of their town and to stop supporting land thieves.

This book, then, is most deeply informed by the perspectives and experiences of the quilombolas of Grande Paraguaçu in their struggle for rights. I lived and researched in Grande Paraguaçu for months at a time, conducting interviews, organizing meetings, and participating in every aspect of the life and work of the community. I did try to understand opposing points of view and listened with respect when I could. Before visiting the quilombola community, I set up an interview in Cachoeira with the primary landowner of Grande Paraguaçu, Ivo Santana. When I arrived at his home, I was greeted by one of his daughters. She entertained a short conversation with me but neither allowed me to record our conversation nor to speak with her father. She told me that the quilombo issue had taken a toll on his heart and that he had grown quiet and reserved since it began. Santana rarely left his room, and he spoke with few people. She said he felt betrayed by the community and had grown depressed throughout the years. His lands had been passed on to his children, and they were now the ones involved in the legal dispute with the quilombolas. After my research in the quilombo was discovered, I was cut off from the rest of the landowners.

Information on the legal and political process of quilombola recognition comes from structured interviews with government officials in INCRA, the Palmares Cultural Foundation (FCP, Fundação Cultural Palmares), the Ministry of Culture, the Ministry of Health, the Special Office for the Promotion of Racial Equality (SEPROMI, Secretaria Especial de Políticas de Promoção da Igualdade Racial), and other government organizations involved in the quilombo process. When interviewing government officials, I had to be very careful and calculated with my questions. I knew I would not be given very much time. I learned that reading government websites before my meetings was crucial so that I could tell when I was just getting an institutional script. When this happened, I had questions prepared to engage the individual work and opinions of that particular person. However, I had to be careful with my words when I was expressing my own opinions or views of the quilombo clause. Some government officials were more critical of the clause than others, but they all said they supported it wholeheartedly. If they sensed that I was critical of it in any way, they would politely engage my discussion but would not see me again for another interview.

During my interview with the regional coordinator of INCRA, I felt he was speaking by the script, and I decided to tap into his sense of social justice. I reframed Amélia's statement about the injustices she found in the quilombola process into a question in order to see how the coordinator would respond. I asked him if he thought the quilombola legal process was just. He gave me a confused look and replied, "Just?" As soon as he did that, I sensed that I had lost him. He gave me a politically correct statement and then quickly wrapped up the interview:

> Just? I don't understand. I don't know the context of these words.
> I'm totally in favor of [the quilombo constitutional article], or else I wouldn't even be here. I wouldn't be here doing this work that I do. Of course I defend it. I believe in it and I think it's fair. Anyway, I'm saying this because of the constitutional conditions.

The regional coordinator was a difficult interviewee. He refused to speak with me after this interview and worked to block my access to other INCRA researchers. Although I was still able to conduct interviews with other INCRA employees, his mistrust significantly delayed my work in the beginning. If it were not for Anita, I might have lost access to the organization altogether.

Information regarding issues of social justice and injustice, land abuses, workshops, and community empowerment comes from conversations and structured interviews with representatives of NGOs such as Koinonia's Observatório Quilombola, the Pastoral Commission of Fishermen and Women (CPP, Comissão Pastoral de Pescadores), the Association of Lawyers for Rural Workers (AATR, Associação de Advogados de Trabalhadores Rurais), and the National Coordination for the Articulation of Rural Black Quilombo Communities (CONAQ, Coordinação Nacional de Articulação das Comunidades Negras Rurais Quilombolas).[8] While NGO leaders also spoke optimistically about the quilombo clause, they were more open about the conflicts they encountered.

These organizations connected their work to a social justice purpose. They understood that in many rural black communities people did not know some of their fundamental citizenship rights and needed guidance. Topics such as citizenship, cultural inclusion, black resistance, and quilombola identity all needed to be engaged and workshopped with communities so people could understand the demands of cultural recognition and the legal aspects of the quilombo process. NGO work was a matter of empowerment and consciousness raising. For CONAQ, work with quilombolas was specifically about connecting their communities to a larger black-movement initiative of racial equality and affirmative action. But more importantly, NGOs are dedicated to helping quilombo descendants through the procedures involved in recognition and rights acquisition by teaching them to use the quilombo clause to their advantage. All of these narratives came out of conversations I had with organization leaders but also observations of their work in the field, organization publications, and reflections on their work and presence as described by quilombolas.

Throughout this book, I include several full transcripts of conversations, debates, narratives, and personal moments of clumsiness that I believe, in Scheper-Hughes' words, "give the reader a deeper appreciation of the way ethnographic 'facts' are built up" (1992, 25). I have been influenced by Richard Price's writing technique in *First-Time* (2002), where he structurally distinguishes his interview narratives from his own theoretical and historical analysis. While many interviews are simply integrated into my analysis, others are included in full. These full narratives are inserted in places where I want the reader to focus on the process by which people are reconstructing or remembering emotions and experiences. Several of these narratives recount the different ways people in the community remember how the quilombola process began in Grande Paraguaçu. I pay special attention to these stories because through their selection of events they illustrate the different meanings of *quilombolismo* within the community. For a process that is complicated by a lack of understanding and acceptance of the contemporary definitions of the quilombola, these narratives also tell more personal stories of the social impacts of the quilombo process.

Price accentuates his analysis of historical memory and narrative construction by using different fonts to illustrate the oral testimonies of the Saramakas in Suriname. In doing so, he offers several layers of critique of historiography and the way the past is reimagined and remembered in a maroon community. I hope to demonstrate recursively the many layers and stories (individual, intellectual, political, and social) that contribute to the production of the quilombola community (lived and conceptual), stories that cannot always be neatly synthesized within one theoretical critique. Politically positioned and socially aligned, I aim to reflect "self-conscious and serious partiality" in my writing, to borrow Clifford's expression (1986, 7), while at the same time lending an empathetic ear and supportive pen to the quilombolas of Grande Paraguaçu.

Throughout this book, I weave together social narratives of the colonial quilombo with the legal processes of quilombola recognition and representation. I use the story of Grande Paraguaçu as an example of the ways in which memories of African ancestry, slavery, and colonial oppression get reinterpreted within a lived experience of racial discrimination and political marginalization. While my work is critical of nostalgic represen-

tations of blackness and African ancestry, I am most committed to illustrating how the quilombolas of Grande Paraguaçu represent themselves
to each other, to society, and to the state, even if these representations are
at times partial, contradictory, or supportive of a nostalgic narrative. In
the end, my goal is to illustrate the multiple layers of conceptualization,
"truths," and embodied life that make up the quilombola identity and the
process of cultural recognition.

ONE

Black Heroes

REWRITING BLACK RESISTANCE AND
QUILOMBO HISTORY

In 2008, while conducting preliminary research for my fieldwork in Brazil, I came across a video online provocatively titled "Fraud in False Quilombo of Bahia." It was a recording of a report broadcast on the *Jornal Nacional* on May 14, 2007. *Jornal Nacional* is a prime-time news program on Brazil's largest broadcast network, Rede Globo. The network's programs air to a national audience of more than a hundred million people every day. *Jornal Nacional* was called to investigate Grande Paraguaçu, a recently recognized quilombo-descendant community in the Iguape region of Bahia. In a segment designed for prime-time television, the reporter approached random people in the streets of Grande Paraguaçu and asked them specific details regarding the written history and cultural traditions of the community. In strategically edited interviews showing residents who negated or simply could not explain quilombo and slave ancestry, the report set out to prove that the people of Grande Paraguaçu were not the descendants of a quilombo and were lying about their identity to steal land. Brazilians who knew little about the quilombo process or its history understood from the *Jornal Nacional*'s report that Grande Paraguaçu had engaged in fraud and government deception, a charge that had economic, cultural, and emotional implications for its residents.

The reporter opened by explaining that the quilombo process was initiated by a group of residents in Grande Paraguaçu that claimed to be the descendants of slaves who were persecuted and sought refuge. But immediately he made clear that proof of fraud could be seen from the outset in the petition for cultural recognition that these residents submitted to the Palmares Cultural Foundation. Flashing a highlighted document on the screen, the reporter proclaimed that "not even the eldest residents

know that at one point their community was called Freguesia do Igaupe."
The image turned to an older woman leaned over her window. She was
identified only as Arlinda Pereira, *aposentada* (retired woman). "Have
you ever heard of the Freguesia do Iguape?" the reporter asked. "No," she
responded, shaking her head. "You don't know that name?" the reporter
asked again. Dona Pereira simply repeated "No" without any further comment as her image was cut from the screen and the reporter moved to the
next interview.

The second person interviewed was Eronildes da Rosa, identified also
as an *aposentado* (retiree) who was eighty-six years old and "witnessed
the town's birth." "Has there ever been a quilombo here?" the reporter
asked, pushing a microphone under da Rosa's chin. "No. No. This is the
first time I've ever heard of this," da Rosa responded as though he had
been asked that question many times. "Have you ever had slave relatives?"
"No. No. No," da Rosa affirmed. "Your grandmother?" "No. No." "Your
great-grandmother?" "No. No. No." "Nobody was ever a slave?" the reporter restated, making sure that the public clearly understood da Rosa's
negation of slave ancestry. "No," da Rosa said, shaking his head. To anyone
watching, da Rosa's denial of quilombo and slave ancestry was important
because he is a black man who could have been seen as an elder and thus a
source of historical memory in the community.

After da Rosa's interview, images of official documents signed by the
Palmares Cultural Foundation were shown, with portions highlighted
where the quilombolas of Grande Paraguaçu declared that they continued
to practice African traditions such as *maculelê*.[1] Using these documents,
the reporter approached two unidentified young men sitting on a side-
walk and asked if they could explain how maculelê was danced. "Maculelê?
I have no idea what that is," one man responded, smiling. "Grande Paraguaçu does not have that," the other man said.

In a final interview, the reporter sat in the home of the private landowner, Ivo Santana. Unlike others, Santana was formally (and very specifically) introduced as a "long-time private landowner" in the region claimed
by quilombolas whose "family purchased the land 150 years ago." Santana
held up his land title for the public to see. "These people who call themselves quilombolas, their descendants actually came here after being af-
flicted by a drought in the *sertão* in the decade of the [19]30s," he claimed
with certain exasperation.[2] "But they were not slaves?" the reporter asked.
"No. They were not slaves. In fact, slavery had already ended." And with
that statement the report underscored Santana's claims to have the real

and documented rights to the land. The interview was a reiteration of the reporter's opening statement that the proof was in the paperwork.

The performance that was expected by the *Jornal Nacional* was that any randomly picked person in Grande Paraguaçu could recite the history of the community exactly as it might be written in a history book. I later came to appreciate that this misrecognition or nonrecognition, in Taylor's words (1994), of quilombo descendants was a common and widespread issue. The *Jornal Nacional* report was premised on the idea that certain residents of Grande Paraguaçu had falsified documents in order to obtain cultural recognition and land as quilombo descendants. However, the audience wasn't given much information about the people interviewed. When I began my fieldwork two years after the report aired, I learned that the reporter gained access to the community under the dishonest claim that he was producing a documentary. I discovered that the two unidentified men who denied knowledge of maculelê were outsiders who did not actually live in the community but instead in a nearby town. Moreover, I soon became aware that with a population of more than three hundred families, not every person in Grande Paraguaçu identified as a quilombola or signed the petition to participate in the change. The Palmares Cultural Foundation only required that a majority of residents sign the petition for quilombola recognition. Da Rosa was one of the residents who did not sign the petition. He did not self-identify as a quilombola, and he maintained a strong alliance to the private landowners in the area.

Finally, I met Dona Arlinda Pereira, whom the *Jornal Nacional* reporter had introduced only as "a retired woman." Dona Pereira is the mother of one of the most active quilombola leaders in the community. She was also the town's esteemed *parteira* (midwife). Retired at the time I met her, Dona Pereira was even granted an official recognition by one of the doctors in the community for having delivered 1,088 babies in her lifetime. A placard hung proudly in her home marking a history that spoke for itself. So while according to the *Jornal Nacional*, da Rosa "witnessed the town's birth," I learned that Dona Pereira had in fact birthed it. Still, none of this information was made available to the audience by the *Jornal Nacional* report. Without any information on the interview subjects, the report painted an oversimplified and partial image of an ignorant, lying community.

The *Jornal Nacional* report had a major impact on the quilombolas of Grande Paraguaçu. Whether the claims of fraud were legitimate did not matter. The report brought public charges against the community that im-

plicated the work and authority of two major government institutions—
the Palmares Cultural Foundation, which had granted Grande Paraguaçu
a certificate of cultural recognition as an official quilombo-descendant
community, and INCRA, which was in charge of the land regularization
process for quilombo-descendant communities. After watching the *Jornal
Nacional* report, I wondered why the Globo network was so interested in
discrediting this particular community and what social conditions allowed
for the network's success. I saw that in order to obtain a clear understanding of the quilombo-descendant conflict, I would need to better understand the meaning, past and present, of *quilombo*. More importantly, I
would need to know how history itself, especially black history, was understood and employed within the social and national imaginary of Brazil.

ON DOMINANT HISTORIES

To disentangle narratives of history from lived experiences requires
first thinking about history as a sociocultural construct rather than a series
of linear facts or truths set along a timeline (Sahlins 1985). This allows us
to think about the representations of historical narratives through certain
symbols and signifiers rooted in a particular culture and power structure
(Clifford 1988, 260; Said 1979). By understanding history as a sociocultural
construction, we make visible the storyteller and his narrative. Eric Wolf
has taught us that "History" with a capital "H" is a dominant and dominating narrative that populations learn in schoolbooks as one big "tale of
unfolding moral purpose" (1982, 5)—a tale reduced to conquest, with winners and losers, heroes and villains.

Since the late twentieth century, scholars have questioned dominant
histories and argued for a new history that includes the voices and narratives of the so-called people without a history, of populations beyond
the white elite (Price 2002; Said 1979; Slenes 2010; Sweet 2003; Wolf 1982).
These scholars have taught us that dominant historical narratives, particularly those told by the winners, the colonizers, the elite, are sustained
throughout generations. But how do these narratives affect living populations? Just because scholars have expanded the voices and subjects of history does not mean that dominant histories are decentralized. Nor does
it mean that previously unrepresented narratives are always empowered.

What better example of this than the conflict that descended on Rigoberta Menchú, a Quiché woman, who wrote and published a historical account of her life only to be accused of lying by white anthropologist

David Stoll (Arias 2001). In the beginning of her memoir Menchú writes, "This is my testimony. I didn't learn it from a book, and I didn't learn it alone. I'd like to stress that it's not only *my* life, it's also the testimony of my people" (Menchú and Burgos-Debray 1984, 1). Menchú specified that her story was an embodied narrative of her past and present life, but even though it was her own, it was not constructed alone and belonged also to her people. Menchú won the 1992 Nobel Peace Prize and received international attention for her bravery and prose, but her accomplishments would not go uncontested.

In his controversial book titled *Rigoberta Menchú and the Story of All Poor Guatemalans* (1998), David Stoll questioned whether Menchú had told the truth about certain aspects of her life. Stoll compared Menchú's narrative to his own research in Guatemala. When the stories did not match, he tagged hers as fraudulent, using his anthropological authority to determine truth and authenticity. Even after all of the critical writing that scholars produced at the end of the twentieth century to include the voices of the excluded and after many scholars wrote in defense of Menchú (Arias 2001), History with a capital "H" reared its dominant head. It seemed that there was still an extant difference between the written subaltern and the speaking subaltern (Spivak 2010), a difference defined by the right to authority, the right to have a voice, and the right to embody a history.

It is important to analyze how dominant histories act as hegemonic discourses—powerful social narratives accepted and continuously recreated by a majority of society. If the *Jornal Nacional* report can teach us anything, it is that a dominant historical narrative regarding quilombos is alive and well in the social imagination. Here I reflect specifically on twentieth-century historical writings of slave revolts and colonial quilombos in order to examine the discourse of a black "heroic history" (Sahlins 1985), at times romantic and at times tragic. I describe just one of the extant conflicts laden in the process of granting tangible rights to quilombo-descendant communities in contemporary Brazil: the problem of dominant history, particularly a quilombo historiography that was produced throughout much of the twentieth century.

In the case of quilombolas, written history acts as a rubric of authenticity, a model of the "real" to which black communities are compared and held accountable when it comes to the distribution of rights. Throughout nearly the entire twentieth century, quilombo history was a heroic history in which historians focused on major slave revolts, battles, and leaders and especially on Palmares, the largest and most successful quilombo. Palmares became a model of African culture, community, and resistance used for thinking about all quilombos during the colonial period. For nearly a hundred years, real slave resistance seemed to exist only in warring, fugitive slave camps that were isolated from and in constant battle with society (Lara 2010). Although historians began to rewrite quilombo history by the end of the twentieth century, today rural black communities are still authenticated according to a heroic history of African cultural resistance. I am not arguing that black Brazilians do not have real historical claims to African ancestry (Funes 1996, 467–493). Instead, I argue that the problem of what is "real" (real history, real ancestry, real cultural identity) is inherent in the new "quilombo descendant" political identity. Despite the conceptual labor of anthropologists and historians, modern black communities seeking to identify as the descendants of quilombos must learn to describe their everyday embodied practices in ways that connect to a dominant quilombo historiography.

The intensity of the slave trade in Brazil set the stage for a black population that lived, worked, and resisted in multiple ways. However, twentieth-century historians created a prevailing and primarily masculine narrative of black rebels and heroes who fought to form African communities in Brazil. Quilombos became symbolic spaces where blacks could be free to practice the traditions of their African homelands. It is a deeply rooted narrative that has become part of how Brazilians think of Brazil as a *mestiço* nation of racial democracy where the idea of Africa plays an important role (Sansone 2003). While Africa and quilombos are important symbols of the Brazilian national identity, these symbols are especially important in the Recôncavo Baiano,[3] making it a particularly interesting place to examine the influence of quilombo history on the lives of quilombo descendants.

SLAVERY AND THE RACIAL GEOGRAPHY
OF THE RECÔNCAVO BAIANO

Brazil was one of the largest slave traders in the Atlantic world, trafficking more than five million African slaves from 1501 to 1866, primarily from the West African coast (Eltis and Richardson 2010). One of the last nations in the West to abolish slavery, Brazil maintained the intensity of its slave trade until abolition in 1888, with new Africans still taken to Brazil throughout much of the nineteenth century (Slenes 2012; Sweet 2003). More than three million enslaved Africans were taken to the sugar plantations of the Brazilian Northeast, where the population quickly became predominantly black, both enslaved and free. Bahia was one of Brazil's four "great slave markets" (Arthur Ramos 1939/1980, 16); there, slave ships landed to sell and distribute Africans to other regions, especially during the early part of the colonial period. In the first half of the nineteenth century, Salvador had an estimated population of more than fifty million people, 40 percent of whom were enslaved blacks, with anywhere from eight thousand to ten thousand Africans arriving in Salvador each year (Schwartz 1996a, 374–375). With thousands of new Africans arriving in Brazil continuously throughout the duration of the slave trade, the impact of African cultural practices, especially West African traditions from present-day Angola, Congo, Guinea, Benin, and Nigeria permanently marked the racial and cultural landscape of Brazil, especially in the Northeast (Arthur Ramos 1939/1980, 12).

In the Bahian Recôncavo, the intensity of the sugar economy and the slave trade led to the emergence of a region that is primarily African in its cultural practices and historical memory. This history provides the foundation for understanding how the quilombolas of Grande Paraguaçu have come to identify the land and region as a significant part of the their cultural ancestry and present identity.

Situated in the Vale do Iguape, Grande Paraguaçu sits along the Paraguaçu River, at a point where saltwater from the Bahia de Todos os Santos (Bay of All Saints) mixes with the freshwater of the river. Grande Paraguaçu is in the heart of the Bahian Recôncavo, a region of the Northeast that has been romanticized for its beautiful landscapes and visibly dominant black presence. Historically the slave trade brought hundreds of Bantu Africans from the Congo, Zaire, Cabinda, Angola, Mozambique, and Zanzibar who were sent to sugar and tobacco plantations throughout the region (Carneiro 1991). Originally inhabited by indigenous tribes, particularly the Maracás, the Vale do Iguape was significantly transformed by the arrival of the Portuguese. The region provided rich land for agriculture and was an important entryway, by way of the Paraguaçu River, into the interior of Bahia. Indigenous groups were systematically removed from their lands and were replaced by massive *engenhos*, or sugar mills, and enslaved Africans.

In 1531, Martim Afonso de Souza's expedition, charged with stimulating the cultivation of sugarcane in the area, settled along the Paraguaçu River and established what later became the city of Cachoeira. Santiago do Iguape, first called Santiago on the Paraguaçu, was formed as a parish town of the Catholic Church in the late sixteenth century (Schwartz 1985, 80). Rule over the lands of the Recôncavo was granted as *sesmarias* to Dom

Alvaro da Costa, son of the second governor general, as a prize for having led the war against the indigenous tribes of the region (Tavares 2001). Since the late fourteenth century, the Portuguese crown used sesmarias, a system of royal land grants, as a strategy for controlling the distribution of lands and promoting the cultivation of "unoccupied" lands (Holston 2008, 118).

The Law of Sesmarias required the productive use of land. After a certain period, lands that were not successfully cultivated would have to be returned to the crown and became reassigned as *terras devolutas*, devolved lands (ibid.). The sesmaria system was riddled with problems that had lasting effects on landownership in Brazil. The crown awarded many land grants, often with little knowledge of what lands were legally occupied and whether they were actually productive. Authorities frequently duplicated grants, causing violent conflicts between people claiming rights to the same lands (120). The impact of the sesmaria system will become more important as we move into the land conflicts involved in the quilombo process of Grande Paraguaçu. Most of the land in the Recôncavo was privately owned. Due in part to protections from the Law of Sesmarias, sugar mills were maintained within the same families through inheritance (Schwartz 1985, 96). It was not uncommon for an heir of a deceased owner to temporarily administer his engenho or for planters to claim multiple ownerships (96).

Strategically located on the Atlantic coast, the Bahian Recôncavo was the nucleus of the sugar economy, contributing significantly to the economic growth of the colony. Cachoeira became the second wealthiest and most important city, after Salvador, to the economic success of Bahia for more than three centuries (Schwartz 1985, 81). Remnants of the hundreds of engenhos, *senzalas* (slave quarters), and churches that defined the colonial period are still a visual part of the landscape of the Recôncavo. The major economic success of the Recôncavo, like the rest of Brazil, is due to the forced labor of enslaved blacks. Stuart Schwartz indicates that more than half of the population of the Recôncavo was made up of enslaved blacks in the early part of the eighteenth century: "The proportion of slaves in the Recôncavo exceeded 60 percent of the captaincy, and in parishes like Matoim, Santiago do Iguape, and Santo Amaro da Purificação slaves were more than 70 percent of the residents" (1985, 87).

In 1563, Santiago do Iguape had an estimated 792 free men and women and 2,212 slaves (88). While the Recôncavo is known for its large landed elites, engenho families that owned large stretches of agricultural lands in the region, blacks made up a significant part of the social life and landscape. They worked the sugarcane fields, fished, learned the forests, and developed their own social and cultural life alongside the white elites.

In the early eighteenth century a letter sent by the Câmara da Vila de Nossa Senhora do Rosário do Porto de Cachoeira, a governing council of the city, announced the existence of a quilombo in the fields of Cachoeira. The letter was given to the governor of Bahia, Dom Rodrigo da Costa, who ordered the immediate destruction of the quilombo (Pedreira 1973). Slave escapes and rebellions were common in the area and instilled panic among the *senhores de engenhos* (plantation owners) and other authorities of the crown. The fear of fugitive slaves prompted severe punishments for those who were captured. Paradoxically, as the punishments worsened, so too did the incidence of quilombos and rebellious slaves (Schwartz 1985). Goulart, Cysneiros, and Ferreira Reis describe this tendency in the growth of black resistance: "Throughout the seventeenth century, the union of fugitive blacks in regimes of *mocambos* [or quilombos] multiplied and spread throughout the exuberant forest of the area" (1972, 259).

The proximity of the capital also intensified the insurgency of fugitive slaves in the Recôncavo. Hausas and Nagôs, as Yorubas were called in Bahia, from the engenhos of the Recôncavo fled into the Atlantic forest and waited there for blacks from the capital (ibid.). The significant concentration of slaves in the Recôncavo made the region highly susceptible to rebellions (Albuquerque and Fraga Filho 2006). Slave resistance in the Bahian Recôncavo was neither isolated nor episodic but rather was systematic and even organized with blacks in the city of Salvador. João Reis (1988) argues extensively in his lifetime research on slave rebellions that fugitive slaves maintained complex relations among various members of society, a survival strategy that provided quilombos with security and power.

The large numbers of enslaved blacks in the Recôncavo, particularly Yoruba and Fon/Ewe from West Africa (Wimberly 1998), influenced the cultural life of the region. By the time of abolition, the majority of slaves in the Recôncavo had been freed, and the African-born population began to decline significantly. Still, the large sugar plantations of the region took advantage of the limited opportunities for blacks in the labor market and maintained their captive labor for many years to follow. After abolition quilombolas maintained their quest to live autonomous lives, and many remained on the lands occupied by their ancestors, often finding refuge in the *terreiros de candomblé* (candomblé houses) that had multiplied throughout the region. Candomblé houses provided more than just spiritual support for blacks; they also provided social services, refuge, and community (ibid., 78). The candomblé of the region combined the practices and deities of various African cultures and thus attracted many devotees. Ceremonies persisted and grew regardless of the police persecution that endangered the lives of those practicing candomblé during and after abolition (79). Blacks had to develop strategies for practicing candomblé safely. One of these means was to include Catholic elements in ceremonies so as to distract the attention of authorities. These included decorating terreiros with images of saints and disguising the names of African deities with the names of Catholic saints. Although these practices began as a form of survival and resistance, they later led to the syncretism of the two religions that came to define the face of much of the Bahian candomblé of the following centuries.

Carneiro contends (1991) that Bantus from present-day Angola, Namibia, Zambia, Zimbabwe, Mozambique, and Congo introduced capoeira and samba to the Bahian Recôncavo. Now a popular martial art, capoeira was as much a pastime as it was a form of defense for blacks in the colonial period. Much of the repression that blacks experienced for practicing capoeira, even after abolition, diminished as the practice was assimilated into Brazilian high culture. In 1973, Mestre Bimba described the earlier repression:

> The police pursued *capoeiristas* like they hunted rabid dogs. Believe it or not, the punishment that they inflicted on two capoeiristas who were arrested while fighting was to tie one wrist to the tail of one horse and the other to a second horse parallel to the first. The two horses were then let go and made to gallop to the police station. (In Teles dos Santos 1998, 125)

Presently what are called Angolan capoeira and regional capoeira make up a significant part of the culture of the Recôncavo; the regional form of capoeira developed in the mid-twentieth century and combines other cultural influences such as Eastern martial arts. Like terreiros de candomblé, capoeira groups served the important role of providing community, refuge, and cultural survival. In the process of teaching capoeira, *mestres*, or masters, perpetuated the use of African instruments and songs, contributing to the survival of African and especially Angolan culture. At the end of the seventeenth century, when Brazil emerged as the world's largest sugar producer, 90 percent of slave importations came from Central Africa, largely from the port of Luanda (Sweet 2003, 16). Sweet points out that it seems to have been at this time that Angola became the primary referent for Africa in Brazil, leading to the common expression "Whoever says sugar says Brazil and whoever says Brazil says Angola" (ibid.). Although Angolans were not the only Africans taken to Brazil, the importance of Angola as a symbolic point of origin and cultural ancestry remains a major part of black identity, especially quilombola identity, in Brazil.

There is a strong belief that quilombos grew and gained support from candomblé houses, capoeira groups, and samba groups; *samba de roda* is a more traditional form of samba practiced primarily but not exclusively in candomblé ceremonies. These cultural forms are among the many forms of resistance that enslaved Africans demonstrated during the colonial period. While the lived reality of quilombos is only approximated through documents written by colonists who feared and sought to destroy them, historians argue that the predominance of slaves and fugitive slaves in the Recôncavo helped to shape the social, religious, family, dietary, and musical life of the region (Reis and Gomes 1996).

In Bahian history, the Recôncavo stands out as a historical center of sugar and tobacco production as well as a site of Afro-Brazilian cultural patrimony, as Schwartz has noted: "The Recôncavo gave Salvador its economic life, it stimulated the settlement and development of the Sertão, and its planters dominated the political and social life of the captaincy throughout its history. To say 'Bahia' was to say 'the Recôncavo,' and the Recôncavo was always *engenhos*, sugar, and slaves" (1985, 97).

It is important to the dominant historical narrative to emphasize that where there were sugar mills, there were slaves. And where there were slaves, there was also resistance (Reis and Gomes 1996). But if this history of slavery and resistance in the Recôncavo does not belong to the quilombolas of Grande Paraguaçu, as the *Jornal Nacional* unabashedly claimed on primetime television, then to whom does it belong? How is it that a major broadcast network is empowered to walk into a black community in a region whose history is defined in large part by slavery and resistance and proclaim that residents do not have slave and quilombo ancestors?

REMEMBERING QUILOMBOS

Historians and anthropologists have written extensively about African origins, religious, linguistic, culinary, and kinship survivals in colonial Brazil. However, no body of research provides a stronger example of these affirmations than resistance and quilombo studies. In the twentieth century, "resistance" became a way of starting to think about enslaved Africans as agents and participants in society. In the beginning of the century, however, resistance was primarily summed up as violent rebellions. Quilombos were described as battle sites and slaves as romantic and tragic heroes in an unfolding moral quest to reconstruct Africa in Brazil. The militant focus of resistance history was in part a consequence of the documents used to remember quilombos. These were primarily the books, journals, and travelogs of military men focused on recapturing fugitive slaves (Price 1996, 53). However, I argue that the romantic narrative of quilombo history also came from a twentieth-century desire to fit the characters of black history within a larger national narrative of a Brazilian multiethnic society.

It may seem contradictory that I would critique a resistance narrative that was formed to counter a dominant history of slave owners and colonists (R. Anderson 1996, 546).[4] I want to be clear that I think quilombo history is important to the overall story of Brazilian history and identity and particularly black identity. However, the government has created a series of policies that use quilombo history and ancestry to determine cultural recognition and the distribution of land rights for modern black communities. In order to understand the pressures of authenticity and proof that these communities experience, we must first understand (and interrogate) the dominant historical narratives of truth to which they are compared and held accountable.

THE PALMARES EFFECT

In 1692, the Conselho Ultramarino established what became the most popularly remembered definition of *quilombo*:[5] "any habitation of five or more black fugitives residing on land that was uninhabited and uncultivated" (Schmitt et al. 2002). This definition reflected the crown's attitude toward these groups not as communities but as fugitives and criminals of the state—"threat[s] to the Portuguese plantation" (Kent 1996, 172). But quilombos have been imagined beyond the limited view of the Conselho Ultramarino. For the twentieth-century historian, quilombos were the closest idea to reconstituting "African societies in a new environment and against consistently heavier odds" (ibid.). Historians have even highlighted linguistic connections between the Brazilian terms *quilombo* and *mocambo* and the West African Bantu term *ki-lombo*, meaning war camp (Gomes 2005, 11), and the Ambundu term *mu-kambo*, or hideout (Kent

1996, 174; Munanga 1996). Often the term *mocambo* is used interchange-
ably with *quilombo*, especially in Bahia (Gomes 2005, 10). While *mocambo*
and *quilombo* have different meanings throughout Africa, in Brazil these
terms were used consistently in connection to fugitive slave communities
(ibid.).

One particular quilombo, Palmares, took center stage in Brazilian history for its size and duration. The heroic memory of Palmares was constructed primarily from the 1930s into the 1970s, when intellectuals like
Arthur Ramos (1939/1980), Edison Carneiro (1966), Clóvis Moura (1959),
Décio Freitas (1973), and Raimundo Nina Rodrigues and Homero Pires
(1932) wrote elaborately about Palmares as a unique symbol of black militancy and African cultural survival, a conglomerate of intricately organized mocambos in the states of Alagoas and Pernambuco that were in
constant battle with both the Portuguese and Dutch crowns.

Palmares became the most important example of African resistance
in the history of Brazil (Funari 1996). But before twentieth-century scholars reimagined Palmares as an African heroic narrative, it was a source of
considerable anguish for the Brazilian colony. Sebastião da Rocha Pita, a
plantation owner in Bahia, wrote about the great mocambo in 1724 in a
collection of ten books titled *História da América portuguesa* (Lara 1996).
The sections where Palmares is discussed focus on announcing to the public the menacing "condition and principles of those enemies," the laws by
which they lived, and the damage they caused the colony (81). Da Rocha
Pita highlighted the "glorious" and "useful" outcome of the war that was
waged on the "negros dos Palmares" (ibid.). In her analysis of Da Rocha
Pita's writings, Lara (1996) highlights the rhetoric used to describe Palmares, noting that quilombos were commonly described in terms of how
destructive and threatening they were to the colony.

Following the writings of the Brazilian anthropologist and eugenicist
Nina Rodrigues, R. K. Kent contended that if Palmares had not been destroyed, the Portuguese may have been faced with "a number of independent African states dominating the backlands of 18th century Brazil" (Kent
1996, 187). Here his tone is cryptic, emphasizing the terror and chaos this
would have created in the historical order of things. Reinforcing the sentiment of fear surrounding quilombos in the colony, Kent writes, colonists complained that Palmarinos raided nearby villages, "kidnapping
and raping white women" (182). Thus quilombos, especially Palmares, in
the seventeenth century were not heroic symbols of resistance but rather
threatening spaces of insubordination that needed to be destroyed. In fact,
destroying quilombos and recapturing fugitive slaves was the primary re-

sponsibility of the *capitães do mato*, the bounty hunters of the forest (Mott 1996).

While much of what has been written on Palmares focuses on its grandeur and militancy, historians actually know very little of the day-to-day life of Palmares. The story that often gets repeated is that Palmares was a fully functioning community; it has even been described as a republic (A. Nascimento 1980, Funari 1996, Schwartz 1996b), a state (Kent 1996), and a nation (Funari 2003) with its own economy or system of trade, sociocultural guidelines and norms, and military. Palmares is said to have had a population of anywhere from ten thousand to twenty thousand escaped slaves, Indians, and poor whites, including former Portuguese soldiers, who lived in the nine villages that made up Palmares (Funari 2003, 84; Schwartz 1996). The main chief of Palmares was Ganga Zumba. Zumbi was Ganga Zumba's nephew and the last leader of Palmares (Lara 2010). Although documents recognize the diverse residents of Palmares, Lara notes that most historical texts agree that all of the blacks of Palmares were people from Central Africa, mostly from Angola (9). Palmares was to some extent maintained by its fame, but its popularity ultimately led to its defeat.

Funari has described Palmares as the most threatening and threatened quilombo of the seventeenth century (1996, 26–51). In 1685 the governor of Pernambuco hired the *bandeirante* (roughly, bounty hunter) Domingos Jorge Velho to destroy Palmares and to capture Zumbi. In 1694, after forty-two days of siege, Macaco, the capital of Palmares was defeated and hundreds of quilombolas were killed. Zumbi fled, only to be captured and beheaded a year later (32); his head was displayed in public as a reminder that "slaves should obey the slave system and not defy it" (34).

Palmares and its leaders Zumbi and Ganga Zumba were immortalized in historical texts. They became the cultural agents that Africanists have used to reimagine quilombos as true African societies in Brazil (Reis and Gomes 1996, 11). We might consider, for instance, the way Arthur Ramos introduces Palmares in his classic 1939 work, *The Negro in Brazil*:

> Palmares was the first great epic of the Negro in Brazil. This was no mere
> quilombo like so many others, which had been set up by fugitive slaves
> more or less sporadically. Palmares has become the great case in point
> of the effort of the Negro in Brazil to organize a state. It was a nation
> in itself, permeated with African traditions, created within the larger
> structure of Brazil. It was, moreover, a desperate reaction to the cul-
> tural collapse which the Negro was experiencing under the slave hold-

ing regime. . . . This extraordinary experiment in communal life endured . . . for over half a century. . . . The whole venture was so utterly
incredible that even to the present day its story is enmeshed in legend.
(1939/1980, 42)

Ramos' introductory paragraph is representative of the language that
most scholars were using to describe Palmares at the time. Adjectives such
as "epic," "great," "extraordinary," and "incredible" emphasized the distinction between Palmares and what Ramos called more "sporadic" quilombos. Ramos creates an image of Palmares as something that was such
an "extraordinary experiment" that it had to collapse and probably could
never exist again. In his description of archetypes, Northrop Frye (1957)
outlines romantic and tragic quest myths. In each there is a hero who is
on some quest to restore or establish a greater good. But the fate of the
hero depends on the mythos or the narrative structure of the quest myth.
Arthur Ramos' text on Palmares seems to come straight out of these arche-
typical structures. He describes Palmares as a romantic venture in which
the black hero is desperately fighting to restore his cultural life, to right a
wrong that has been dealt by an unjust slave system, but in the end the hero
fails. As in all tragedies, the hero must fail, even if his quest was honorable.
Society continues as it was and is not redeemed. The hero is immortalized
as a symbol of hope (Frye 1957, 215). Abdias do Nascimento has made this
heroic tragedy much more literal: "The feats of that cluster of *quilombos*
(military communities) called Palmares were heroic to the point of min-
gling with legend, and catapulted the republic into history as the Black
Troy" (1980, 42).

Throughout much of the twentieth century, focus on Palmares over-
shadowed writing on other forms of slave resistance and created an image
of resistance as exclusively large-scale and militant (Lara 2010). The authors imagined Palmares not only as a militant society but also as an "isolated and isolationist" one where fugitive slaves wanted to "recreate a pure
Africa in the Americas . . . alternative societies where everyone was free and
the same, as would have been the case in Africa, a considerably romantic
Africa" (Reis and Gomes 1996, 11).

Brazilian historian Sílvia Lara shows that for nearly a hundred years,
Brazilian historiography reproduced the image of quilombos as isolated
camps, politically and socially removed even from the "world of slavery"
such that fugitive slaves only came in contact with the world outside of the
quilombo if it was in battle or if they were recaptured (2010, 1). Less visibility was given the numerous and more widespread forms of resistance

that took place daily in the farms, sugar mills, and big houses throughout Brazil. For nearly the entire twentieth century, then, quilombo history was one of heroes and battles that said little about the everyday lives of ordinary individuals, not to mention women and families.

Since the 1990s, however, historians have been more concerned with the everyday lives of escaped slaves, the ways they interacted with enslaved Africans, indigenous people, and other groups as well as their "conditions of survival and political organization" (2). A central purpose of this new historiography is the understanding of the enslaved subject as a member of the slave-holding society, a person who did more than just engage in violent battle but also formed relationships and learned to negotiate within this social structure to survive. The historiography is now clear that quilombos were not isolated war camps hidden in the forest (Reis 1988). In many cases, these communities lived near urban centers and engaged in commerce with nearby plantations and even indigenous communities (Slenes 2010, 112). Brazilian historians have been working to balance the extraordinary memory of Palmares with other forms of resistance, but that has not been easy.

It is this historiography of quilombos and all of its complexities, with agreements and disagreements between scholars, that rural black communities now find themselves having to connect with their real and immediate needs for land and security. Although scholars have been working since the end of the twentieth century to rethink the role of quilombos in Brazilian history, the discourse that prevails in social and political imaginaries continues to be the one of quilombos as extraordinary African enclaves isolated in the middle of the forest and existing only in a distant past. The accusation of Grande Paraguaçu as a fraud was premised on this extant imaginary.

FROM HISTORICAL REFERENCE TO CULTURAL SYMBOL

Palmares was also cemented as a primary symbol of black resistance within social and political realms. Abolitionists in the late nineteenth century already used the idea of the *quilombo* to talk about a range of racial inequalities in land distribution, labor, and education (I. Leite 2012, 253). Following abolition, Palmares and its leaders Ganga Zumba and Zumbi quickly became symbols of "political militancy" (Gomes 2005, 33). Decades later, in the 1930s, the Brazilian Black Front (Frente Negra Brasileira) employed the concept of *quilombismo* as a way of denouncing a national whitening ideology (*branqueamento*) that developed out of eugenicist ideas of black inferiority (I. Leite 2012, 254).[6] In the 1970s the new Unified Black Movement (Movimento Negro Unificado) would take the concept even further and make quilombismo official in a 1978 manifesto that created Black Consciousness Day. The text reveals much about the symbolic importance of the quilombo:

> We, Brazilian Blacks, proud of descending from Zumbi, leader of the Black Republic of Palmares, . . . come together after 283 years, to declare to the Brazilian people our true and effective date: November 20, National Black Consciousness Day! The day of the death of the great Black national leader Zumbi, responsible for the first and only Brazilian attempt to create a democratic society, free, in which all people—Blacks, Indians, and Whites—achieved a great political, economic, and social advance. An attempt which was always present in all quilombos. (In A. Nascimento 1980, 153)

In this statement, Unified Black Movement leaders officially connected quilombo history to postabolition Afro-Brazilian struggles. Palmares became the historical-social object of black consciousness and Afro-Brazilian historical memory—and a real way of making claims to citizenship and a place in Brazilian society past and present.

In 1980, the black activist, scholar, and politician Abdias do Nascimento further developed the idea of quilombismo in an article titled "Quilombismo: An Afro-Brazilian Political Alternative," one of the only writings calling for a separate black nation in Brazil as a response to the violent injustices that blacks suffered throughout history. The paper opens with a demand that "the Brazilian black people . . . win back their memory" of more than just slavery (142–144), a memory that reaches as far back as black Egyptian ancestors:

> In my country, the ruling class always, and particularly after the so-called abolition of slavery (1888), has developed and refined myriad techniques of preventing Black Brazilians from being able to identify and actively assume their ethnic, historical and cultural roots, thus cutting them off from the trunk of their African family tree. (141–142)

Nascimento contended that a history of domination and violence created African resistance and cultural affirmation in the form of quilombos. For him, quilombos were African enclaves in Brazil, but they were also powerful symbols of resistance to racial oppression. Nascimento emphasized that the quilombo, past and present, represented the black Brazilian's refusal to be enslaved—no matter whether the "master" carried a whip or idealistic views of racial democracy. Therefore, according to Nascimento, since blacks continue to live in a situation of violent oppression, "at the margins of employment," and within an "imposed residential, racial segregation" (150), a *quilombist* ideology is relevant and urgent. Nascimento coined the term *quilombismo* to emphasize a necessary reaction to a history of black oppression that would only continue if left unquestioned. Thus, *quilombismo* is an "ethnic and cultural affirmation" of a history of resistance, a memory robbed, as well as political empowerment and strategic insubordination—Nascimento called this a point where the "'illegal' and 'legalized' form a unity" (152). Here he gives us a glimpse into the future by asserting that the term *quilombo*, once a criminalized and persecuted organization, would become a social and political mechanism of mobilization and demand for rights.

Nascimento helped redefine the quilombo in the language of black militancy during a historical moment of political repression and dictatorship when any suggestion of a Brazilian racist state was violently silenced (Marx 1998). Abdias do Nascimento later became a member of the National Constituent Assembly that drafted the 1988 constitution (I. Leite 2012, 254); he was essential in writing the quilombo descendant into the constitution as a way of including Afro-Brazilians in the new distribution of social, cultural, and political rights. A tireless activist in the twentieth century, Nascimento planted the seed for a twenty-first-century quilombola movement, setting quilombola land rights in the pages of the constitution so that black communities would rise up to defend and demand those rights. The terminology has changed from *quilombismo* to *quilombolismo* to emphasize the newly defined *quilombola* identity that black communities who identify as the descendants of quilombos have taken up as their own, but the quilombola movement continues to use the language of quilombismo and black justice as first written by Abdias do Nascimento.

While the literary and social narratives of Palmares are important to the recognition of a black history of resistance and culture, these narratives are also attached to the misleading ideas that quilombos were isolated and isolationist, pure ethnic societies. This idea of quilombos is unsupported by historical writings since the 1990s, but it also allows for the misrecognition of quilombola communities as modern versions of Palmares. Quilombos were as much a part of society in the seventeenth and eighteenth centuries as their descendants are today. Moreover, quilombo descendants identify with a range of black ancestors who are not limited to the leaders of quilombos. When Nascimento wrote his 1980 essay "Quilombismo" he wanted to create a new Afro-Brazilian praxis, a way of describing and enacting black history and black experience in Brazil. At the same time, he seemed to anticipate the difficulty of this new praxis when he wrote that black historical memory had been "systematically assaulted by Brazilian Western-inspired structures of domination for almost 500 years" (141), making it very difficult for blacks to reclaim this history as their own.

The story of Palmares was brought to life for the masses in Carlos Diegues' 1986 film *Quilombo*. Diegues reproduced the utopic mythos of Palmares (Price 2003, 216), but more importantly he gave the heroic leaders of Palmares a more contemporary form. Diegues brought to life the sense of a black struggle for freedom and justice with which a society beginning to recover from twenty years of authoritarian rule and repression could identify.[7] In 1996 Zumbi became more than just a reference for the black movement. Zumbi was officially deemed a national hero and his name was included in the *Livro dos heróis da pátria* (Book of Heroes of the Fatherland) in Brasília (Lara 2010, 3). But one year before Zumbi was deemed a national hero, President Fernando Henrique Cardoso addressed the country and called for the interpretation of Palmares as a multiethnic state that struggled for freedom and thus served as a model for a democratic Brazil (Funari 2003). Cardoso's statement brings this discussion of dominant historical ideologies full circle, signaling the appropriation of Afro-Brazilian history and black resistance within a national narrative of racial democracy and one mestiço identity.

It is evident in the prevailing national memory of quilombos and Palmares that the heroic illustration of African resistance is valuable to the Brazilian national identity, as is the image of the noble Indian (Alcida Ramos 1991), but only when framed in support of a unified racial democracy. This becomes clear in the attempt to reimagine Zumbi as the leader of a multiethic society and in the constant reproduction of Palmares as a noble yet tragic attempt to form a separate African society. An example is a statement Funari cites from an interview with the Brazilian historian Evaldo Cabral de Melo: "Palmares was destroyed and I prefer that it was so. It was a black polity and if it had survived, we would have in Brazil a Bantustan" (2003, 88).

The lesson of Palmares is that it was a utopia, a cultural experiment, in Arthur Ramos' words, but is no longer a reality. For the mestiço nation it is more valuable that Palmares be remembered as an ethnic democracy rather than an independent black state. But decades of historical and political discourse describing Palmares as an African enclave and symbol of black resistance in Brazil cannot simply be erased. After years of archeological research on the land sites of Palmares, Pedro Funari found (1996) that the social and emotional significance of Palmares was just as great as the archaeological objects found, if not more so. He argues that research on Palmares cannot ignore

> the difficulty of interpreting the material culture of the quilombo and its appropriation by social groups. The issue of the negritude of Palmares is a passionate one, and as we study quilombos, we are dealing first and foremost with the symbolism of the mocambo. . . . "Land of Heroes" . . . is a common expression used to describe Palmares. But digging for heroes is a particularly difficult task. (47)

The adoption of a romantic and tragic memory of Palmares within the discourse of the national identity is not a unique story. In fact, it came several decades after the appropriation of the "noble Indian" as the official ancestor of the Brazilian modern state (Alcida Ramos 1998). During the height of the whitening ideology's prominence, indigenous peoples, unlike blacks, were included as part of the national imaginary. In the early twentieth century, intellectuals were consumed by a romantic nostalgia for indigenous ancestors. *Indigenismo* in Brazil held that "the Indian should be considered the supreme symbol of national identity" (Peirano 1981, 19). Indigenous peoples were featured in literary and art works as ancestral relics, noble savages, and warriors belonging to a romantic past from which modern Brazil developed. These ideals were most notably illustrated in works such as José de Alencar's famous novels *O guaraní* (1857) and *Iracema* (1865). The Indian provided an idealized image of a heroic and complex culture, an archetype for a nation trying to assert its own identity apart from Europe (Peirano 1981; Alcida Ramos 1991).

However, the idealization of the Indian as a heroic ancestor also depended on the tragedy of his demise. The noble Indian, in the imagination of the state, was a dead Indian (Schwarcz 2006)—a self-sacrificing, warrior who bravely resisted but, like Zumbi, failed and perished in the modern state. Building from a lifetime of research on indigenous communities, Alcida Ramos writes, "We should not . . . underestimate exoticism; it is a powerful rhetorical tool which can be put into action at politically crucial times" (1991, 158). While the Indian was imagined as a romantic symbol of the nation, she contends, living indigenous communities still face forced marginalization and precarious living conditions, their lands systematically occupied by a paternalistic and exploitative state. What is more, just because the nation benefited from a romantic narrative of a primitive and passive "Indian" does not mean that indigenous communities embraced this identity and form of inclusion within the national imaginary (Hale 1994, Alcida Ramos 1991).

Like indigenous communities, rural black communities are fighting for the right to reclaim quilombo history in their own words, memories, and lived experiences. The discourse of the heroic, isolationist quilombo is complex. Although institutions like the *Jornal Nacional* can employ this dominant narrative to discredit black communities in a powerful use of the exotic, the narrative also provides a language of struggle and pursuit of justice around which communities can rally.

The *Jornal Nacional* changed the lives of the quilombolas of Grande Paraguaçu by propelling them into a fight for authenticity. The report publicly accused the community of fraud, questioned the legitimacy of their cultural recognition, and dismantled the oral histories of its residents. Although not a legal entity, the media used a dominant discourse of historical truth to interrupt the legal process of land acquisition for Grande Paraguaçu. The *Jornal Nacional* was able to publicly label the quilombolas there as perpetrating fraud because of a dominant narrative of quilombo history that is supported by twentieth-century historical writings. This narrative imagines the quilombo as a symbol and heroic experiment that was both romantic and (necessarily) tragic.

The impact of what I call the "Palmares effect" on resistance history is that it has led to the assumption that all blacks who resisted slavery were rebels bent on destroying modern European society in the fight to re-create an African one. While heroic narratives of resistance serve an important social and cultural function of broadening the experiences of blacks in the colonial era, these narratives become difficult and even detrimental when applied to contemporary public policies. Thus it is important to restate that I am not interrogating the validity of black heroes and grand legends. Rather, I believe it is important to look carefully at the impacts these historical imaginaries have on the rights acquisition process of living communities. Like Menchú, some black Brazilians are attempting to speak to their own historical memory. They are using the memory of the quilombo, but their stories are not the same. Still, their narratives of everyday life are no less authentic than the stories documented by historians. While the conflicts and struggles faced by quilombo descendants are due in part to the contentious historical memory of colonial-era quilombos, this is not the only issue. The "quilombo descendant" is, after all, a political category immersed in a Brazilian history of national identity formation and racial exclusion. Understanding the significance of a quilombo descendent cultural and racial identification also requires understanding the history of racism and black identity in Brazil.

TWO

Black Identities

CONCEIVING BLACKNESS AND

QUILOMBOLISMO

I met with Valmiro Silva in a cold, dim office behind the famous Igreja do Carmo of Salvador. The church sits quietly in the middle of Pelourinho, a historic neighborhood and tourist trap in the upper city (*cidade alta*) of Salvador. When Valmiro told me to meet him there, I warily agreed. I usually avoided tourist traps, and I always felt Pelourinho was one of the most intense. Tourists flocked into Pelourinho by the hundreds every day. They photographed everything from food stands to elaborately dressed *baianas* and strategically centered capoeiristas. Few of them knew of the darker history of Pelourinho. Its very name means "pillory," the whipping post that was installed in the middle of the neighborhood during the colonial period. Slaves were tied and publicly whipped in Pelourinho to serve as examples to any black person who thought about disobeying the system. The very ground that tourists walked, with their newly purchased Havaiana flip-flops, is popularly known as Cabeça de Negro (Black Man's Head) because the sporadically placed rocks that make up the winding streets of Pelourinho are said to look like the heads of black people. Meeting Valmiro to discuss the meaning of "quilombo descendant" in a place that itself carries multiple significations reminded me of the complexity of thinking about blackness and racial injustice in Bahia—a place imagined as the black mecca of Brazil for its predominantly black population and rich Afro-Brazilian culture.

Valmiro had been a black-movement activist for most of his life; he was also a sociologist and professor working on completing his doctorate at the time we met. Sitting at a small metal desk in the middle of the room, Valmiro leaned forward with a serious glare. We had been talking for nearly an hour about his past research with Rio das Rãs, the first legally recognized quilombola community in Bahia, when I asked Valmiro what he thought about the term "quilombo descendant." By the time I spoke with Valmiro, I had already interviewed several people working in different government organizations and NGOs involved with quilombolas. The more I thought about their narratives, the more blurred the term became. Each individual offered his or her own interpretation of "quilombo descendant," but all seemed to converge on a few common ideas: African resistance, Palmares, and reclaiming a black history forgotten or erased. Valmiro's response was not different:

> History books only want to teach that blacks were slaves but ignore everything else we were and accomplished. We also resisted slavery and formed thriving communities like Palmares. The term *quilombo* remembers Palmares and a history of resistance, which is why it cannot just be replaced by another term like *negro*.

Valmiro used the example of *negro* because I asked him if he thought "quilombo descendent" created confusion, as it seemed to be defined in the same way as other terms for black identity. For example, terms such as "Afro-Brazilian" and *negro* were also often used politically within a discourse of African cultural resistance and memory. In a 2004 interview, the journal *Estudos Avançados* asked the Brazilian anthropologist Kabengele Munanga the question "Who is *negro* in Brazil?" Munanga responded:

> It seems like it would be simple to define who is black in Brazil. But in a country that developed a desire for whitening, it is not easy to define who is black and who isn't. . . . The concepts of *negro* and *branco* have an ethno-semantic, political, and ideological foundation, but not a biological content. Politically, those working in organized black movements qualify as black anyone with this appearance. It is a political qualification that approaches the North American definition. (52)

By comparing the political use of the term *negro* (which he interchanges with *afro-descendente*) to the use of "black" or "African American" in the United States, Munanga highlights primarily the ways in which blacks have imbued these terms with notions of black cultural and racial affirmation and political resistance. Also, by stating that the concepts of *negro* and *branco* do not have a "biological content," Munanga is not denying the physical indicators of blackness or whiteness—that black bodies that are historically, socially, and politically marked as such exist. Continuing his response, Munanga explains that defining blackness in Brazil is only problematic when it comes to discussing affirmative action policies. This seems to be when the rhetoric is such that everyone has African ancestors and anyone can identify with that ancestry as a way of demanding rights—and "regardless of how light the person's skin color might be, no one can come and deny that" (52). But irrespective of this presumed fluidity in black identity, Munanga argues (2001) that national statistics do not leave any doubt of the gravity of the situation of black exclusion at all levels of society, most of all in education and economic attainment; this is where blacks are massively overrepresented among those living in poverty and underrepresented among those in higher education.

Approaching Valmiro with a question about the difference between the terms *quilombola* and *negro* was important because these terms are in fact not very different, socially or ideologically—that is, the same people who will identify as *quilombola* as a political affirmation will also identify as *negro*. However, these two terms do carry distinct legal positioning. Following Valmiro's response, I asked, "So, theoretically anyone who identifies as *negro* can also identify as a *quilombola*?" Sitting back in his chair with a deep sigh Valmiro responded:

> Yes, we can pass through a moment where everyone wants to identify as *quilombola*, just like we can pass through one where the term is forgotten and replaced with another. In the meantime, we use it because it is already in the language of the constitution.

Although Valmiro seemed a bit annoyed by my last question, his response highlighted the fundamental value of the term "quilombo descendant"—its presence in the constitution. Earlier in the month I had interviewed Carlos Marinho, a lawyer from the Association of Lawyers for Rural Workers (AATR). Answering the same question I asked Valmiro, Carlos explained the power of a constitutional article. He said that no matter how confusing or broad the article for quilombo rights in the constitution, the importance was that it was in there. Developing a legal process of rights distribution based on an extant constitutional foundation was easier than creating one out of thin air, according to Carlos. While I agreed with Valmiro that we could not take lightly the particular value of identifying as "quilombo descendant" versus *negro* or *afro-brasileiro*, I did not think that the term was as flexible as he made it seem. I sensed that Valmiro was mostly reacting to my question as an intellectual problem—a problem of social categories that are continuously reimagined. As any good anthropologist would, I understood Valmiro's message, but I still was not convinced.

Like Munanga, I maintain a critical ear toward a narrative of flexibility or fluidity when discussing blackness, especially in the context of the quilombo-descendant identity. The concept of quilombo descendant seemed flexible and open in its interpretation, but having previously interviewed the director of the Palmares Cultural Foundation, I knew that it was not flexible in its application. After all, there are bureaucratic procedures and "experts" in place for the legal identification of quilombolas. Just because anyone can self-identify as a quilombo descendant does not mean the government will grant rights to everyone who does so—but why not? Before we can understand how black lives are delegitimated in their demand for rights and justice, we must first understand how black identity has been conceptualized and imagined within the Brazilian state.

Black identity—as a political and intellectual imaginary—has been formed along with the development of the Brazilian modern nation, first through exclusion during a period of eugenics and whitening ideology, and then through integration and assimilation within a politics of racial democracy. Blackness came to be integrated within the national identity through a culturalist framework of African ancestry and inheritance that respected a dominant ideal of racial democracy in the mid-twentieth century.

Building from this analysis, the quilombo-descendant identity becomes a new category of blackness that fits within a discursively distinct culturalist framework that emphasizes the cultural recognition of difference in the late twentieth and early twenty-first centuries. Within this politics of cultural recognition, anthropologists become key experts who help establish the official boundaries and parameters that allow the government to identify the authentic and legitimate subjects of a quilombo-descendant identity; these parameters are primarily drawn along the lines of ancestry and traditional cultural practices. While blackness has been excluded and included within various intellectual conceptualizations of a national cultural identity, what has been consistently left out are the everyday experiences of racial exclusion and racial violence that blacks have lived throughout the history of the nation. By focusing on a multicultural politics of recognition for quilombo descendants, this new public policy specifically replaces a discourse of racial exclusion for one of ethnic and cultural identification, creating a rubric of authenticity that will be used not only to define quilombo descendants but also to exclude embodied experiences of blackness and racial injustice that do not fit within it.

THE "PROBLEM OF BLACKNESS" IN BRAZIL

*Abolition was a façade: juridical, theoretical, abstract. The
ex-slaves were driven to the brink of starvation; they found only
disease, unemployment, complete misery. Not only the elites, but all
of Brazilian society, closed the avenues through which blacks might
have survived; they shut off the possibility of a decent, dignified life
for the ex-slaves. They created a fabric of slogans about equality
and racial democracy that has served to assuage the bad national
conscience. Abroad it presents our country as a model of racial
coexistence; internally the myth is used to keep blacks tricked
and docile.*

(ABDIAS DO NASCIMENTO, "THE MYTH OF RACIAL DEMOCRACY"
IN LEVINE AND CROCITTI 1999, 379)

Abdias do Nascimento made this statement in a publication for the
progressive journal *Cadernos Brasileiros* on the eightieth anniversary of
abolition. In this piece against the myth of racial democracy, Nascimento
decried the complete absence of any systemic action taken after abolition to integrate the lives of blacks within Brazilian society as equal members and fellow human beings. The idea here is clear: abolition may have
legally freed blacks from bondage, but black existence is still confined by
a systemic oppression that is negated by a "fabric of slogans" about racial
equality. Nascimento's words are powerful and rightfully angry. Blackness has been imagined and treated as a social and national problem in
Brazil since abolition. Nascimento's reflection vividly highlights not only
that there is an important disconnect between dominant narratives of
equality and everyday, lived experiences of racism but more importantly
that dominant narratives have a real bearing on existence, especially when
it comes to the conceptualization of black lives throughout the history of
Brazil. In this way, a myth, a national story, of racial democracy can have
a real impact on black lives, keeping them, in Nascimento's words, tricked
and docile.

Although prior to abolition there were already many manumitted
and free-born blacks in Brazil, the "Golden Law" of abolition permanently changed the legal and social status of all blacks within the nation
(Schwarcz 1999). Slavery ended in part due to the abolitionist movement's
increasingly persuasive appeal to the elites that slavery damaged Brazil's
international image as a modern nation; European powers had abolished

slavery more than five decades earlier and had been pressuring Brazil to do the same (Viotti da Costa 2000). Still as Gomes da Cunha and Gomes observe, "In many cases, liberty did not mean the reversal of slavery. In others, the subjection to subordination and dehumanization that defined the experience of captivity was refashioned within new social relations of labor, hierarchy, and power" (2007, 11). While abolition did not by itself fully improve the quality of life of the former slave population in Brazil, it did signal the beginning of a new set of sociological questions about the impact of slavery on Brazilian society, economy, and culture. At first, the question of how to classify the new social and political status of former slaves and their descendants was a scientific and legal problem.

Before racial democracy became a dominant narrative, eugenics and racist science dictated social and political ideologies. Eugenics was a significant social movement in Brazil that had a profound impact on liberal political models and the construction of the modern nation-state (Viotti da Costa 2000; Schwarcz 1999). The late nineteenth century and early twentieth century was a time when scholars were working and writing to prove to the outside world that Brazil could be a modern nation despite its dark population (Caulfield 2003, Graham et al. 1990; Stepan 1991). Peirano describes this national self-consciousness as a struggle with European ideologies of race: "For the entire century following independence in 1822, the Brazilian self-image had to be asserted by opposing, struggling with, or accepting the European view of the country, a view which was predominantly negative" (1981, 18).

In the nineteenth century Brazilian intellectuals began experimenting with European eugenics, taking up Francis Galton's fundamental ideas about human capacity as a function of heredity. In particular, Brazilian scholars sought to understand how miscegenation, and the masses of black and indigenous Brazilians, led to the underdevelopment of the nation (Schwarcz 1999, 5). Among the most prominent eugenicists in Brazil were Renato Kehl, the father of the Brazilian eugenics movement (Caulfield 2003, 164), and Francisco de Oliveira Vianna, a juridical consultant and cabinet member of the Getúlio Vargas regime of the 1930s and 1940s. Vianna was central to the installation of immigration policies that would increase the entry of white Europeans and diminish that of all other races, most of all Africans and Asians (166). An earlier well-known eugenicist was Raimundo Nina Rodrigues, a psychologist, physician, and anthropologist. Nina Rodrigues' research influenced theories in medicine, anthropology, and history, particularly those emerging out of the Brazilian Northeast. Like his European contemporaries, Nina Rodrigues contended that miscegenation would eventually lead to a degenerate Brazilian race. He warned that the Brazilian identity would become predominantly black or mestiço, most of all in the northern regions, unless the nation interfered (Telles 2004, 26).

A student of the Italian criminologist Cesáre Lambroso, Nina Rodrigues vehemently advocated for separate criminal laws by race in his first book, *As raças humanas e a responsabilidade penal no Brasil* (The Human Races and Penal Responsibility in Brazil, 1894), and later that year in an international journal article titled "Negro Criminals in Brazil" (Correa 2005). The Nina Rodrigues School, an important medical group in the Bahia School of Medicine, became famous for correlating insanity, criminality, disease, and overall biological degradation with miscegenation, giving rise to "purification eugenics" in the 1920s (Schwarcz 1999, 235). It is important to note that one of the most insistent and prolific eugenicists in Brazil was an anthropologist producing knowledge in Bahia, a region with one of the largest black populations in the nation.

Faced with a multiracial society, eugenicist theories eventually had to be molded to fit the demographic reality of Brazil. The Brazilian population was defined by miscegenation, a fact that included much of the elite. For that reason, Brazilian scholars did not simply replicate European eugenics but rather molded their own racist model to fit the desired face of the Brazilian population—and to save their own identities from the degradation ascribed by Europe (Schwarcz 1999). Elites imagined that miscegenation would eventually pass through a process of whitening, or branqueamento, leading to a "healthy mixed population growing increasingly whiter both culturally and physically" (Peirano 1981, 20).

The concept of branqueamento, which gained popularity as early as 1912, helped to position the mestiço as a new national identity, one that would become whiter as black people were slowly eliminated from the reproduction of society. Peirano explains, "The optimistic conclusion was that the black population was becoming progressively less numerous in Brazil for several reasons, including a supposedly lower birthrate, higher incidence of disease, and the social disorganization of the black population" (ibid.). In a paper prepared for the First Universal Races Congress in London in 1912, João Batista Lacerda, the director of the Brazilian National Museum in Rio de Janeiro, predicted that "by the year 2012 the Negro population would be reduced to zero and the mulatto to only three percent of the total" (Stepan 1991, 155). Vianna reiterated Lacerda's prediction, claiming that over time "the mulatto strain would be filtered out and whites would develop a clear biological predominance over Negros and mestizos" (ibid.). São Paulo was probably the most aggressive state in its attempt to create a dominant white population, primarily through immigration, labor, and land policies that favored white Europeans (Weinstein 2003). Although São Paulo still has a large black population, it is also one of the most visibly racially divided states in the country (Andrews 1991). Bahia, like much of the Northeast, became known for its Afro-Brazilian population and culture despite eugenicist predictions of white predominance.

The theory of branqueamento spoke strongly to the influence of blackness on the Brazilian identity. The idea, or hope, was to eventually white out all black influence, "black genes" and black culture. As described earlier, indigenous peoples were also subject to racial discrimination during this period, primarily through a national romanticism that turned them into exotic symbols of the nation while simultaneously rendering them invisible as living communities. But blacks at that time were not included within the national imaginary or desired, even nostalgically, as part of the new Brazilian identity. Neither image was any less damaging. Brazilian romanticism reflected a desire for nativism that was never open enough to include the masses of blacks and mulattos (A. Guimarães 2001, 123). Blacks were seen as a social problem that needed to be fixed—or whitened. Over the course of three hundred years, blacks went from being property, excluded from humanity and citizenship, to becoming an undesired genetic, legal, and cultural problem.

It is important to emphasize the roots of eugenics and branqueamento in the formation of the mestiço identity and simultaneously in the degradation and attempted erasure of the black identity in order to fully understand the historical development of race thinking in Brazil and the people who were involved in producing this dominant mind-set. The whitening thesis is a reflection of the "race problem," and the problem of blackness, as imagined and perpetuated by the white elite in the early twentieth century; it illustrates the contradictory terrain in which racist theories and racial identities took root. While the whitening thesis led to a more favorable view of miscegenation, one that did not end in a degenerate race, it still depended on the idealization of whiteness and on the authority of the elites to control the face of a multiracial society—an authority that only grew stronger into the twentieth and twenty-first centuries.

Toward the end of the nineteenth century, there were also black intellectuals who were thinking and writing about the "race problem" but through the lens of the black experience in Brazil. Ana Flávia Magalhães Pinto's 2010 book on the nineteenth-century *imprensa negra* (black press) in Brazil is one of few publications that showcases black resistance as early as the nineteenth century, a period that has received little attention in the literature on black history and resistance. Pinto analyzes a sample of eight journals published in various Brazilian cities, such as *O Homem de Cor* (published in Rio de Janeiro in 1833) and *O Progresso—Orgão dos Homens de Cor* (published in São Paulo in 1899), to illustrate some of the earliest roots of black consciousness and social organization. Through the publication of these journals, black intellectuals joined together to speak out against racial injustice and to defend the talents and intellect of blacks beyond the pseudoscientific theories of race. For example, in *O Homem de Cor*, free blacks and *pardos* (brown, mixed-race) publicly denounced racial discrimination as early as 1833, fifty years before abolition, speaking to a growing discourse of democratic values of liberty for all and citizenship rights for blacks (Pinto 2010, 17).

Pinto demonstrates how black press journals denounced the racist rhetoric of newspapers during the height of whitening immigration policies; these newspapers portrayed blacks as primitive—the antithesis of a civilized and modern society. By defining blacks as stupid and barbaric, Pinto argues, whites maintained "possession over the insignia of civilization" (128). Blacks may have been legally free, however, they still did not have the liberty to define their own humanity. In *O Progresso*, black intellectuals responded to these images and to immigration policies, denouncing the "intolerance and prejudice dispensed toward blacks" and arguing that "immigration policies were just a pretext for the exclusion of blacks in the labor market" (ibid.). Pinto's research on black press publications reveals an important element missing in the history of racist ideologies in Brazil, that is, the ways black intellectuals witnessed and responded to the formation of a modern Brazilian nation that, not only left them out but also, taught citizens to believe that blacks were inherently unfit to be part of a civilized society. The activism of the *imprensa negra* ended in 1937 when Getúlio Vargas censored all political expression and shut down all political organizations (Butler 1998, 11). Still, it is important to recall the significance of black intellectuals during the nineteenth century; by working together to speak back to racist institutions, they helped pave the road for future black resistance.

THE CULTURE OF BLACKNESS IN BRAZIL

The mid-twentieth century was a time of transition for race thinking in Brazil. Anthropologist Mariza Peirano refers specifically to the 1930s as "a major ideology-producing period" (1981, 16). It was during this period that Brazilian intellectuals and politicians in search of modernity invented the idea of racial democracy, an image of Brazil as a utopic society where three ethnic groups, Portuguese, African, and indigenous, live and interact equally. While much of the creation of racial democracy has been attributed to Gilberto Freyre, throughout much of the twentieth century racial democracy was a matter of national policy, beginning with Vargas' Estado Novo of 1937–1945 and continuing through the military dictatorship of 1964–1985.

The First Republic of Brazil was overthrown by the Revolution of 1930, which placed Getúlio Vargas as the new leader. Although the Vargas regime is remembered as a somewhat paradoxical period of both progressive and regressive politics (Stepan 1991), it was clearly an anti-oligarchic, nationalistic, corporatist, and ethnically and morally homogenizing regime (Caulfield 2003, 166). During Vargas' Estado Novo, new social groups were incorporated into the state, particularly the urban, industrial working class and previously marginalized ethnic and racial groups. Florestan Fernandes recounts the sentiment of a white matron at the time who indignantly expressed how "Negroes' insolence had grown slowly and had become habitual and intolerable only after the enactment of Vargas' Labor Laws" (1969, 154). Vargas encouraged the study of Brazil's African and Indian heritage "as nationalist folklore" (Caulfield 2003, 166) while at the same time "encouraging whitening and repressing ethnic diversity through immigration and educational policies" (ibid.).

Stepan describes how new state apparatuses were designed to create a "homogenous consciousness of nationhood," "mobilize patriotism," and "level ethnic disparities" (1991, 164). Under the ideology of the time, explicit racist language and exclusion were to be avoided, especially after Brazil joined the Allied forces in the war against Nazi Germany in 1943. It seemed that although whitening was still the national goal, the mass numbers of African, Afro-descendant, and indigenous people in Brazil had to be reckoned with, even if just for the sake of the nation's international image. By the 1930s, the most widely accepted solution to Brazil's race problem was cultural miscegenation. The belief in the mestiço as an ideal and "cosmic race," to borrow Vasconcelos' classic term (1925/1997), became the dominant political ideology and intellectual fantasy.

As Vargas worked to nationalize Brazil through public policies, scholars and artists were completely reimagining the modern Brazilian identity through experimentation in literature, social science, music, and art.

Cultural cannibalism, or *antropofagia*, became a dominant concept in the Brazilian modernist movement. Modernists argued that the Brazilian identity needed to be reborn out of the absorption and transformation of cultures—in particular European cultures. Cannibalism as a metaphor highlighted the violence that came hand in hand with cultural assimilation (Bastos 2006, 102). Still, as Guimarães (2001) argues, it was uniformity, racial and ethnic, that was desired and politically mandated: "Anything else was repressed and feared" (124).

By the end of the nineteenth century, Nina Rodrigues reflected on the threat of a culturally divided country:

> "[Even] the most reckless and improvident Brazilian cannot fail to be impressed by the possibility of a future opposition, which can already be seen, between a white nation, strong and powerful, probably from a Teutonic origin, which is forming in the southern states, where climate and civilization will eliminate or overpower the Black Race; [and] on the other hand, the Northern states, [where] mestizos [are] vegetating in the sterile turbulence of a living intelligence, but associated with more determined inertia and laziness, discouragement and sometimes subservience, and thereby threatened to become submissive pasture to all noble holdings and small dictators. (In Guimarães 2001, 124)

Nina Rodrigues describes the perils of a future nation that is racially and regionally divided, and he reminds the nation that forming a uniform, white state is the only path to power and modernity.

Appearing during the formative 1930s, *Casa grande e senzala* (1933), published in English as *The Masters and the Slaves* (1956), gained immediate popularity among Brazilian intellectuals thirsty for a different narrative of the past. Its author, Gilberto Freyre, a student of Franz Boas, emphasized the cultural contributions of the "Indian" and the "Negro Slave" to the Brazilian identity. He was one of three important scholars who would help rewrite Brazilian history and the national identity in the twentieth century; the others were Sérgio Buarque de Holanda and Caio Prado Júnior. Freyre's main contribution was to reimagine the black subject from an inferior race and outsider to the "civilizer" within the triad of the three races. In *The Masters and the Slaves*, Freyre places the "material and moral culture of Negro slaves" above that of the Portuguese and even the Indian. Responding directly to a historical placement of black culture at the bottom of the order of cultures in Brazil, Freyre writes,

For nothing could be more unscientific than to speak of the inferiority of the African Negro in relation to the American Indian. . . . Nothing is more absurd than to deny to the Sudanese Negro, for example, who was brought to Brazil in considerable numbers, a culture superior to that of the most advanced native . . . it was precisely by all these evidences of a material and moral culture that the Negro slaves show that they came from more advanced stocks, and that they were in a better position than the Indians to contribute to the economic and social formation of Brazil. At times, in a better position than the Portuguese themselves. (1956, 281)

Freyre begins his two-hundred-page section on "The Negro Slave in the Sexual and Family Life of the Brazilian" by comparing African culture to "American Indian culture." Thus he begins by first addressing what he calls an unscientific exclusion of an advanced African tradition within the nation's romanticist narrative of ancestry. Throughout the chapter, Freyre emphasizes African contributions in hygiene, diet, adaptability, labor, and more. "Once in Brazil," he writes, "the Negroes became in a sense, the masters of the land: they dominated the kitchen, preserving in large part their own diet" (287). Using Boas as his intellectual foundation, Freyre argues against eugenicists, demystifying eugenic measures of intelligence as unsubstantiated theories: "The testimony of anthropologists reveals for us traits in the Negro showing a mental capacity that is in no [way] inferior to that of the other races: 'considerable degree of personal initiative, a talent for organization, and . . . imagination, with technical skill and thrift,' as Professor Boas puts it" (295).

Instead, Freyre argues that it was the institution of slavery that not only degraded the Brazilian identity but also the richness of African culture: "At times what appears to be the influence of race is purely and simply that of the slave, of the social system of slavery, a reflection of the enormous capacity of that system for morally degrading masters and slaves alike" (322).

Conversely, Freyre's work, as many scholars have already noted, is problematic and difficult to read for the ways it reduces the rape of black and indigenous women to sexual affinity and the way it equates the enslavement of blacks with cultural "adaptability." It is difficult to comprehend (or even hear) Freyre's contributions to a more positive discourse of African culture when comments like the one about a "morally degrading" slave system are combined with endless romantic-erotic musings about "the mulatto girl who initiated [the white, Portuguese male] into physical love and, to the creaking of a canvas cot gave [him his] first complete sensation of being a man" (278).

Freyre's work has been criticized for its positivistic and elitist view of slave relations with little regard for the violent, often coercive, power relations in which Africans were held in Brazil (Skidmore 1972; Reis 1988; Rosa-Ribeiro 2000). Undoubtedly, Freyre imagined Brazil as one big family, even while two massive branches of that family were enslaved, used, and executed without moral question. A rough sketch inserted at the back of *The Masters and the Slaves* (468), illustrating a plantation in Pernambuco, looks more like a quilombo than a plantation, with blacks frolicking freely with whites throughout the big house and the land, playing, dancing, conversing, and even embracing in a hammock. Freyre produced an erroneous, and long-lasting, image of a more benevolent slave system and integration of blacks in Brazil, an idea that to this day contributes to the negation of a historical and extant black racial oppression (Caldwell 2007; Goldstein 2003; Hanchard 1994a; Marx 1998; Perry 2013; Telles 2004; Twine 1998; Vargas 2011).

I discuss how Freyre shifted the conversation about African culture in Brazil not to negate the damaging nature of his interpretation but rather because we also see in his writing a clear shift in the discourse on the influence and place of African culture, from a racialist theory of black inferiority to a positivist narrative of African cultural tradition. Prior to the 1930s, blacks were not part of the Brazilian intellectual imaginary except in the form of a race problem. Scientists and scholars turned blacks into an undesirable genetic mark that needed to disappear; Freyre was writing against this dominant discourse by describing African culture as valuable to the Brazilian identity. However, he glossed over and even rationalized racial violence and oppression using a theory of cultural miscegenation. Other scholars of the time followed a similar style of writing about African culture, a form of writing and inquiring that almost exclusively focused on finding and building a grand, romantic narrative of the roots of "Mama Africa" in Brazil (Maio 2001, 128), a cultural origin story that was "good to think with" as a matter of nationalist folklore.[1]

The problem of race became the problem of culture and the anthropological preoccupation with origins. The Brazilian anthropologist Arthur Ramos (1939/1980, 177) wrote that there were two interesting questions about the history of slavery: the number of Africans actually taken to Brazil and their places of origin. Ramos lamented that many of the documents that proved the cultural ancestry, "the races and tribes," and cultural practices of blacks during the colonial period had been destroyed with the passage of abolition (178). All that was left were the "studies made by foreigners who visited Brazil during the colonial and empire period"—research that, according to Ramos was "prejudiced" and conducted in "bad faith" (177). Ramos elaborates on the importance of all Negro studies, even those on "the biological problem":

> Studies on the Negro present a diversity of angles, demanding the treatment of specialists in various scientific fields. . . . The question of cultural anthropology is extremely significant: the religion, traditions, folklore, and material culture of the Negro. The biological problem embraces matters of social heredity and racial crossings. . . . The sociological [deals with] the influence of the Negro in the social life of Brazil and the problems of class relationship, and, lastly, the social and political aspect . . . of the Negro in his reaction to the problems which confront him. (178)

It is clear in Ramos' language that even in the late 1930s blacks continued to be imagined as scientific objects of inquiry; the need to measure black crania was replaced with the desire to find and document the origins of a newly imagined "Negro" humanity. The same rhetoric can be seen in North American anthropological thinking of the time.[2] Ramos goes on to commend what he calls the "careful," "thoughtful," "intellectually honest," and "devoted" research of Nina Rodrigues, "the first in Brazil to devote a solid work of investigation to the Negro." Like Freyre, Ramos paused to recognize the importance of Nina Rodrigues' research to the anthropological understanding of blacks, only commenting in passing (and in forgiveness), Nina Rodrigues' "unfortunate" beliefs in the "inequality of races" and "degeneration of mulattoes." Ramos defends Nina Rodrigues as "prone to explain difficulties in terms of race, where today we prefer to think in terms of cultures" (179).

In fact, Edison Carneiro has observed that the vindication of Nina Rodrigues' research and scholarship became "the fight of [Ramos'] life" (Carneiro and Ivy, 74). This proclamation of culture over race not only became the accepted national mentality but also laid the foundation for discussing blackness in Brazil for years to come. During the transitions from eugenics to whitening to racial democracy, there was still no place for denouncing racial injustice and a history of antiblack violence among the white intellectual elites. Instead, these issues were systemically excused and rationalized and then simply replaced by theories of culture. After the 1930s, for better and for worse, black Brazilians became honorary members of the Brazilian racial democracy. Writing about African culture became part of writing about Brazil, and engaging in African cultural practices became part of being Brazilian (DaMatta 1991, 1995). Blacks became part of the intellectual cultural imaginary and as a result lost the legitimacy to denounce racism and racial exclusion.

With the end of Nazi genocide in Europe and the rise of the African American civil rights movement in a racially segregated United States, Brazil's claim to racial democracy drew strong international attention, often from North American scholars and black civil rights leaders (Frazier 1942; Herskovits 1943; Landes 1947/1994; Pierson 1942).[3] Violent racial conflict in the United States allowed Brazilian intellectuals and politicians to point with pride to their own country as an example of racial harmony (Telles 2004, 41). During the 1950s,[4] black intellectuals positioned themselves to use racial democracy and a surging intellectual interest in African ancestry as mechanisms for social and political mobilization (A. Guimarães 2004, 271). Black activists re-created their own spaces of cultural identification and intellectual production, particularly in connection with an empowered idea of Africa and African cultural tradition — "Africanness replaces, or at least significantly challenges, whiteness as a source of dignity, respect, and self-esteem for Afro-Brazilians" (ibid.).

The transition to black politics came with the birth in 1978 of the Unified Black Movement (MNU, Movimento Negro Unificado) (Telles 2004, 46). Led by black activists and intellectuals such as Abdias do Nascimento, Leila Gonzalez, José Correia Leite, and Francisco Lucrécio, the MNU grew stronger together with other pan-Africanist movements throughout the diaspora. The negritude movement, which emphasized the beautiful and innate values and traits of black people, and Marcus Garvey's "back to Africa" campaign, which placed a "mother Africa" at the center of all black identity, had a significant impact on the foundation of the MNU and earlier black organizations such as the Black Experimental Theater (TEN, Teatro Experimental do Negro) and emerging *blocos afros* in carnaval throughout the country (Marx 1998, 20; Pinho 2010, 75). Still, the MNU was working in a difficult political climate. The 1964–1985 military dictatorship once again brought, at a high cost of civil liberties and personal freedom, a strong commitment to national unity and racial democracy. In a 1970 report to the United Nations, the Brazilian government declared that racial discrimination did not exist in Brazil.

Around the same time, the Brazilian National Security Council, in its executive advisory role, labeled studies of racial discrimination in Brazil "subversive" (Marx 1998, 172). Race and racism had become taboo as research subjects, and they were seen as divisive topics to the nation. Scholars could write about blackness and organize around African culture as long as their research and initiatives contributed to the nation's image as a unified, multiethnic democracy. The MNU declared a Black Consciousness Day within the dictatorship's repressive intellectual policies, precisely because its manifesto was couched in the language of culture and racial democracy. In the service of supporting an image of racial unity, it is significant that Zumbi was reimagined from a fugitive criminal of the state into a democratic leader of a "free" multiracial society (Nascimento 1980, 153).

The manifesto illustrates the tactical way in which black activists were able to affirm the integrity of a black history of resistance, through the use of Zumbi as essentially the father of the only true Brazilian democracy and still sustain the obligatory multicultural discourse. The MNU and other black organizations used cultural inclusion and an African ethnic group identity as a strategy in pushing for the political and economic equality of blacks in the late twentieth century and for decades to follow (Butler 1998, 12).

The MNU's emphasis on cultural integration became an important point of discussion among North American scholars who were trying to understand how racial democracy could maintain its ideological and social foothold despite a visible exclusion of blacks at all levels of society (Hanchard 1994a; Twine 1998). Black North American scholars like Michael Hanchard and Francine Twine argued that demonstrations of racism and blatant black discrimination could be seen and heard in everyday interactions with black Brazilians, from the poorest to the wealthiest, even as these same Brazilians maintained a defense of racial democracy and multicultural identity. "I am concerned with how ordinary Brazilians perceive and conceptualize multiple forms of racism," Twine argues. "My aim is to illuminate why nonelite Brazilians, especially Afro-Brazilians, continue to have faith in racial democracy" (1998, 6). As the twentieth century came to a close, it was clear that the idea of racial democracy had been effectively embedded in the delicate social fabric of the Brazilian nation. Hanchard has referred to it as a racial hegemony that impregnated the public sphere and public opinion.[5]

The production and alienation of blackness in the public sphere, Hanchard argues, is also an example of how popular authority constitutes a Foucauldian "regime of truth": "Racist ideologies are facets of publicity and public opinion, insofar as they mark bodies to inform others of the meanings of those bodies in racial terms" (1994b, 179). In other words, even as the black body had been intellectually and politically molded into an inferior subject of the nation, subjecting black Brazilians to exist as partial citizens, racial democracy created a façade of an egalitarian inclusion of all cultures and a unique mixture of the races—a myth that everyone, even the historically excluded, learned to desire. Livo Sansone offers a reflection:

> If racial democracy is a myth—as it undoubtedly is—we are dealing
> with a fundamental myth of socio-racial relations, whose origins were
> inspired by the fable of the magic mixture of the three races. . . . This
> myth is accepted by a large part of the community, which reproduces
> it in everyday relations, articulating it in a series of popular discourses.
> (Sansone 2003, 54)

But Hanchard makes an important point, that myths are not magically sustained, nor as Twine argues are people simply controlled like puppets of an invisible hegemonic structure. Racial democracy is a matter of public policy and a national project of knowledge production.

Debating Race and Racism in the Twenty-First Century

At the end of the twentieth century and the beginning of the twenty-first, the Brazilian government positioned itself internationally against racism. Again responding to international trends, the nation ratified antiracist agreements including the International Labor Organization's Discrimination Convention of 1958 (Convention 111) and the UN's International Convention on the Elimination of All Forms of Racial Discrimination (Telles 2004, 38). However, the Brazilian nation would not officially recognize the existence of racial inequality in Brazil until 2001, when Brazil participated in the World Conference against Racism, Racial Discrimination, Xenophobia, and Related Intolerance (2002). Together with other participating UN countries, Brazil recognized that

> despite efforts undertaken by the international community, governments, and local authorities, the scourge of racism, racial discrimination, xenophobia and related intolerance persists and continues to result in violations of human rights, suffering, disadvantage, and violence, which must be combated by all available and appropriate means and as a matter of the highest priority.[6]

In a significant change of tone from its 1970 letter to the United Nations declaring that racism did not exist in Brazil, the Brazilian government not only internationally recognized the existence of racism,[7] but it also allied itself with other UN member nations in a promise to take strategic political action against it. The conference set the stage for the implementation of a series of political and social actions to end racial inequality in Brazil, initiated in the final years of the Fernando Henrique Cardoso administration (2001–2003) (Htun 2004).

At first, individual universities like the federal universities of Rio de Janeiro in 2001 and Brasília in 2004 implemented their own quota systems for black, brown (pardo), and indigenous students as a way of enacting the promise of the world conference within the higher education system (Sousa and Nascimento 2008). However, it would not be until 2012 that a comprehensive Lei de Cotas (Quotas Law) would be created as an educational policy for the entire nation.[8] Conversations about racial inequality, beginning with education, and the possible implementation of affirmative action policies threw Brazilian scholars into a bitter debate over the appropriateness of race-based policies in Brazil. Anthropologists were among the most vocal proponents and opponents in these debates. Bailey and Peria go as far as to compare the quota debate to a form of "culture wars" within Brazilian academia (2010, 592).

Anthropologists in Brazil remain divided along the lines of race between those who believe that racism is a systemic and real social issue in Brazil and those who believe that race does not exist and therefore social inequality represents a class issue and not a racial one. Pro-quota scholars claim that their antiquota colleagues refuse to recognize the extant and well-documented problem of racial inequality at all levels of society (Munanga 2001). For example, in 2001 the Institute of Applied Economic Research (IPEA, Institute de Pesquisa Económica Aplicada) published a report on racial inequality in Brazil in the 1990s. The report showed that in 1999, blacks represented 45 percent of the population but 64 percent of the poor and 69 percent of the indigent population (Henriques 2001).

The 2006 "Manifesto in Favor of a Quotas Law and a Statute of Racial Equality," addressed to the Brazilian Congress and signed by nearly fifty pro-quota scholars, describes a historical pattern of racial inequality in Brazil that has existed for "four uninterrupted generations" in which blacks and pardos continue to be overrepresented among those with the least formal education, lowest salaries, highest unemployment, least access to health care, and worst living conditions. For their part, antiquota scholars argue that inequalities are solely class-based and that treating them at the level of race reinstated the scientific racism of the early twentieth century (Bailey and Peria 2010; Fry et al. 2007; Maggie 2005).[9] They have also argued that race-based quotas force Brazilians into a US-style white/black system that is inappropriate for Brazil's more fluid multicultural society (Lessa 2007).

The affirmative action debate illustrates one main intellectual issue that has complicated conversations about race and racism in twenty-first-century Brazil: the problem of whether race should be included as a category of difference within the Brazilian national identity. This remains a problem of a racial democracy ideology that continues to uphold the mestiço identity at the level of social relations and everyday interactions (Munanga 2001; E. Nascimento 2007). In this sense, the cautioning words of Brazilian scholars maintain that Brazil is not like the United States because Brazil never officially instituted a binary black/white system through segregationist policies and a "one-drop rule" of racial identity. Furthermore, these scholars uphold that Brazilian racial identity is primarily fluid and thus does not lend itself to the fixed racial categories on which affirmative action policies depend.

The idea of racial fluidity in the color continuum as a way of identifying racial groups as color categories is an important point of contention in studies of Brazilian race relations. In the Brazilian census, race is coded according to specific color categories except for the one ethnic category for indigenous people; the categories include *branco* (white), *preto* (black), *pardo* (brown), *amarelo* (yellow, or Asian), and *indígena* (indigenous) (Sousa and Nascimento 2008). There has been extensive research on the census and a critique that these categories fail to account for the multiple ways Brazilians place themselves all along a color continuum.[10] But scholars have increasingly critiqued the defense of racial fluidity, arguing that the color continuum acts as another mechanism for racial domination by diffusing racial identities into ambiguous color categories, thus keeping with a Brazilian idealization of assimilation and the mestiço (Caldwell 2007; A. Guimarães 1995; Perry 2013).

Putting into question the color continuum is a significant development in Brazilian race studies that is largely led by black scholars who are speaking to the Brazilian black experience and racial democracy through their own narratives of identity formation and encounters with racial injustice (Costa 2010; Lima 2006; Perry 2013). These scholars, as Munanga did earlier, point out that the argument for a fluid Brazilian identity that does not conform to racial binaries, primarily of black and white, seems to grow loudest when it comes to discussing real political reforms for racial justice and race-based policies. "It has not been difficult for poor black people to decipher who is black in Brazil," writes Perry, "since they see and feel race and class structures in their everyday lives, *na pele* (in the skin). Nor do policy makers, development agents, and the police have much difficulty deciding who is black" (2013, xix). Here Perry illustrates how a discussion of racial fluidity represents an intellectual disconnect between multicultural theories of flexible identities and the immediate reality of racial discrimination that black Brazilians, like other black communities across the diaspora, experience on a daily basis.

These critical race scholars defend an intellectual and activist position aiming to study and reveal the structures and everyday lived experiences of antiblack discrimination, exclusion, and violence across the black diaspora (Marx 1998; Munanga 2004; E. Nascimento 2007; Perry 2013; Twine 1998; Vargas 2011). What is more, these scholars are decentralizing a social science field, particularly an anthropological field, that has primarily been constructed by the white, intellectual elite with a voiceless black subject as the scientific object of inquiry, as Ari Lima observes:

> As anthropologists . . . , black academics observe their "natives" and themselves from the Establishment's ethnographic perspective and defend their field's cultural and political agenda in terms of the very sociopolitical context in which they are either completely negated or assimilated as *evolved* beings (Fanon 1983). Their ethnic consciousness, which has been entirely fashioned by outside forces, is forced to imagine or ignore only that which the reality of the field permits. (2006, 83)

Liberal democratic values of multiculturalism and racial democracy continue to be defended within a social science and anthropological discourse of racial fluidity, some anthropologists go as far as blaming research on race and racism as "dangerously divisive."[11] Undeterred, critical race scholars are defending the urgent need to speak to racial injustice and an everyday reality of blackness that has historically been left out of the field.

Since the end of the twentieth century, "blackness" became a way of talking about black social experience throughout the African diaspora (Torres and Whitten 1998; Wade 1997). Although blackness can be understood in multiple ways, there are certain characteristics commonly ascribed to the overall concept of blackness. Paul Gilroy (1993) described diasporic black cultures as sharing a discourse and memory of slavery, African legacy, and the experience of racism and racial exclusion. Abdias do Nascimento defined black cultures as a "creative unity" of the cultures of Africans and their descendants throughout the diaspora, "which may not be entirely African or African-inspired, but that are specific to the black communities of their homelands" (1989, 26). In Brazil and Bahia in particular, blackness has not lost its primary referent of Africa (Pinho 2010; Sansone 2003). Patrícia de Santana Pinho (2010) refers to the persistence of Africa as a social, cultural, and national symbol in Brazil as the "myth of Mama Africa," an idea that black people are as much connected to each other by their local experiences of blackness as they are by an imaginary of where their blackness comes from and what it looks like. Here, in Taylor's view (2004), "imaginary" is used as a social imaginary or socially shared and accepted ideas about people and spaces. Although few Brazilians have visited the continent, "Africa" is used to describe the historical past of Afro-Brazilians as a homeland of cultural preservation and tradition.

The social contentiousness of blackness as simultaneously an ethnic group category and a racial identity and experience is an important issue for the quilombo-descendant identity in public policy and social discussion. The new quilombola identity is gaining strength at a time when affirmative action demands are challenging multiculturalist ideologies, most of all racial democracy. Although the residents of quilombo-descendant communities are diverse in their skin colors, reflecting the social reality of Brazil, they are nonetheless marked by blackness through their identification with the quilombo, a space embedded in a narrative of African cultural tradition, defined by a political affirmation of black resistance, and rooted in the history of the slave state. The quilombo-descendent category was born out of the political and ideological formation of black identity through the birth of the Brazilian nation.

THE POLITICS OF BLACK CULTURAL RECOGNITION

The 1988 constitution marked a pivotal moment in Brazil's democratization process. One of the ways the new government sought to reinstate democratic values was by extending citizenship rights to more groups (Van Cott 2000). It was during this period that the political recognition of different cultures and ethnic groups became an important part of the multicultural state. Rather than focusing on assimilation and integration, on a single, unified mestiço identity, as had been the tradition throughout most of the twentieth century, the state recognized the need to respect and protect difference.

The politics of cultural recognition throughout most of Latin America has largely been used for the protection of indigenous cultures and land rights. Only a few nation-states, including Brazil, have mentioned special rights for Afro-Latinos in their constitutions. Some of those collective rights are the official recognition of ethnic and racial diversity, the right to difference, land rights, and the recognition of indigenous languages (Hooker 2005). Multicultural policies were part of the process of relegitimating Latin American nations after years of authoritarian rule such as Brazil's twenty-year dictatorship. The 1988 Brazilian constitution was hailed as progressive because in Title I it denounces all forms of discrimination by "origin, race, sex, color, and age." The constitution includes Afro-Brazilians by declaring the right to lands for a group called *remancescentes de quilombos* (literally, "remnants of quilombos"). Quilombo descendants were named in a brief, temporary article of the constitution without any provisions for the actual distribution of rights or even for the identification of quilombo descendants; it wasn't until much later, in 2003, that provisions for recognition and land distribution were introduced.

The constitution primarily made important concessions for indigenous groups. According to the Fundação Nacional do Índio (Funai), indigenous groups are officially defined as ethnic groups with distinctive cultural practices and historical ties to their lands. Indigenous land protections were made part of the permanent body of the constitution, and indigenous rights to culture, language, and land use were explicitly stated and defined throughout several articles. In contrast, the constitution did not mention the culture of quilombo descendants or the nature of their land rights. It created the "quilombo descendant" identity as a political category, but it failed to define them and therefore left them with "quilombo ancestry" as the only constitutional basis for collective rights.

Still, the language of the constitution is, after all, just that, a discourse—a political promise. Regardless of the constitution's more detailed, rhetorical inclusion of indigenous communities and its relative silence on black communities, neither group has had its rights to land fully granted or respected. Alcida Ramos comes to a similar pause in her analysis on the rhetoric of indigenism in Brazil:

> Why should the Brazilian state bother to guard the rights of aboriginal populations in order to occupy what was—and still is—considered to be national territory? The answer, to my mind, is that Indians are not simply good to conquer and rule; they are also very good for making whites reflect upon their self-image. Like a convenient mirror, the Indi-

ans, despite themselves, help reinforce white faith in the superiority of European origins. (1991, 156)

Protecting "indigenism" as a multicultural concept of the state is different from granting and protecting rights. Indigenous communities might have their land rights detailed in the constitution, but even in the twenty-first century, these communities still do not have ownership of their own land titles. Their titles are still held by a patriarchal state that has defined "Indians" as "relatively incapable" by law for more than a hundred years (Alcida Ramos 1991, 160). With the advent of quilombo-descendent rights in the constitution, rural black communities are now bound by similar measures of cultural exoticism and ethnic authenticity, which can also be held up against a mirror of white normativity that defines the Brazilian nation.

Charles Hale (2005) has called the turn to the recognition of cultural difference for indigenous and Afro-descendant communities "neoliberal multiculturalism," a concept he uses to describe a new politics of cultural recognition that trades a long-seated homogenizing discourse of *mestizaje* for one of difference. "In part taking the rise of cultural rights activism as an inevitable given," Hale explains, "and in part actively substituting a new articulating principle, the emergent regime of governance shapes, delimits, and *produces* cultural difference rather than suppressing it" (13). While Hale uses Central American examples, Guatemala, Costa Rica, Nicaragua, and Honduras, to illustrate neoliberal multicultural policies in practice, he articulates a political trend that can be seen throughout contemporary Latin America, particularly in Brazil.

Hale argues that Latin American governments are granting black and indigenous communities collective rights rather than violently forcing assimilation; however, in doing so they also create and control the standards of recognition. As long as these communities meet the requirements set forth by government policies, the promise of collective rights is maintained and communities are driven to work with the system rather than against it. The neoliberal government, in turn, "reduc[es] the potential for chaos and conflict, and lock[s] the community into a mindset that makes it more difficult for expansive political alternatives to emerge" (2005, 18).

Cultural recognition grants black and indigenous communities the right to difference, even self-identification, without necessarily changing the unequal structural distribution of rights. Juliet Hooker contends that cultural recognition for Afro-descendants depends on a black culture that can be specifically defined and visibly identified as a distinct ethnic group with its own cultural practices, language, and relationship to the land; these are the standards that make up the "appropriate subjects of collective rights" (2005, 291). This is where the twentieth-century imaginary of quilombos and black culture as African tradition affects the recognition process of quilombo descendants. Although the language is different, the discourse of cultural recognition in Brazil still depends on the narratives of national identity formation established in the twentieth century.

Once again, social scientists are central in reconceptualizing intellectual constructions of black communities for the purpose of facilitating their inclusion or in this case their recognition from the state (O'Dwyer 2005). Just as anthropologists have worked to conceptualize the role and integration of indigenous communities in Brazil, they are now tasked with making sense of quilombo-descendant rights for Afro-Brazilians within the multicultural rhetoric of the nation. Here anthropologists are borrowing from a rubric of indigenous cultural recognition and land protection as a way of reimagining rural black communities as ethnically differentiated communities deserving of rights and cultural preservation. The cultural recognition of quilombo-descendant communities focuses solely on the ethnic formation and authentication of these communities without recognizing or engaging the racial discrimination that these communities experience on a daily basis. As agents of the state, anthropologists are producing knowledge about new quilombo-descendant communities that reflects an extant caution in the field (and nation) about whether a discourse on race and racial exclusion is a legitimate discourse within a Brazilian intellectual production (Lima 2006; A. Nascimento 1989; Ribeiro 2004).[12]

DEFINING THE CULTURAL PARAMETERS
OF "QUILOMBO DESCENDANT"

The "quilombo descendant" mentioned in the constitution needed a face that could be connected to living communities. At first, the official definition reflected Nascimento's idea of quilombismo as a form of resistance that could be applied to contemporary black experiences. In 1994, the Palmares Cultural Foundation defined "quilombo descendant" as "any black rural community composed of descendants from slaves, who survived through subsistence agriculture, and with cultural manifestations linked to the past" (in I. Leite 2012, 251). The concept of "rural black community" already existed as a political unit of focus in the government since the early 1980s (French 2009), so the term was easily employed in the definition of "quilombo descendant."[13] In interviews with representatives of the Palmares Cultural Foundation and INCRA, I was told that rural communities became the primary focus of quilombo rights because of the perceived inviability of dealing with dense, urban spaces. However, as O'Dwyer (2005) explains, rural black communities, as they had been studied and conceptualized by anthropologists, already seemed to match the ideal of an ethnic community and specific land practices that the quilombo-descendant category would require.

Since 1994, the definition of "quilombo descendant" has changed and was rewritten with the help of anthropologists. In a 1994 statement to the Ministry of Culture, the Brazilian Anthropological Association (ABA) declared that the "quilombo" had assumed a new social and academic definition, which was elaborated particularly within nongovernmental organizations, autonomous working groups, and the black movement. According to the ABA, these groups used the term *remanescente de quilombo* as well as *terras de preto* (black lands) to designate a legacy of cultural and material inheritance that relates to a sentiment of belonging to a specific place or group (Pacheco de Oliveira 1994, 81). Experts in the cultural politics of their nation, the members of ABA knew that the government needed specific boundaries that identified quilombo descendants as distinct groups deserving of collective rights. Anthropologists applied Frederick Barth's theory on ethnic groups and boundaries as a strategy for molding the quilombo descendant into a new political, ethnic identity. The choice of Barth's theory of culture reflects a dominant intellectual tradition of cultural anthropology in Brazil since the mid-twentieth century.

In the twentieth century, the concept of culture as diverse and relativistic to individual human groups became central to anthropology (Stocking 1966). Franz Boas had declared for the world of science as early as the 1890s that race did not exist as a biological fact; he was the first to famously propose a shift from an evolutionary fixation on race to a focus on cultural difference when thinking about human diversity (Boas 1921). By the end of the twentieth century, anthropologists were consumed by culture — and those studying Brazil were no exception (Clifford and Marcus 1986). Brazilian anthropology was heavily influenced by Boasian cultural relativism and European, especially French, anthropology more broadly. Anthropology in Brazil was not established as a separate field of study until the middle of the twentieth century along with the creation of national museums and universities and an overall preoccupation with the modern state (Peirano 1981). Social science scholars wanted to establish a field of their own that would use ideological tools borrowed from European traditions and apply them to an understanding of "Brazilianness" (37). Culture and citizenship became central concepts during Brazil's democratization period illustrated primarily in the creation of a Ministry of Culture and provisions for indigenous rights in the 1988 constitution. Anthropology in Brazil began as an intellectual field in the service of the nation, as anthropologists were primarily tasked with helping to conceptualize the modern national identity.

In the beginning, Brazilian anthropologists primarily focused on the "point of contact" between indigenous groups and national society (Peirano 1981, 74). Alcida Ramos (1991) explains that Indians represented a mirror to the modern Brazilian and were used to reflect the progression and transformation of a culture. Unlike their European and North American counterparts, who studied indigenous groups as disappearing, primitive societies that needed to be documented and preserved, Brazilian anthropologists studied indigenous groups in their relationship to the nation. In the 1970s, Darcy Ribeiro, an anthropologist who also worked for the Indian Protection Agency, a precursor to Funai, came up with an alternative to the concept of assimilation when thinking about relations between indigenous people and the state. Ribeiro coined the term "ethnic transfiguration," which Mariza Peirano defines as "the process by which tribal populations confronting the national society develop the ability to survive as ethnic groups through a series of changes in their biological stratum; . . . culture; and the form of relations they maintain with the society that surrounds them" (1981, 75–76).

Ribeiro understood the issue of "contact" as distinct levels of integration that did not end in ethnic assimilation or a complete fusion of indigenous culture with that of national society (D. Ribeiro 1970/1982, 434). Instead, he found that Indian integration represented a form of *acomodação* (accommodation) "that represents a specific ethnic representation, with an increasing participation in the economic life and institutional spheres of national society" (435). In other words, indigenous people in Brazil could simultaneously become integrated in Brazilian society and economic and institutional life while at the same time maintaining a strong ethnic group identity.

Around the same time that Ribeiro was rethinking the impact of contact between indigenous groups and the nation, Frederick Barth (1969) outlined a theory of ethnic boundaries that helped redirect anthropological focus from the cultural contents of groups to their boundaries, or characteristics of belonging, that unified them and distinguished them from the rest of society. Barth argued that ethnic groups established themselves through social processes of incorporation and exclusion, maintaining themselves despite changing participation or membership. Specific boundaries that distinguished quilombo descendants as separate groups from their colonial-era ancestors and other black Brazilians, who were conceptualized as a color category but not a separate ethnic group, was exactly what anthropologists needed to create a case for quilombola land rights. Thus, similar ideas that were used to rethink the integration of indigenous groups in the twentieth century were also employed in the construction of an ethnic group identity for rural black communities now defined as quilombo descendants in the twenty-first century. Before land rights could be determined there needed to be a collective unit of rightful bearers. The ABA applied Barth's theories in establishing the specific characteristics of authenticity for quilombo-descendant communities. The hope was that by defining modern quilombo descendants as ethnic groups, anthropologists could help improve the chances of Afro-Brazilians in obtaining similar multicultural and political rights as indigenous peoples (Arruti 2005; O'Dwyer 2002).

In 2011, the ABA signed an official partnership agreement with INCRA to support the land regularization of quilombo descendants and other public policies for quilombolas through the professional collaboration of anthropologists such as through the publication of research (ABA 2007). The ABA organizes its research subjects into topical committees. There is a specific Quilombos Committee (Comité Quilombos) that publishes statements on the academic, political, and social situation of quilombo descendants. This discussion on the role of the ABA in defining the quilombo-descendant identity largely comes out of the contributions of the committee's Working Group on Quilombos.

FORMING ETHNICITY AND DOWNPLAYING RACE IN QUILOMBO-DESCENDANT IDENTITY

In reviewing the expanded emphasis on cultural attributes in Brazil's attempts to redress previous discrimination, it is interesting to see the role anthropologists play in restructuring the focus of the quilombo-descendant identity. Prior to 2003, anthropologists were essential in determining which communities could and could not be recognized as the descendants of quilombos. During the Fernando Henrique Cardoso administration of 1995–2003, quilombos could only be granted cultural recognition after a detailed anthropological study was conducted by the Palmares Cultural Foundation to determine whether the residents had proof of ancestral ties to the land. When President Lula granted quilombo descendants the right to self-identify in 2003 through Decree 4.887, based on ILO Convention 169, the government restructured the quilombo process in Statute 56 so that anthropologists would no longer be responsible for determining cultural identification. Anthropologists would now work for INCRA and be in charge of researching and documenting land use.

Leading up to the government's restructuring of the quilombo recognition and land process were a series of anthropological discussions and meetings aimed at rethinking the definition of "quilombo descendants." In order to make Article 68 of the constitution more applicable to the language of cultural recognition, the first thing the ABA did was encourage a conceptual shift from race to ethnicity when doing research on quilombos (O'Dwyer 2002). The rhetorical shift was part of the process of highlighting the cultural practices of quilombolas and of grounding cultural practices in land use. Once again, the idea was to focus on a historically accepted rhetoric of *cultura negra*, or black culture, as a collective difference within the multicultural nation (Guimarães 2004, 276).

According to the ABA, rural communities based their identities on their historical ties to the lands they had worked as sharecroppers since the 1950s. The ABA argued that the government should not treat quilombo descendants as though they were archeological or biological artifacts that could be visibly and materially linked to one common ancestor. Instead, they emphasized that modern quilombo descendants were ethnic groups organized around their own rules of membership and belonging, just like any other traditional community in Brazil (Pacheco de Oliveira 1994, 81). This was an important contribution by the ABA because it officially set the theoretical ground for the legal adoption of self-identification as the official method of cultural recognition. Finally, the ABA stated that quilombolas lived communally and therefore should be granted communal land titles. If the Ministry of Culture implemented its recommendations, the ABA would provide experts to produce any necessary anthropological reports to assist in implementing Article 68 (82).

In 2003, the government took up the recommendations of the ABA and officially defined the "quilombo-descendant community" as a "self-identified, ethno-racial group with their own historical trajectory, a specific relationship to the land, and the presumption of a black ancestry connected to forms of resistance to historical oppression" (Araujo 2007). Immediately one would notice the dramatic change in definition from 1994 to 2003, with the FCP's definition being race—and labor—specific (highlighting blackness and subsistence agriculture) and the anthropological definition being intentionally broad and racially nonspecific and introducing the idea of the ethnoracial group. The Palmares Cultural Foundation's definition is not necessarily clearer or more "authentic"; however, it is interesting to note that it directly identifies "rural black communities" and "descendants of slaves" as the clear subjects of quilombola identity, an identification that approximates the narratives of identity that I heard in Grande Paraguaçu and other quilombola communities. The ABA definition, on the other hand, avoids specifying a black subject, instead vaguely pointing to "a presumed black ancestry."

Considering how African cultural traditions and ancestry have been incorporated into the dominant ethos of the nation, "black ancestry" does not necessarily speak to racially excluded black bodies and lives. While the ABA aimed at expanding the recognition of life experiences and oral histories that could count as *quilombola*, this new definition only applied in theory. In practice, the Palmares Cultural Foundation would still be required to document specific ancestral histories and cultural practices, and INCRA would be required to write a detailed anthropological report proving that these cultural practices were necessarily connected to the land in question. In fact, this official definition of "quilombo descendant" reflects the confusing dualisms that I sensed in my interviews with government representatives and Valmiro. Politically the quilombo-descendant identity was supposed to be open to self-identification, but in its application it was rigidly fixed to ideological boundaries and an unforgiving bureaucratic process. When it comes to enacting the distribution of land rights granted in the constitution, the definition closes and becomes bounded by cultural theories of ethnic groups and parameters subject to the validation of experts and to the dominant historical narratives of the nation.

Although they are still characterized as black communities and defined by their African cultural traditions, the policies that were established to identify quilombo descendants downplay their racialized identities and bodies and instead focus on the documentation of cultural practices and the validation of an inherited ancestry. Officially identified as cultural groups and ethnic communities, rural blacks could demand more than just land rights. They could apply for a series of social programs that would improve everyday life in their towns. For example, quilombo descendants are given priority when it comes to infrastructural developments such as running water, waste management, electricity, paved roads, and building construction.[14] They are also eligible for funding for schools, health services, and support for local job opportunities and artisan initiatives. Finally, these communities can apply for support from the federal Pontos de Cultura (Culture Points),[15] an initiative that provides financial support for certain activities that are seen as maintaining and enriching the cultural traditions of a community. Because quilombo-descendant communities are defined through African ancestry and culture, these traditions could include capoeira and maculelê classes, candomblé houses, and the artisan agricultural production of *dendê* (palm oil) and *farinha* (manioc flour).

CONNECTING EMBODIED LIVES AND CONCEPTS

Although the Palmares Cultural Foundation was the first to define quilombo-descendants as communities, the ABA strengthened this connection by emphasizing the ethnic group. The political use of the ethnic group as an organizing concept for quilombo descendants did one important thing: it established quilombo descendants as members of ethnic communities with identifiable boundaries—common ancestors, cultural practices, and traditions—that differentiated them from the rest of society, at least on paper. Barth wrote of ethnic groups, emphasizing social boundaries or criteria for determining membership and exclusion as defining characteristics (1969, 15). While Barth is describing boundaries that were seemingly created organically at the moment of contact between members and nonmembers, in the case of quilombo descendants these boundaries had to be determined and formalized by the government because there was never a point at which quilombolas established their own boundaries of membership and exclusion from other black Brazilians or from a broader national society. On the contrary, quilombolas consistently define themselves in connection to a shared, lived experience of blackness in Brazil and as equally deserving citizens of the nation.

Therefore, how do people connect an everyday lived reality to an anthropological concept? How did groups who were not previously differentiated by political ethnic boundaries become quilombo-descendant communities? One quilombola leader, Rosinda Nascimento, would express the following during a community meeting in Grande Paraguaçu:

> We always knew about our culture and could explain the traditions of our ancestors; it is just that we never connected our culture to the word

quilombo. We never knew to connect our lives and experiences to that word.

Part of my initial interview process in Grande Paraguaçu was to ask quilombolas how the quilombo process began in their community, including when they had first heard of quilombos. I learned that most people had not heard of quilombos until the political process began in their own town. A few people had read about quilombos and Palmares in elementary school. But mostly, residents of Grande Paraguaçu learned about the constitutional provision for quilombo land rights and subsequently the new political definition of "quilombo descendants" at a meeting in a nearby town that had just obtained cultural recognition. The reconceptualization of the quilombo thus was not just politically significant; it was also important in providing a way for modern rural black communities to identify with this colonial identity. People knew about their ancestry and cultural practices, but they did not connect these to the word *quilombo.* For the quilombolas of Grande Paraguaçu, as is true for all social groups, culture is embodied and lived in practice, as habitus (Sahlins 1983). O'Dwyer notes that the concept of ethnicity is attributed to quilombo descendants precisely because of their habitus (2005, 12), a certain way of living, working, worship, and even producing knowledge that are tied to notions of African ancestry and tradition.

But what if a group of people does not automatically know how to communicate or connect this habitus to broader concepts of African culture, quilombolismo, and multicultural rights? Anthropologists have shown us that culture is taught, learned, embodied, and always changing (Benedict 1934; Boas 1928; Clifford 1988; Csordas 1990; Mead 1928); it is not an object that we can hold but rather an everyday practice and way of thinking and speaking about the world (Bourdieu 1977; Mauss 1973). But few researchers have discussed the issue of "not knowing"—the fact that often people cannot describe their everyday habitus in a way that connects it to larger concepts of culture and ancestry, a condition that extends beyond quilombolas and black communities. In Peru, Tanya Golash-Boza interviewed Afro-Peruvians about their African ancestry. She reports that she expected to find emotional narratives of African ancestors and slavery, but instead she discovered that interviewees were "embarrassed" and "ashamed" because they did not know a lot about their ancestry (2011, 49). Unlike in Brazil, the situation of Peru is one where the dominant narrative of mestizaje has made invisible the lives and experiences of black Peruvians. Golash-Boza illustrates how Afro-Peruvians consequently maintain a stronger connection to their local histories and struggles such as with land tenure and not with a broader memory of slavery or African ancestry (45). The same problem occurs in Brazil, where for decades, African ancestry and cultural traditions were not taught as part of school curricula.

Valmiro observed that when blacks were included in discussions of Brazilian history, it was only with regard to slavery. It was only recently, in 2008, that the government passed Law 11.645 requiring the implementation of studies in African, Afro-Brazilian, and indigenous culture and history in all school curricula.[16] The law was a success for black-movement leaders who had been fighting for changes in the education system for many years. Not only had the quilombolas of Grande Paraguaçu not had access to a formal education on African culture and tradition, but most of them had also not been exposed to the history of quilombo resistance, much less to the refashioning of that history by late twentieth-century historians. The historical narratives that the quilombolas of Grande Paraguaçu described were those of their community—local struggles related to their everyday forms of labor, interactions with the land, and their lives in the Recôncavo. Most of the stories I recorded from the quilombolas in Grande Paraguaçu and surrounding communities were not detailed histories of ancestry or even explicit recitations of race theories; rather, they were expressions of anger at racial discrimination, at intimidations and threats by landowners, and frustration at constantly having their rights overlooked. However, I could tell that community members were learning that the only way their petition for land would move forward was if they dictated the history of their lives in ways that made sense to the researchers, political leaders, and activists who worked on the quilombo issue.

Brazilian anthropologist Maurício Arruti interprets the appearance of "not knowing" differently. He argues that what may appear as lack of understanding in quilombo-descendant communities actually might be an "incorporated" silence. He argues that for black elders, silence regarding lived experience "is an incorporated ethos . . . [that reflects] a fear and a permanent state of caution with words, which have the capability of reviving people and histories" (2005, 212). Arruti's work is significant in illustrating how culture is lived and remembered in the modern quilombo. He warns that quilombo descendants should not be punished for their inability to describe their ancestry or the history of the community. What may seem to be ignorance, Arruti contends, may instead be an incorporated silence about a history that was surrounded by punishment and violence. Arruti appears to connect to a broader observation made by Sahlins, that "the very experiences of the past are the way the present is experienced" (1985, 59). Thus, silence is a reflection of the embodiment of history for people who have not historically been part of written traditions.

My first experience with silence came when I interviewed Dona Andira, the mother and grandmother of two quilombola leaders. I was already living in Grande Paraguaçu when I went to visit her home. She was sitting in a blue rocking chair on the porch, staring out into the street. I walked up to Dona Andira accompanied by her granddaughter, Marisa. "This is Elizabeth, Vó," Marisa introduced me in almost a whisper so as not to startle her grandmother. "She wants to talk to you about your life." "Boa tarde, Dona Andira," I said. "Will you tell me about your life as a *marisqueira*?" Dona Andira turned and looked at me for a second and then looked down at her hands. She remained silent. And then she cried. I didn't know why Dona Andira started to cry. It wasn't a hysterical cry, just quiet tears that rolled down her cheeks. Startled, I turned to Marisa for some clue. Marisa's look was soft and fixed on her grandmother. She turned to me and said, "It's okay. She's been like this lately. She is sick and has been losing some of her memory. Ever since she had a stroke, she hasn't quite been herself. She doesn't say much, especially when anyone tries to talk to her about her life." I bent down and stroked Dona Andira's hands, which were tightly grasped in her lap. We were all silent for what felt like an eternity.

I did not yet know how important my first meeting with Dona Andira would be for understanding the lives of the people in Grande Paraguaçu and the embodied experience of blackness more broadly. Dona Andira's silence was enlivened by her tears. She reminded me how real her life and memories were, even if she did not speak them at that moment. I am reminded of the discomfort and confusion I felt sitting with Dona Andira as she silently cried to herself. It is this uncomfortable unknown of an embodied, physical, and emotional reality that reveals so much about the quilombola issue. The embodied experiences of quilombolas cannot adequately be accounted for in the political boundaries of the quilombo-descendant identity—a concept that is restricted by a specific historical and anthropological narrative of what culture and ancestry look like, how they function, and how they are communicated. The quilombo-descendent category cannot account for the embodied experiences of rural black communities because it does not privilege embodied forms of knowing. Tears and silence might demonstrate an important moment of personal reflection for Dona Andira, but they will not earn her cultural recognition and land rights. Embodied narratives are not always comfortable or logical;

they are not clear and concise; in fact, they are often contradictory and seemingly mundane.

In this sense, embodied narratives are sincere but not authentic (Jackson 2005). Jackson is interesting here in the way he thinks about blackness by interrogating authenticity through an idea of sincerity: "Authenticity is a way of spying on the real by privileging structures over agents, hard and fast systems over slippery sensibilities" (85). He asks what happens when "we are not afraid to grope around clumsily in the darkness of the real, a reality beyond our vain attempts at search-engine certainty and scientific transparency" (ibid.). Jackson argues that the real is unknowable, ungraspable, and that is precisely why we come up with overarching frameworks to enclose it and understand it.

This understanding pertains to the idea of blackness as a way of thinking and talking about the everyday experiences of being a black Brazilian, *na pele*. Here the question, or problem, of authenticity and what is a real or true identity becomes the primary issue for black communities settling into a new political identity of blackness, that of the quilombo descendant. In this sense, not knowing for Rosinda Nascimento demonstrates a process of understanding and connecting her everyday life as she knows it to a new concept of ethnic identity. On the other hand, Dona Andira's silence might reflect a feeling of fear or sorrow at impending changes, a fear of losing a way of life. While identities can be fluid and performative, creative and contradictory, once an identity is incorporated into the state apparatus and used for the purpose of distributing or withholding rights, as is the case in policies of cultural recognition, all fluidity, contradiction, and silences are called into question. This is when culture, an amorphous glob of "everything people do," turns into a rubric of parameters used to authenticate and delineate the boundaries of the real.

The everyday lives of the women and men of Grande Paraguaçu reflect experiences of labor and struggle in their relationship to the land. Quilombolas understand their lives as embodied and connected to a broader experience of blackness in Brazil. Embodied narratives may or may not always meet the standards of political processes for cultural recognition; nevertheless, these lived experiences are a significant part of quilombola self-identification and the fight for racial justice.

THREE

Black Lives

"WE ARE QUILOMBOLAS!"

W hen I first arrived in Grande Paraguaçu, I was welcomed by blaring white signs pasted on the walls of some homes that declared, "We are not quilombolas." As I walked around the town, it did not take me long to see other homes with hand-painted signs that loudly responded, "We are quilombolas with a lot of pride" and "I know what it is: that is why I am a Quilombola" and "I am a Quilombola until the end." I was taken aback by the sparring signs, which seemed to yell at each other in the quiet and almost empty streets of Grande Paraguaçu that afternoon. At that early stage in my research, I was not exactly sure what to expect. By then I had been told in numerous interviews that Grande Paraguaçu had been bitterly divided since the *Jornal Nacional* report aired between those who strongly identified as quilombolas and those who refused the title. The signs felt like a powerful reminder of how little I still knew about peoples lives in Grande Paraguaçu. Although I had arrived in the town armed with historical and anthropological definitions of quilombos and quilombo descendants, these signs told a different story, one that I would have to understand in practice.

Here I lay out the geographical, cultural, and social make-up of Grande Paraguaçu in order to understand the day-to-day life of the quilombolas who live there. While there are specific parameters to the definition of *quilombo*, quilombo descendants also play a central role in defining their own identity, history, and cultural practices. Because the politics of cultural recognition make bureaucratic structures overly focused on the performance of specific cultural narratives and traditions, I highlight primarily the various labor practices and embodied forms of knowing that represent everyday life and struggles for quilombolas. The quilombolas of Grande Paraguaçu locate their most valuable memories and sense of

3.1. *Quilombola home. The writings on the wall read, "We are quilombolas with a lot of pride" and "I know what it is: That is why I am Quilombola." Photograph by the author.*

3.2. *Declaration at the entrance of a home in Grande Paraguaçu. The paper reads, "We are not Quilombolas, No." The second "o" in "Quilombolas" is replaced with an icon of a face with its tongue sticking out. The rest reads, "Conselho Pastoral dos Pescadores— CPP. Maria José, Marcos Brandão, GET OUT!!!!!!!!" The CPP is an NGO that supports fishermen and women as well as the quilombolas of Grande Paraguaçu in their fight for land rights. Photograph by the author.*

3.3. *Door of the home of a quilombola leader. "I am Quilombola until the end."*
Photograph by the author.

belonging and personhood within their everyday engagements with the
land. Quilombolas describe lives that are embodied; they point to physical, black bodies that are actively interwoven with the production of a particular space. The quilombola lifestyle is most essentially dependent upon
active and able bodies that can interact with the land. While quilombola
lives are connected to the struggles of marginalized black communities
throughout Brazil, a connection that is made through references to experi-

ences felt "in the skin," quilombolas illustrate through impassioned narratives of unrelenting yet deeply satisfying labor their desires for a secure life and future in the mangroves and forest.

ANCESTORS AND BELONGING

Seu Miguel dos Santos, an active quilombola and self-identified elder of the community, called me *minha neta* (my granddaughter) on the day we met. It was a name he would use throughout my stay and for years after. When I met Seu Miguel in my second meeting with the community, he was eager to tell me the history of Brazil and Grande Paraguaçu's place in that history. He said it was his dream to have this history, as he remembered it, written down before he lost the ability to tell it. We agreed to meet for a tour of the Convento de Santo Antônio do Paraguaçu, which Seu Miguel described as the most important monument that proved the history of Grande Paraguaçu. The Convento de Santo Antônio is a Franciscan monastery that sits at the edge of town overlooking the Paraguaçu River. On the day we met to tour the monastery, I walked over to Seu Miguel's home early in the morning. He asked me to wait a minute while he finished feeding his canary. As I stood there watching Seu Miguel carefully changing the water in the cage, he looked into the cage and said,

> Sometimes I feel like our lives here in the quilombo are like the life of this *canarinho* [little canary]; we have the right to be free, yet we are not. Some of us are fighting for freedom, but others here do not want to leave the cage. Like this little canary, they are trained to believe that they would not know how to live outside of the cage. That is what these landowners have taught us to believe so that we never demand our rights.

Seu Miguel's words were filled with lament, and it would not be the last time I would hear him speak with pain and sorrow of the conflict that had divided his community. He continued:

> The color of our skin is sorrow. The black person has suffered a lot. And they say there was no slavery here, that there are no quilombos here. That is a lie! There are quilombos all around here where slaves fled when they arrived. They fled to the Boqueirão and Caonde, deep into these forests you see all around you. Those are our ancestors!

3.4. *Convento de Santo Antônio do Paraguaçu, 2009. Photograph by the author.*

Seu Miguel expressed a strong desire to teach the history of the community most of all to the youth. And true to his beliefs, Seu Miguel spent the greater part of his days surrounded by children, telling stories and teaching traditional songs during youth capoeira classes.

As we walked toward the monastery, Seu Miguel noted that most of the homes surrounding it were vacation homes that belonged to people living in Cachoeira and nearby cities. He mentioned this because many of these homes were pasted with signs that read, "Não Somos Quilombolas" (We are not quilombolas). Seu Miguel explained that the signs were posted by people who worked for the landowners, and every time the community took the signs down, they were immediately replaced. Since the homeowners were rarely in town, the signs could stay up for months or even years, a situation that highlighted the conflict in the community for anyone passing through—or for reporters eager for a story.

Walking around the massive property of the monastery, Seu Miguel narrated the history of the space and reminded me to record, photograph, and document everything. He said the quilombolas of Grande Paraguaçu consider their ancestors the enslaved blacks who built the monastery at the end of the seventeenth century. According to community history, during the monastery's construction, many blacks fled into the surrounding forest. There they formed the quilombo of Boqueirão and occupied areas named Boqueirão, Alamão, and Caibongo Velho that were chosen for their prime locations near water. Seu Miguel explained that Grande Paraguaçu was one of the most important points of arrival for slaves during the colonial period. It was from there that slaves were distributed throughout Cachoeira and other areas in the Recôncavo. Pointing toward the dense lands behind the monastery, he described how escaped slaves planted potatoes, beans, and manioc root all throughout the region. After abolition, these blacks returned to the town center, where only the white owners of the engenho had previously lived.

While Seu Miguel took me through every part of the monastery that was open to see, there was one part that especially stuck with me. It was a nook enclosed by metal bars along one of the lower walls in a side section of the monastery. We could only see the top part of the nook because the rest was under water. "Isso é o salão do mar," Seu Miguel explained. Quilombolas believe that under the monastery there is a *salão do mar*, literally a "room in the ocean," that once served as a prison for insubordinate slaves. Because the prison was built under the monastery in the water, when the water from the river would rise, prisoners would slowly drown. The skeletons of these victims are said to have been found with chains around their necks and feet. The quilombolas tell this story as an example of their historical connection to the region and to the suffering that makes them deserving of land rights. I have not been able to find written sources about the salão do mar, but it is, nonetheless, reflective of the popular memory of slavery in the region, as it is a story that every quilombola knew well.

My tour of the monastery with Seu Miguel was more than just historically informative; it revealed a great deal about the passionate commitment that the quilombolas have for their land and the ways in which the stories of the land are interconnected with their own lives and notions of belonging. I remember thinking, as I watched Seu Miguel, a man with more than eighty years of life, carefully climb over boulders to show me the salão do mar, "Where was this history and example of embodied knowledge in the *Jornal Nacional* report?" And yet I was only at the very beginning of the story.

Because I was interested in how quilombolas constructed and communicated their identity as a group, many of my interviews were conducted collectively as community meetings held in the meetinghouse. The meetinghouse was a space that the quilombolas had built for the community to congregate around any and all issues related to its political, social, and cultural life. The bare, red-brick building was little more than four walls with two window cutouts and a gray cement floor. It was still under construction after the community's first meetinghouse was destroyed in the middle of the night by unidentified men.

During one community meeting at which I met with a group of about fifteen people to talk more about the history of Grande Paraguaçu, Marta Santos, a middle school teacher, asked for the chance to speak. Recognizing the importance of what she was about to say, one of the male quilombola leaders picked up my recorder and walked over to where she was sitting. Holding the recorder close to her mouth, he gave her a nod as though to say, "Go ahead. Now you can speak to the world." A small but strongly built woman, Marta, unlike everyone else, had not grown up in Grande Paraguaçu but in the nearby town of Maragogipe. She moved to Grande Paraguaçu when she was in her twenties to teach middle school. After living there for a couple of years, she fell in love with the community and decided to settle there and start a family. She had now lived in the community for more than twenty years. Marta began by affirming that what she was about to read was a historical pamphlet that told the true story of the Convento de Santo Antônio and proved the history of the quilombo in Grande Paraguaçu. As she began, people around the room sat up, and many demanded that everyone be silent so they could hear her speak.

MARTA: What I have here in this pamphlet is the history of Grande
    Paraguaçu.
CROWD: Yes, that is important. Good!
MARTA: Here it says that the Convento de Santo Antônio was the first to
    be established in Brazil after independence from the custody of Por-
    tugal through the decree of independence signed on April 12th of
    1647 by Father João de Napolis, general minister of the Franciscan
    order, signed on April 18th of that year by the Papa Inocêncio X. . . .
    The Convento de Santo Antônio do Paraguaçu was founded in
    1649 after independence at the request of the residents of the Fre-
    guesia do Iguape, being that the lands were donated by Father
    Pedro Garcia to the custody of Brother João Batista. During those
    years the monks lived in a small chapel constructed by them in the
    Pontal that has now disappeared. This is the history of our monas-
    tery, but the most important part is the following. It says here that
    many years passed of continuous labor where under the orientation
    of Brother Daniel de Grande Paraguaçu, *slave labor* [Marta em-
    phasizes "slave labor," pausing to acknowledge people nodding in

agreement around the room], lent by plantation owners removed rocks, worked wood, made the *gamasa* [mortar], and laying down rocks and bricks, built this monument.

ANTÔNIO DE JESUS, QUILOMBOLA LEADER: The proof is there! The monastery is there for anyone to see.

MARTA: This pamphlet here is more than twenty years old. It proves that the monastery was constructed with slave labor donated by the plantation owners.

MIGUEL DOS SANTOS: Hold onto it! Don't let it go!

MARTA: This here has everything. It is our proof. I have had it for a long time. It was distributed in the school but thrown out because they did not recognize its value. I want to photocopy it because with time it will get ruined. I will not lend this to anyone. If someone needs proof, I will take the time to make a copy myself. I will not give this to anyone because I think this is the only copy in Grande Paraguaçu.

CROWD: Yes, make a copy of that! Take care of it! Don't let it go! That is our history!

MARTA: They say there is no quilombo here. This is proof! It is all written right here for anyone to see.

As she talked, the group grew loud and agitated. Marta spoke louder, adding to the excitement. People spoke out in amazement and concern for the pamphlet. For the quilombolas this one pamphlet was a document of hope—the only apparently official document they had of a historical narrative that was consistently denied to them. The history and presence of the monastery is one of the most contentious issues in Grande Paraguaçu's land dispute. While the quilombolas use it to prove that they are the descendants of slaves, others use it to prove that a quilombo could never exist in that area. The counterclaim hinges on the erroneous yet dominant historical narrative that quilombos were isolated in the middle of forests and did not exist in populated areas. Many quilombo-descendant community members do not know how the bureaucratic process of recognition works, but they understand that documents are official proof. For the quilombolas of Grande Paraguaçu, it did not matter who wrote or published the pamphlet. What mattered was that it was a document that told the history of slavery in their town. It was a document that for them proved, because the monastery is still standing, that their ancestors were slaves and because of that, they are the descendants of a quilombo.

It is not difficult to understand how this one pamphlet could be so valuable to the community. The *Jornal Nacional* accused the community of not having any slave ancestors but also of not knowing the history of their own town. As evidence, the reporter pointed out that Dona Pereira did not know that the community was once called Freguesia do Iguape. If the *Jornal Nacional* reporter had asked Marta or Seu Miguel, they would have known, and they might even have educated him. But that is the nature of dominant histories. They are wielded by the powerful and privileged as weapons used to disempower and dominate. For quilombolas, not knowing—or in some cases, not agreeing with—the dominant history of their ancestors carries greater consequences than it would for others. There is a bureaucratic process set up for identifying the validity of quilombola claims to land, and gaining validity depends on proving applicants' "understanding" and thus authenticity. Whether the reporter knows the history of his ancestors is inconsequential; his home and livelihood do not depend on his historical understanding and knowledge of self. The quilombolas of Grande Paraguaçu have learned that it is not enough to embody their history, to know it in their skin; they need documents, their own proof; they need to take back the narrative.

Although they had gone into the quilombo process optimistic and excited about their inclusion in the constitution and their right to finally own their land, after the *Jornal Nacional* report aired, the quilombolas of Grande Paraguaçu became defensive. They felt cheated, discriminated against, and disrespected. They had been accused of fraud on national television without any defense from the justice system. Their knowledge and lives—their years of labor and commitment to the land—were negated and delegitimated. By having their knowledge and relationship to their land questioned, the quilombolas also felt that their very personhood was attacked. The quilombolas of Grande Paraguaçu were not going to let that stand, nor were they going to allow it to happen again. The pamphlet was a material authority that put written history on their side and supported their struggle. The pamphlet, like Seu Miguel's mission to document the history of Grande Paraguaçu, became part of a long journey in taking back their knowledge, history, and land.

LIFE, LABOR, AND CULTURE IN PRACTICE

Grande Paraguaçu sits between the rich Mata Atlântica (Atlantic forest) and the Paraguaçu River. It is a coveted region of the Recôncavo Baiano. More than three hundred families in Grande Paraguaçu subsist on *mariscagem* (shellfishing), fishing, and agriculture. They harvest *man-dioca* (manioc or cassava root), *piaçava,*[1] *estopa* (a cottonlike fiber), dendê, *licurí*, and *castanha* (cashew fruit), as well as small mollusks, clams, crabs, oysters, and mussels in the mangroves. Schwartz describes the coastal life of the Recôncavo:

> Lands along the coast were often *mangues* [mangroves] or saltwater swamps, a problem for the planters anxious to appropriate every inch of possible cane lands, but salvation for the slaves who depended on the crabs, the *siri*, the blue *guaiamu*, and other crustaceans. (1985, 77)

While the people of Grande Paraguaçu spend their time in various forms of labor, their most significant resources come from the mangroves and the forest. Typically, while the men are working in the forest, women and children can be found working in the *manguezal* (mangrove, mangue). Women who work in the mangroves harvesting shellfish are called *maris-queiras*. The mangroves and Atlantic forest surround all of Grande Para-guaçu and the Iguape region. During my time in Grande Paraguaçu, there was only one way of knowing what work was like in the mangroves and the forest, and that was to go to work.

LIVING THROUGH THE MANGUEZAL

The first day I visited the manguezal, Marisa picked me up at Antônio's house at 6 a.m. Luciana and Luis, two of Antônio's children, came with us. Both were just under fifteen years old and were said to be very knowl-edgeable of the manguezal. We walked straight to Lúcia's home just a few houses down the street. "*Embora*, Lúcia! The siri won't wait for you to fin-ish your coffee," Marisa yelled from the street. We waited a few minutes while she gathered her gear. Lúcia was another marisqueira and quilom-bola. She and Marisa were good friends and often worked together. The manguezal was about a forty-five-minute walk down the dirt road just out-side the community. It was the rainy season, so the road was muddy and covered with potholes filled from the incessant rain. We cut through some small farms and larger *fazendas* (ranches or estates).

The walk didn't feel so long because Marisa and Lúcia were talking to me about the land conflict and showing me the lands that were under dispute. They pointed to lands that once were covered with fruit trees of all varieties but that were now barren, "destroyed by *fazendeiros* [landowners] to keep people from taking their fruit," Marisa lamented. "We used to be able to collect fruit freely for our families, but now most of the land is cleared and used for grazing cattle. They would rather have these lands empty than to allow us to enjoy fruit from their trees. It's so sad," Lúcia added. Before arriving at the mangrove, we stopped at a small river that looked more like a creek. Marisa said the river had mostly dried up because of deforestation in the area. We cleaned our muddy feet in its water, and Marisa and Luciana changed their clothes. "This is where we always stop to change," Marisa commented. "We change into our older work clothes and leave our clean clothes here by the river. When we leave the manguezal, we will stop here again to bathe and change back into our clean clothes."

When we arrived at the manguezal, Marisa and Lúcia sat down to change out of their sandals and into their work shoes. Marisa explained that the mud in the manguezal was filled with sharp and painful things that could easily cut your feet even if you were very careful. They all had special shoes, actually old tennis shoes, that they used to protect their feet. Marisa brought an extra pair for me. She apologized that the shoes were not a matching pair. One of the shoes had grown so worn it had an exposed staple on the inside, making it unwearable. Before we could put on the old shoes, Marisa had to soak them in the river so they would soften. These shoes were worn only for going into the mangrove, and even though they were rinsed after each workday, they still dried hard from the mud. Shoes on and tools in hand, we descended into the manguezal. I had no idea what to expect. I will admit that when I saw the opening into the short, thick trees with wide roots and black mud, I was a little worried about what I would encounter.

As soon as we walked in, I lost my bearings. The ground under me grew soft, and my steps grew weak. My feet and legs were sucked into the ground with force each step I took. "Walk on the branches, but be careful because they are slippery," Marisa yelled from already deep in the manguezal. I struggled to find and walk on the roots of the trees. They were good signs of firm ground but were coated in mildew and so slippery they were no easier to walk on than the mud. There were also short root sprouts that stuck out of the ground and, I quickly learned, also indicated firm ground.

I moved slowly, my eyes glued to the ground, terrified of falling into one of the crab holes Marisa warned me about. "If you fall into a crab hole, you can be buried up to your chest. It happens to us all the time, and then someone has to pull you out." I never sank in that deep, but to my utter terror, I did sink down to my knees a few times. One young girl who came with us, Niara, who wasn't a marisqueira, also sank into holes several times. She stayed close to me so we could pull each other out if needed. Everyone else went straight to work. It's not difficult to imagine that I was left behind pretty quickly. Juliana and Luis moved through the mangroves running after crabs like experts. I was amazed at their precision. I was mostly amazed because Antônio had told me that he did not allow his children to work in the mangrove often. Even Marisa said she was surprised that they were allowed to come with us that day. Antônio had already explained to me that he was working hard so that his children could go to school and have a different life, one that was not as hard as working in the forest and manguezal.

I struggled to catch up with Lúcia so I could film her working. She was so fast and determined it was difficult to get a still shot. Marisa and Lúcia ran after all sorts of crabs, siri, *aratu*, and *caranguejo*. Some crabs such as the medium-size, dark-blue caranguejo live in deep holes that require careful attention to find. Other crabs like the large, red aratu live high up in the mangrove trees. Aratus could be heard in the quiet of the manguezal running furiously from trunk to trunk. To catch these, marisqueiras used sticks to knock them down and then scrambled to catch them on the ground before they ran away. Lúcia, Marisa, Juliana, and Luis plunged their arms into the mud wherever they saw a crab stop. They dug into the holes and homes of caranguejos, which were famous for giving the most painful bites known to the community. Marisa and Lúcia wore gloves, but gloves did not protect the rest of their arms, which were also deep in the hole. Lúcia was bitten on the arm once before. She said it was incredibly painful, but she still kept working. Unlike the rest of us, Lúcia did not wear old tennis shoes. She said they hurt her toenails and made her clumsy while navigating the mud and slippery branches. She had long made her own footwear—special socks hand sewn out of two layers of what Lúcia referred to as resistant and impenetrable fabric.

When Lúcia and Marisa went after caranguejos, they usually kept their arms in the crab holes, digging and feeling around until they captured the creatures. Sometimes they had to lie down in the mud on their sides to get their arms in deeper. At times Lúcia would dig in so far I thought she was going to be sucked in. When they finally caught their victims, they rinsed them off in muddy water and threw them into a bucket or straw bag. We were in the manguezal for more than an hour. Admittedly, it wasn't a normal workday. The women were there to show me what their work was like. Marisa explained:

This time we all stayed together because we came mostly to show you how we work, but normally when we get here we all split up and get lost from each other. When we are ready to go home, around one or 2 p.m., we call out to each other or whistle so we can all leave together. The water usually begins to rise around 3 p.m., so we have to be out before that starts to happen. Otherwise we have to swim out. We also didn't go very far out this time because it is your first time. You would not be able to handle going farther out. We normally walk out into the middle of the bay. We go all the way out to that island I showed you while we were walking out here. It's very far.

On most occasions, marisqueiras worked eight to ten hours in the manguezal, depending on the tide and the time of day they began their work. Women needed to be well aware of the time of day and the time the tide rose so they didn't get trapped in the mangrove. On a normal work-day, women walked out for miles into the middle of the bay or river without even noticing how far they had gone. It usually took an hour to walk back to the nearest mangrove exit. When the tide began to rise, it only took minutes for the manguezal to disappear under water, leaving only some of the taller trees as markers of the mangue's presence. Marisqueiras were usually aware of the time they should make their way out of the mangrove, but just in case someone was not paying attention, they whistled at the end of the day to alert all of the women that it was time to leave. All of the women were usually counted at the end of a workday to make sure no one was left behind.

Mariscagem was described as difficult labor. Although it was an important source of food for families, it offered little income. When they left the mangue, women carried several kilos of mariscos home on their head, and then went straight into cooking it and separating out the crabmeat. A couple of kilos of crabmeat, or *catado*, sold in the city for about seven or eight reais (three to four dollars). It was a lot of work for very little money. No one survived on mariscagem alone, at least not any more. Mariscagem was used to feed the family, and what could be sold was sold for supplemental income.

Reflecting on the labor of mariscagem, I asked Marisa if pregnant women worked in the mangrove. She laughed and said, "Claro!" (Of course!). Marisa continued:

I came to the mangue all throughout my pregnancies, up until the day before I gave birth. The day before I gave birth my mother told me not

3.5. *Woman separating crabmeat after a day of mariscagem. Photograph by the author.*

3.6. *Children helping their mothers separate crabmeat. Photograph by the author.*

to come to work because I would be giving birth soon. I went to work anyway. The next day when I woke up I knew that would be the day. I told everyone I wasn't going to work because I would give birth that day, and sure enough I gave birth that afternoon. But it's not just me. We are all mangue babies. All of our mothers worked in the mangue throughout their pregnancies. *Não é grande coisa. Isso é tão normal* [It is not a big deal. That is so normal].

I found the expression "mangue baby" very interesting, as I was still trying to understand the meaning of *quilombola*. Marisa explained that a mangue baby was a person whose entire life, even before birth, was rooted in the mangroves. She was someone who had grown up working in the manguezal with her mother and who had learned to step lightly, balance on the roots, and identify crab holes. A mangue baby knew the exact movements of the tide and when to enter and leave the manguezal at different times of the day. Her entire body was accustomed to the mud of the mangrove, and she joked that the mud did wonders for her skin. Thinking about Marisa's words, the "mangue baby" represents one example of the embodied lives of quilombolas. Marisa described the mangue baby as someone who not only carried the mangue on her skin every workday but who also understood the movements, needs, and dangers of the space. While thinking about the expression "mangue baby" to understand the embodied lives of quilombolas, it is important to not essentialize or romanticize this idea; to do so would lead us dangerously close to the reproduction of a primitive black subject that is no different than the animals and the trees of the environment she or he inhabits (Alcida Ramos 1998, 64). The women I interviewed in Grande Paraguaçu all spoke of their lives as difficult and *sofridas* (of suffering). Mariscagem was arduous work that took a toll on women's bodies, especially their backs, which grew weak from hours of bending over to dig, and their hands, legs, and feet, which were frequently bitten and scarred by crabs and other animals. Although they never painted a romantic picture of their lives, the women of Grande Paraguaçu were nonetheless proud of their embodied knowledge of the mangue. The manguezal was an important part of their lives and memories.

It took us a little over forty-five minutes to return to the manguezal entrance. Marisa and Lúcia smiled at each other noting that we had not gone very far at all. We were covered in mud, and as I walked on firm land, I noticed the mud in my shoes. We walked back to the river, as promised, to wash ourselves off and change clothes. The kids immediately jumped in the water and washed their entire bodies. Juliana even washed her hair. The water was freezing. I washed off my feet and noticed a medium-size scrape on my ankle. My toenails were black, and it was impossible to get all of the mud out of them. Marisa said I would have to use lemon juice to get it all out. Marisa took off all her clothes and also bathed in the river. Lúcia had a bar of soap she used to bathe and to wash her dirty clothes. We hung out and enjoyed the river for a few minutes and then made our way home. As we walked back along the winding dirt road, Marisa explained that it was a good walk because it was winter, so it was cool and breezy. "During the summer, the walk back home from the mangue is terrible," she said. "The sun is so hot on our heads it is really miserable." As she spoke, I tried to imagine a pregnant woman walking back in scorching summer sun with pounds of *mariscos* (shellfish) on her head.

THE TIME DONA ANDIRA SPENT
THE NIGHT IN THE MANGUE

Dona Andira was a marisqueira for nearly seventy years. Like most of the quilombolas, Dona Andira started working in the mangroves with her mother when she was just a young girl. When she had her own children, she also took them into the mangroves at young ages. It was what she knew best. At eighty years old, Andira experienced a stroke that impaired her walking and memory. The stroke eventually led to her permanent retirement from the manguezal, a forced retirement that threw her into a deep depression. But just months before her stroke, Andira was still working daily. It was not until she was forced to spend the night in the mangroves that she understood that life was changing for her. I was told this story during a second visit with Dona Andira. Marisa had come along to help me talk with her grandmother. Most of the story was recounted by Marisa with Dona Andira interjecting in moments when she seemed to feel a strong recollection of what she thought and felt that day. Andira sat in her blue rocking chair, just as she had the first time I met her, and listened quietly as Marisa narrated her story.

> Like I said, when we go out to the mangue we never stay together but we try to stay close. If we get lost, we whistle to find each other before going home. But Andira knows the manguezal better than anyone else in the community. That day she decided to go further out from the rest of the group to take advantage of another area.
>
> It was a little after one o'clock, and Andira went out for miles, thinking that the bay was going down at that time and would not rise until much later. After hours of working, she looked around and noticed that the bay was rising. She was almost entirely surrounded by water that was rising very quickly. By that point she was so far out in the middle of the bay, there was no way she would make it out of the manguezal, especially since she did not know how to swim. Andira called out to her companion dog and hugged the dog tight.

Before our conversation began, I commented to Dona Andira about all of the stray dogs I had seen in the town. She corrected me, saying that they were not strays. "Each dog belongs to a marisqueira. They are our best friends and trusty work companions," she said. Dona Andira explained that dogs helped them dig up *sururu*, small crustaceans that look like black, oval oysters. Sometimes the dogs caught crabs, too. But they were most useful as companions, to keep women company when they were separated from the rest of the group.

> MARISA: When the water was almost up to her chest, she scrambled and found a low branch that had not been covered by the water and that was still low enough for her to climb up.

DONA ANDIRA: The Lord put that branch there for me. [She laughs.] It
was like it was waiting for me. I climbed up on the branch with my
little dog and prayed that it would rain so I could drink some water.
I was so thirsty. When it started to sprinkle rain, I gave thanks for
the rain and drank as much as I could. I did not know what to do. I
was scared to call out because I had heard that there was a man who
raped elderly women, so instead I slept. I actually slept very well,
and when I woke up I could hear the roosters. I also heard two men's
voices approaching in a canoe. I called out for help. "Hey canoe, hey
canoe," I yelled. They heard me and asked who I was. I said, "I'm
lost. Are you going to Grande Paraguaçu?" They said yes and told
me to hold on because they were going to get me. They carried me
into the canoe, but we struggled to get the dog in. Can you believe
she wanted to stay? Crazy dog! At first I hesitated to get in the canoe
because it was so nice and clean and I was so dirty and covered in
mud. I knew they were not really going to Grande Paraguaçu, but
they felt bad for me and wanted to take me home. They offered me
bread, crackers, and some coffee, but I just wanted water! I was so
thirsty I drank two liters of water all by myself that day.

MARISA: While she was sleeping in a tree, everyone here at home was
dreading the worst. We were up all night looking for Andira with
no luck. Antônio went to the manguezal in a boat but couldn't find
her. He was so upset. We were all in disbelief when we heard she had
not returned home because she knew the manguezal better than
any of us. I was already in mourning because I thought she surely
had drowned. If she knew the manguezal better than me, how could
she be lost? I thought she was dead. And then, when she got home
she didn't even tell anyone! Can you believe that? [Andira laughs
at Marisa's alarm.] We all cried and laughed. We couldn't believe
that she was so calm like nothing had happened! The next time you
decide to spend the night in the mangue, please let us know first!
[Marisa grasped her grandmother's hands tightly, smiling and looking into her eyes.]

DONA ANDIRA: When I got here, the streets were empty. I was so tired. I
just showered, had some breakfast, and went to sit by the window.

At this point, Dona Andira barely spoke any more, saying very little
else about the manguezal or her life as a marisqueira. As I carefully attempted to interview her, Marisa explained that Dona Andira was never
the same after her stroke. "She does not like to talk about the life she had

because it makes her very sad to remember now when she can hardly move from her chair." Marisa explained it to me through the idea of the mangue baby. She told me that the mangue was all Dona Andira ever knew. She was born and raised in the mangue, and that is where she raised her own children and grandchildren. As Marisa and I spoke, Dona Andira sat quietly between us staring out into the street.

Dona Andira's story quickly fused into a discussion of quilombolismo and land rights. Marisa extended Dona Andira's sadness to the threats being made by landowners and the prospect of losing their homes. The memory of Dona Andira's night in the mangue became a story the quilombolas told frequently to illustrate how deeply their everyday lives were intertwined with the manguezal. In her explanation of collective memory, Sally Cole describes how "social memory is produced through the dynamic interplay of agents . . . and particular contexts" (2003, 95). She argues that individual narratives or stories contribute to the production of collective memory. "Memories are best viewed as a complex outcome," Cole writes, "of the way people's 'moral projects' shape their selection, use, and interpretation of particular events" (ibid.). Dona Andira's night in the mangue was never described as carelessness due to her age or failing health. Rather, it was seen as a representation of changing times in the community and as a symbol of everything they stood to gain or lose in the quilombo process. The story stood as almost an omen because nobody in the community could explain how one of the most skilled marisqueiras could get lost in the mangue. The quilombo political process had thrown the entire community into a tumultuous situation that seemed to be most difficult for the elders.

After Dona Andira, I met two other quilombola elders who also shared a narrative of silence. Their quiet faces reflected a desire to be left alone as well as a sign of caution. Spoken narratives are difficult enough to interpret, so I do not pretend to understand Dona Andira's silence exactly as she experienced it. I can only reflect on the interpretations of others and the understanding that the community was undergoing major changes.

"PROTECTORS OF THE FOREST": LABOR IN THE MATA ATLÂNTICA

Antônio and Sumido took me into the Atlantic forest so I could also get a feel for their work. We started out on the small dirt road that leads to the farinha house and to all the quilombo *roças* (land plots). We walked for about forty-five minutes until the road became loose, white sand. The

3.7. *Seu Miguel looking out into the Atlantic forest. Photograph by the author.*

stretch of sand lasted for about thirty minutes and was extremely difficult to walk with tennis shoes. The morning was cloudy and crisp. The day eventually grew hot and dry while we were in the forest, but I never noticed. The forest had its own climates. Some places were dark, damp, and cool, while others were hot and arid. As we reached the end of the road, which had become more like a trail, Antônio pointed out the various entrances that could take us into the forest. "This entrance we are using today is one of the closest points," he said, pointing to his left. "We'll go in here because you will not be able to handle going in farther on your first visit. This is a good work area, but most are much farther out." We walked into the forest mostly going uphill. We were still on a trail for a short while, but as we walked on, the forest grew thicker and the trail began to disappear and give way to steep rocks, slippery slopes, and winding creeks. We continued our walk, maintaining a rhythm of ups and downs. Sumido asked if my shoes had smooth soles. The ground was wet and slippery, so regardless of how careful I was, I slipped and fell many times, but I got used to it. Besides making sure I did not step on any snakes or other creatures, I had to watch out for sudden slopes, holes, and branches as the trail disappeared.

All along the way, Antônio and Sumido cut piaçava, a fibrous material used for making brooms. Antônio pointed out different types of trees and plants and explained how they were used. He had learned to identify and use medicinal plants from his father. He told me it was a gift that was passed down through the generations. His father learned from Antônio's grandfather, and Antônio would also teach his own son. We saw trees used for making the *berimbau*, a musical instrument used in capoeira. Antônio also pointed out trees used for making furniture and work tools as well as plants that were good for rheumatism, strokes, common pains, and other afflictions. The quilombolas did not cut down trees for furniture or other large industrial uses. They primarily went into the forest for piaçava. Not only did quilombolas not have the tools to cut down and treat such massive trees, but also they saw themselves as protectors of the forest, as Antônio explained:

> Rede Globo accused us of deforestation, but that is impossible. Why would we destroy the forest that we need to survive? Why would we cut down and kill that which puts food on our tables. We do not deforest. We don't even have the means or machinery to be able to do what the fazendeiros and large corporations do to our *mata* [forest].

When we finally reached a common work area, Antônio and Sumido disappeared into the forest. I struggled to find them and realized how deceptive the forest could be for someone who did not know it. I walked around slowly, carefully parting the trees in front of me. When I finally found them, we started back through a different route to see some of the waterfalls hidden in the forest. Antônio showed me a creek where they stopped to rest and eat lunch on a regular workday. There were even some hidden sacks with empty bottles that men left out so that they could drink water when they arrived in the afternoon. The waterfall was distant and painfully difficult to access. We walked on the margins of a steep hillside that rose right above the creek. I had to hold onto the trees to keep from falling or sliding to the bottom. The walk was difficult, to say the least, but it was important. The waterfall was tall and powerful. It was an amazing experience to stand before something that seemed like nothing less than a natural treasure.

As we walked back, the day had grown hot, and the sun beat down relentlessly on our tired bodies. Antônio and Sumido asked me to imagine carrying pounds of piaçava on my back. The narrative was similar to the one told by marisqueiras. The men usually went to work at 4 a.m. and began to make their way back home around 2 or 3 p.m., arriving home between 4 and 6 p.m., depending on how far out they had gone. "This is how we survive," Sumido said proudly. Antônio explained more:

> It is hard work, but we never go hungry, and it is honest. If our stoves ever run out of gas, we can cut some firewood and still have fire to cook our food. When will I ever be able to do that in the city? I would not leave all of this for anything in the world. They say we deforest, but it is a lie. We take care of the forest, and we only take what we need to survive. Why would we kill that which feeds and clothes us?

Sumido and Antônio explained how important the certificate of recognition that they received from the Palmares Cultural Foundation was for the community. Before then, they said, people were thrown off their lands without impunity, and men were even barred from going into the forest to collect piaçava. Sumido recalled how they had to go into the forest and work quietly so they would not be heard by the landowner's *capachos* (henchmen). "If these men caught us working in the forest, they would stop us at gunpoint and call us thieves," Sumido recalled angrily.

As we neared Sumido's small plot of land, the men showed me all of the lands that had been taken away from quilombolas by landowners and areas that had been small farms and were now barren and overgrown by weeds. The trip into the forest, like the manguezal, tested the limits of my body at every creek and slope, but without it I would not have understood the magnitude of the land at stake in the quilombo conflict. The land quilombolas are fighting for is not limited to their homes and farms; it also includes the forest. Because quilombolas largely survive from the forest, bay, and mangroves, moving them to any other location would be detrimental to their lifestyle, sense of self, and sense of belonging. While quilombolas cannot own the mangroves and Atlantic forest because these are national territories, it is understood that they need these lands to survive. Not only do they extract piaçava and dendê for minor income, but they also depend on the medicinal plants, firewood, and fruits of the forest.

Having learned the medicinal properties of plants from his father, Antônio gave me a list of some of the plants his family used: *banho de folha de algodão brabo* (for rheumatism), *erva doce* (for gas), *boldo* (for stomach pains), *banho de aroeira* (for wounds and menstrual pains), *caroço de laranja torrado* (for diabetes), *papa nicolau* (to stimulate abortion or for liver problems), *mutamba* (for hair loss), *capim santo* and *erva cidreira* (for their calming properties), and *araçá mirim* (for dysentery).

In addition to the use of natural resources, the forest was also a spiritual part of the community. The quilombolas told stories of beings that protected the forest. For instance, the Caipora was believed to be a creature (male or female) that protected the forest and animals. It was said that it could cause people to get lost in the forest if they saw it. Therefore, when entering the forest, people were supposed to whistle so as not to be distracted and deceived by the Caipora. Quilombolas also took *fumo* (tobacco twisted into a ring-shaped rope) and *charutos* (cigars) as offerings to appease the Caipora as well as candles to light their way. When Antônio and Sumido took me into the forest, they whistled as soon as we began to leave the trails. The first whistles startled me because they were answered by another quilombola already working in the forest who was practically made invisible by the thick brush. The story of the Caipora, also known as Curupira and Vovô do Mato, is a common folk story told throughout Brazil; it is popularly believed to have originated as a Tupí Guaraní legend (R. Guimarães 1968). Like all folklore, the Caipora story alters slightly depending on who tells it. Some describe the Caipora as an Indian woman covered in leaves, others as a short, indigenous boy, and others as a little man with fire for hair and a green body. The quilombolas have maintained and taught these stories so as to foster respect for the forest.

The Palmares Cultural Foundation and other government organizations charged with observing environmental rights in Brazil have documented the value of the forest for quilombo-descendant communities (Bennett 2008). In my interviews with representatives of the Palmares Cultural Foundation and of the Office for the Promotion of Racial Equality (SEPROMI, Secretaría de Promoção da Igualdade Racial), quilombo descendants were often described as the "protectors" or "keepers" of the forest. Their lives were connected directly to the development and preservation of the lands, so much so that the law came to include this symbiotic relationship in its stipulations for granting land rights. Statute 56 determines that INCRA must identify and describe in detail a community's relation to the environment, including production and sustainability.

When INCRA's report is completed, it must be sent to the Institute of Environment and Renewable Natural Resources (IBAMA, Instituto Brasileiro do Meio Ambiente e dos Recursos Naturais Renovaveis), among other agencies, to determine whether the disputed lands are areas of environmental protection (APAs, Areas de Proteção Ambiental). If they are, such as an important mangrove in Grande Paraguaçu that was declared an APA, then IBAMA has to determine if the community is caring for the area or if the land needs to be officially closed to all extraction. Sustainable

3.8. *Garbage collected from the mangroves. Two weeks' worth of bagged trash is piled to the left of the meetinghouse. Photograph by the author.*

living and environmental protection is required of quilombo descendants and have become part of the language used to describe labor practices within these communities. Many quilombolas in Bahia have organizations dedicated to environmental protection. The quilombolas of Grande Paraguaçu named their organization Amantes da Terra (Lovers of the Land). These quilombolas maintain an artisan fishing association that ensures that the community only practices sustainable fishing. Antônio explained that fishermen and women were taught to only catch larger fish and return the smaller ones to the water to ensure their reproduction.

Similarly, the quilombolas of Grande Paraguaçu formed a group that cleaned the mangroves every weekend. Because mangroves are natural barriers and filters of the ocean and river waters that flow through the bay, they are often filled with litter from passing boats and urban garbage. Quilombolas need the mangroves for their daily sustenance, so they are very concerned with keeping them clean so the pollution does not interfere with the survival of the species on which they depend. Throughout Brazil, hundreds of mangroves have become barren wastelands that are no longer rich in marine life to be harvested. I accompanied one of the cleaning expeditions in Grande Paraguaçu. The quilombola leaders called INCRA to show the agency their mangrove-cleaning project in hopes that they could get some funding to support their work.

In just a few hours of work, we collected five large bags of trash that included large pieces of scrap metal, car tires, and even old shoes. Most of the garbage was obviously from large boats and factories. One of the requirements of cultural recognition is that the community protect and care for the environment. INCRA officials were very attentive and documented everything the quilombolas collected. The area they were cleaning that day was a mangrove that was declared an environmentally protected area. Marisqueiras were no longer allowed to work in this mangrove. Because it was no longer a work site, it became more susceptible to contamination because it was not visited as often as other places. Antônio said the quilombolas took on the responsibility of cleaning the mangroves because the state had refused to do it, claiming that the government did not have the resources to carry out such a large project. The state was also responsible for collecting the community's trash, which was piled up at the entrance of the town each week. Antônio said they were never certain the trash would be collected on schedule. Every week was different. The day INCRA representatives visited Grande Paraguaçu to observe the cleaning project, Antônio made sure to call their attention to the uncollected trash still sitting at the town entrance from the previous week.

BODIES OF LABOR

Labor in Grande Paraguaçu did not end with foresting and mariscagem.[2] During the winter, the community primarily focused on the cultivation and production of manioc.[3] Manioc root is used in the production of various foods, such as tapioca, *beijú*, and farinha, and provided an important staple food for the quilombolas of Grande Paraguaçu. Farinha is a coarse flour made from manioc root, also known as cassava or yucca in other parts of Latin America and Africa. The farinha house (*casa de farinha*) was a small, open structure where the manioc was peeled, cut, and ground into flour to make farinha and tapioca. Every day of the week, primarily women could be seen working at the farinha house. Just the process of peeling and cutting the manioc, divided up among five women, took all day depending on the amount of manioc. Because of the tremendous amount of labor it took, farinha was usually made once a week, but sometimes it could be made every day depending on how many families needed it. One of the changes that quilombolas hoped to see from the cul-

3.9 (top). *Child peeling manioc. Photograph by the author.*

3.10 (left). *Women peeling manioc in preparation for making farinha. Photograph by the author.*

3.11 (right). *Grinding manioc to make into dough. Photograph by the author.*

3.12 (bottom left). *Woman washing manioc dough to make farinha. Photograph by the author.*

3.13 (bottom right). *Women removing excess water from the dough. Once the dough is washed and drained, it is sealed in a special container to dry overnight. After the dough dries, it is baked into crunchy, coarse farinha that is ready to sprinkle on any meal. Photograph by the author.*

tural recognition process was the creation of more income-earning jobs in the community. Quilombolas wanted support from the government so they could sell more of their products, especially farinha and catado, in the surrounding cities. They wanted a more secure way of making an income that would help them develop their homes, farms, and community activities and help them pay for school supplies as well as bus fares for everything that had to be done outside of the community.

I spent a great part of my fieldwork in the farinha house, usually in the afternoons. It was a place where, in addition to work, women and men gathered to talk and gossip about everything going on in the community, from quilombola affairs to conflicts with nonquilombolas, to problems in their own households. The women I observed spent hours sitting on the dirt ground peeling the tough skin off the manioc with small knives. Older children helped their mothers, and younger children hung out and observed. At one point a young woman breastfed her baby while carefully peeling manioc. On an afternoon after I had spent more time in the community, I called attention to what I had long observed as a painful working position. I asked the women if any of them had back pain from sitting on the ground, hunched over for hours peeling manioc. Almost unanimously they yelled out that everyone in Grande Paraguaçu had a "broken back." Joelma Nascimento spoke up about this condition:

> When we are done making farinha, everything hurts, my back, my arms, my hands, my *bumbum* [bottom], even my *pinguelo* [clitoris] hurts! [Others laughed hysterically and threw manioc peels at her.] Everything hurts! It feels like my back is split open when I am done. The nurse at the health post won't even treat me any more. When I go in complaining about my back, she tells everyone at the clinic, "Here she comes again. *Ela gosta!*" [She likes it!] So I don't even go any more, and then she asks why I don't go. I have to work, I tell her. I can't stop working just because my back hurts. My finger is burning just from holding this knife. That's how it is here.

Even though everyone laughed at Joelma's candid response to my question, it was a serious matter. Many people in the community suffered severe back pain from the amount of strain they placed on their bodies throughout the day. Because there was only a health post and not a full-time doctor in Grande Paraguaçu, people often worked through pain and illness. And as Joelma stated, people simply could not just stop working. If they did, they would not have anything to eat. Most people did not make a solid income that would allow them to feed their families without working every day.

Antônio and Sumido had described how people in Grande Paraguaçu lived and survived from the land. Nina, Antônio's wife, had to be forced out of the manguezal by several dislocated disks in her back. One day her back pain became so unbearable that she had no choice but to go to the hospital in the nearby city of São Felix. The doctor told her that her back was "all broken" and that if she didn't stay out of the mangue she could soon lose the ability to walk. The pain in her spine also caused Nina incredible leg pain. Even with such a grim warning, Nina rested for a few months and then went back to work. She worked less frequently, only going to the mangue every couple of weeks, but she never stopped. On a few more occasions the pain return twofold and forced her back into the hospital. When I tried to talk to Nina about her back, she would just look down and say, "*Coisa chata*! [Annoying thing!] It won't let me do anything." Nina was sad that she could not be in the manguezal every day. She was not accustomed to being inside the house all day, and it made her very unhappy.

The people of Grande Paraguaçu worked seven days a week and what must have felt like twenty-four hours a day. When people were not working in the mangue, fishing, making farinha or dendê, cutting piaçava, or making brooms they were at one of the two local water fountains collecting water and washing clothes. For a quilombola, the work she performed in the forest, mangroves, river, and farm was not only part of her cultural identity, it was an extension of her relationship to her own body. Having an able body that could work the land was fundamental to the quilombola's ideal life, but it also determined how she interacted with the world. Having lost their ability to work in the manguezal, Dona Andira and Nina felt that they had nothing to say to me or most other people who asked about their lives. Although these women still engaged in the world, their representations of self became reduced and even silenced without the manguezal. Expressions such as "mangue baby," "Amantes da Terra," and "broken back" speak vividly for themselves, signaling a centrality of the body in an everyday engagement and relationship with the land. While the body, as Csordas notes, is not the object of anthropological inquiry, it is the subject and transformative tool of culture, the ground and mechanism through which everyday life is enacted.

RACIALIZED BODIES OF LABOR AND EXCLUSION

The idea that land and labor are key markers of class difference in Brazil is not new. Research on the unequal distribution of land and the plight of the rural poor has been the subject of numerous research studies (Cardoso 1997, Pereira 1997, 2003). However, land and labor are also key markers of racial and ethnic difference. The racial make-up of the black, rural poor is an issue that has only begun to receive sustentative attention with the recognition of quilombola communities and their fight for land rights. Using data from the 2010 census, the Instituto Brasileiro de Geografia e Estatística (IBGE) found that 16.2 million people in Brazil were living below the federal poverty level. According to the IBGE report, which was commissioned in 2011 by the Dilma Rousseff administration for the creation of a new social program called Brasil sem Miséria (Brazil without Misery), the majority of the people in extreme poverty live in rural areas in the Northeastern region of Brazil and are primarily black and pardo.[4] With these figures to bear in mind, it makes sense that almost two thousand rural, black communities have identified themselves as the descendants of quilombos, uniting around more than just a historical past of slavery and resistance but more importantly around an embodied and collective experience of marginalization and social struggle.

During one of my meetings with Anita Souza, the INCRA anthropologist, she asked me for help in translating the subtitles for a short film she had created about the life of Dona Maria das Dores, one of the first quilombola leaders of Grande Paraguaçu. Dona Maria died in 2008, the year before I began my fieldwork. Although I never met Dona Maria, her story was told repeatedly in the community. She fought fiercely for the community's land title, but in the end she was not able to see it happen. In one part of the recording, Dona Maria speaks before a public audience in defense of quilombola rights:

> Who puts food on the tables of the rich, whether he is a landowner or a wealthy farmer? It is the poor laborer who puts food on people's tables. All we ask is for our rights to be respected; for the love of God, we do not want our children to go through what we have gone through. Do you know why I'm saying this, because I am fifty-nine years old; I am the mother of twelve children and fifteen grandchildren, and I never went to school. I can barely write my own name because all I have had time to do is work and suffer. One thing I wanted to say, just a few things because I do not know how to speak correctly, what I know is how to work, but

speak I will! About the things we experience deep in our skin. God gave us this coarse hair, our skin color, and our origin with a lot of pride, and that is what people have to understand. Our rights cannot exist only on paper or at the bottom of some desk drawer. Let the rights of each person to carry their machetes on their waist and work in the fields planting their manioc be made clear. Go plant your seeds! Plant to survive!

Dona Maria's statement is powerful for the bodily descriptors that she uses to communicate her experience and to connect it to the experiences of others like her. It is important to understand the ways in which a physical body becomes intertwined with a space, as this is the fundamental basis for belonging. In other words, quilombola narratives of labor remind us that spaces are not only produced by structures of reason—in this case, historical and cultural narratives used to define a space as meaningful and purposeful in the past and present (Gupta and Ferguson 1992). Rather, spaces are most immediately and significantly produced by the ways people physically interact with them, the ways bodies stand, sit, bend, lean, walk, eat, breathe, sweat, speak, and hurt within a space. Bourdieu explains, "Bodily hexis is political mythology realized, *em-bodied*, turned into a permanent disposition, a durable way of standing, speaking walking, and thereby of feeling and thinking" (1990, 70). Like her fellow quilombolas, Dona Maria speaks to quilombola rights directly through her own embodied knowledge; she speaks about what she can do and what she cannot: she "did not go to school and can barely write," but she works, puts "food on people's tables," and suffers. She does "not know how to speak" but she "will speak" about what she experiences "deep in the skin." Dona Maria not only emphasizes the centrality of the body (what the body does and does not do) but particularly the racialized body, the black body, characterized by hair, skin, and origin.

Seu Miguel also emphasized the black body when he reflected on the *Jornal Nacional*'s denial of slave and quilombo ancestry in Grande Paraguaçu, lamenting the "sorrow" embedded in the blackness of his skin color. Emphasis on the skin highlights the visible body and the less visible effects of race and skin color on everyday experiences and emotions. Seu Miguel and Dona Maria point to a skin that is impregnated with experiences of sorrow, suffering, struggle, and labor. This is the body that goes into the mangroves and fields to work every day, that carries the machete to plant manioc, and that is fighting for land rights in Grande Paraguaçu.

Yet, this body could also be fighting for land rights in a favela of Salvador (Perry 2013), performing domestic labor in a wealthy neighborhood of

Rio (Goldstein 2003), entering the whitewashed classrooms of the Federal University of Bahia or any other federal university in Brazil, or walking past the mistrusting and violent gaze of the state police. The underlying message is the connection of the quilombola experience of labor and struggle with the experiences of other marginalized black communities throughout Brazil. Similar to the way the terms for *negro, afro-brasileiro,* and *quilombola* share an ethnosemantic foundation, so too do the experiences of marginalization and racial injustice build racial solidarity, as Hooker finds (2009), among black Brazilians in multiple spaces. While the connection to a larger fight for black justice is an important part of quilombola narratives, it does not negate the quilombola's particular connection to a specific land. Thus quilombolas desire the freedom and legal right to work in the mangroves, plant manioc, and live from the forest; however, they want to do these things within a secure space where they can build a future for their children without the constant fear that it might be taken away.

Dona Maria makes a clear demand that cannot be overlooked and is the primary message of the quilombolas (and this book) when she states, "God gave us this coarse hair, our skin color, and our origin with a lot of pride, and that is what people have to understand. Our rights cannot exist only on paper or at the bottom of some desk drawer." Dona Maria's message in this statement is clear: black bodies, black rights. Dona Maria, like Abdias do Nascimento, spoke against ideas and promises of equality that are written in legal documents. For her these are just words on a piece of paper often quite literally stuffed at the bottom of a larger pile of papers in some bureaucratic desk drawer. And just to be clear, this is not a metaphor for exclusion, nor is it an imagined analogy to make a point. Quilombolas are repeatedly told in meetings with representatives of INCRA and other government agencies that there is not enough money, employees are scarce, and the bureaucratic process is long; they are told to be patient because there are hundreds of cases before theirs. When the years pass with no results, quilombolas are encouraged to fight and protest because the bureaucratic structure is broken. Quilombola rights are stuffed in desk drawers, and no doubt every quilombola listening to Dona Maria's words could relate to her statement *na pele.* Dona Maria was demanding rights in action and directly aimed at the black population, which has experienced injustice throughout the history of the nation.

But the government recognizes "a specific relationship to the land, and the presumption of a black ancestry connected to forms of resistance to historical oppression" (Araujo 2007), everything that the quilombolas of Grande Paraguaçu passionately demonstrate and live. Then why, after almost ten years of having received cultural recognition from the Palmares Cultural Foundation as an official quilombo community, did Grande Paraguaçu still not have a land title? I could write page after page about the importance and particularity of an embodied black experience of labor, struggle, and exclusion in the quilombo and the intricate ways that men and women illustrate this experience, but it does not matter if this form of knowledge production and representation is not prioritized and legitimatized in the actual distribution of rights. Just as a focus on the structures of reason—culture as a set of boundaries and rules containing an authentic subject—cannot help us fully understand quilombola lives, we also cannot appeal to reason, or to a multicultural recognition of cultural difference, as a way of changing a racialized power structure that has consistently given less value to the existence and lives of black people. Here I borrow from Fanon's words on "The Negro and Recognition":

> For the Negro who works on a sugar plantation in Le Robert, there is only one solution: to fight. He will embark on this struggle, and he will pursue it, not as the result of a Marxist or idealistic analysis but quite simply because he cannot conceive of life otherwise than in the form of a battle against exploitation, misery, and hunger. (1967, 224)

Fanon's words reflect the clear-headed analysis and emergency call to action that Dona Maria displays in her defense for black, quilombola rights. The quilombolas have united to fight for land rights not because they have suddenly discovered a unique ancestral past but rather because their lives are threatened; losing their lands would mean losing their personhood, their sense of being and belonging in the present and future world. "It is not because the Indo-Chinese has discovered a culture of his own that he is in revolt," Fanon explains. "It is because 'quite simply' it was, in more than one way, becoming impossible to breathe" (226).

For my perception of life in Grande Paraguaçu, I represent a partial truth, a truth that is divided into self-selected stories, expressions, and situations, in an attempt to provide a different snapshot of quilombola lives as less neatly defined and conceptualized. Rather than a list of definitions indicating the different ways people define "quilombo descendant," I provide a sequence of narratives—some spoken, others silent, and many shouted. I went into Grande Paraguaçu prepared with an interview schedule outlining how I planned to interview people about the way they defined their identity and what "quilombo descendant" meant for them. The project failed in the first attempt as I realized that I was only repeating the

3.14. *Woman washing her daughters' hair at a public well in the community. Photograph by the author.*

same method used by INCRA. Because my identity as an anthropologist was a politically important position for the community, especially after being accused of fraud, people worked to answer interview questions "correctly" so as not to be perceived as unaware or ignorant. Thus, the only way for me to get a different narrative was to participate in everyday life, find meaning in silence, and listen to different forms of expression. Joelma's joke about pain in her pinguelo, Nina's annoyance with her "broken back," Dona Andira's silence, Marisa'a "mangue baby" expression, Marta's protection of a single pamphlet, and Seu Miguel's tour of the monastery spoke volumes about the experience of everyday life in Grande Paraguaçu and the incorporated meaning of being black and quilombola.

While the quilombolas of Grande Paraguaçu may not mirror the lives and practices of slaves in the colonial period, they nevertheless embody stories of labor, suffering, and exclusion that include memories of slavery and resistance and that are part of a locally and nationally extant reality and everyday experience of blackness in Brazil.

Grande Paraguaçu is defined by its long history rooted in the sugar economy and slave trade that characterized the Recôncavo throughout

the entire colonial period. The quilombolas of Grande Paraguaçu identify their ancestors as the slaves who built the Convento de Santo Antônio,
holding onto a small pamphlet that summarizes slave labor in the region.
But their labor practices say more about their embodied lives and identities than an origin story of ancestors can. The quilombolas of Grande
Paraguaçu largely define themselves through their relationship and lived
engagement with the land. Although quilombolas subsist from a variety
of productions, the most important forms of labor are found in the manguezal and the Atlantic forest. It is in these spaces that men and women
spend most of their days collecting food for their own consumption and
for minimal income. Quilombolas work nearly the entire day, often ex-
hausting their bodies, particularly their backs, to the point of excruciating
pain. The ability to work in the mangue and forest are an important part
of the quilombolas' valued existence.

For the quilombolas of Grande Paraguaçu, personhood is embedded
in the land. But like the public and the media, the processes of cultural
recognition and rights distribution demand a neatly authentic, ethno-
racial subject, not an embodied one. In other words, the embodied lives
and habitus of Grande Paraguaçu will need to be explicitly grouped, organized, documented, and conceptualized in order to be perceived as something different—something ethnic, traditional, and authentic—even if
embodied practices remain the same. This is the process of becoming a
politically recognized quilombo-descendant community.

FOUR

Black Rights

DOCUMENTATION, PROOF,

AND AUTHENTICITY

T he 1988 constitution propelled Brazil into a new democratic phase in which everyone was considered equal under the law. All forms of discrimination were denounced, at least on paper. Article 68 of the constitution seemed to recognize the labor and land practices of black communities by granting land rights to the descendants of quilombos, communities that, according to the ideology of the time, had resisted in the name of freedom and African cultural survival. However, Article 68 did not define the criteria for deciding who would be considered the legitimate descendants of quilombos. It did not describe how land would be taken away from powerful, landed elites and redistributed to poor blacks. But perhaps most importantly, Article 68 did not make provisions for protecting the rights and safety of the individuals who stepped forward to identify as the descendants of quilombos. Here I review the detailed process of cultural recognition and land distribution carried out by the Palmares Cultural Foundation (FCP) and INCRA. Rural black communities that identify as quilombo descendants must pass through a long, tangled, bureaucratic process of authentication and approval before any rights can be conferred. The process has itself become a hindrance to the very acquisition of rights it is intended to facilitate.

Two government organizations, the FCP and INCRA, bear primary responsibility for quilombo authentication. These organizations are bound by three essential documents that define the parameters of cultural recognition and authenticity for quilombo descendants: Article 68 of the constitution, Decree 4.887 founded on ILO Convention 169, and Statute 56 (N56).

In 2003, Brazil ratified the International Labor Organization's Convention 169 for Indigenous and Tribal Peoples (ILO 169).[1] The Lula administration adopted ILO 169 as a model for quilombo policies and made it the basis for Decree 4.887, which officially granted quilombo descendants the right to self-identification and to a separate culture without persecution from the state. ILO 169 specifically addresses

> tribal peoples in independent countries whose social, cultural and eco-
> nomic conditions distinguish them from other sections of the national
> community, and whose status is regulated wholly or partially by their
> own customs or traditions or by special laws or regulations.

ILO 169 affirms "self-identification" as the legal criterion for granting recognition and rights to indigenous and tribal communities. The conven-tion newly imagined quilombo descendants through the categories of in-digeneity and tribal peoples, making their ethnic identity and authenticity dependent upon their ability to prove not only their cultural and historical connection to the land but a fundamental "difference" that would distin-guish them from the national community. The Palmares Cultural Founda-tion employs Decree 4.887 as a legal mandate for granting communities cultural recognition based on their own self-identification.

Statue 56 is an instructional document that outlines the bureaucratic process that INCRA must follow in determining land rights. It defines qui-lombos as "ethno-racial groups, according to the community's own crite-ria of self-identification, that have their own historical trajectory, a specific relationship to a particular territory, and black ancestors who suffered and resisted historical oppression." The lands occupied by quilombo descen-dants are defined as those "used to guarantee the land's physical, social, economic, and cultural reproduction." I illustrate the important role of these documents in regulating what is and is not determined an authentic "quilombo-descendent community" deserving of rights. Here I reinforce my argument that even though rural black communities have the right to self-identify, they must do so within a limited and limiting set of criteria established within a bureaucratic system that, at the end of the day, is still empowered to determine their authenticity.

The INCRA process is complicated, drawn out, and often stalled by its own requirements. Furthermore, the absence of adequate federal fund-ing and support frequently incapacitates INCRA in its ability to fulfill its own procedures and its ability to defend quilombola communities against attacks by private landowners who often have greater resources. Coming to understand the process led me to appreciate how, on the ground, qui-lombo rights are overcomplicated by bureaucratic procedures that expose communities to violent retaliations and long-lasting land conflicts.

STEP ONE: PALMARES CULTURAL FOUNDATION
AND CULTURAL RECOGNITION

The first step to becoming a quilombo-descendant community is obtaining a "certificate of recognition" from the FCP, the agency in charge of legally assigning cultural recognition to any community that petitions for quilombo-descendent status. Although Decree 4.887 grants quilombo descendants the right to self-identify, they must still submit a series of documents to the FCP that describe their ancestry, history, and cultural practices. A community must present a historical report, written with the collaboration of elders, that describes the history of the community, including the origins of its ancestors, traditional use of land, and religious and labor practices. A community must show signatures from the majority of its residents agreeing to the recognition process. They must present proof that they have formed an association (Fishermen and Women's Association, for example) that will respond for the communal title, if granted. Finally, any documents, including old letters or photographs, that can help prove the community's land claims are also requested.

In an interview with Aline Motta, the regional director of the Palmares Cultural Foundation in Bahia, I asked why so much documentation was required if quilombolas had the right to self-identify. The director responded that in reality the process was pro forma, a matter of precaution against other possible issues such as the accusation of fraud or a third party interested in exploiting quilombola lands for commercial purposes, something that was very common. The foundation could not deny any community cultural recognition unless it was a case of exploitation. The director explained that the process was also a way of making sure that everyone in the community was on the same page about the quilombo identity, that they all wanted it and understood what it meant. Division within the community, she said, was extremely problematic because it weakened the community and exposed it to infiltration. She used Grande Paraguaçu as an example of what she called a problematic community:

> We ask the quilombolas to tell us anything and everything they know
> about the history of their community. We do this in order to see if they
> can communicate their own history. If they can't do it, then nobody will
> be able to do it for them, and the public will punish them for it.

Aline explained that the *Jornal Nacional* was able to deceive the people of Grande Paraguaçu because they were unprepared and divided. The FCP comunidade existem três terreiros de candomblé, a igreja católica, e várias igrejas evangélicas.

Atualmente estamos perdendo a nossa liberdade de ir e vir em busca do nosso próprio sustento devido o grande plantio de eucalipto ao nosso redor e nas nossas terras. O eucalipto tem destruído o resto da Mata Atlântica da nossa terra, e empobrece as nossas roças. Somos impedidos, através de forças policiais, e das empresas (Aracruz e BahiaSul), de caçar, pescar e tirar lenha nas nossas próprias terras.

Portanto reiteramos pedido de certificação como remanescente de quilombos, reconhecendo, delimitação, demarcação e titulação de nossas terras pelo órgão competente.

Assinam:

Associação e Comunidade Afro (A.C.A),

____, RG:____, CPF:____, data de nascimento:____/1918
(86 anos),

____, RG:____, CPF:____, data de nascimento:____/1931.

____, RG: 5.6____, CPF:____, data de nascimento:____/1923.

____, RG:____, CPF:____, data de nascimento:____/1930.

DEPOIMENTOS

Fazenda:
Vitória da Conquista – Ba
Depoimento de ____ e N____

____, 84 anos, filha de Marcimina Rosa de Jesus e Rui Roseno Manelo dos Anjos, sua mãe teve 13 filhos. O avô materno nasceu e criou no Boqueirão, o sogro também. Quando criança fazia boneca de barro para brincar, as crianças tinham medo de fantasma. As festas mais comuns eram religiosas. Santo Antônio, Bom Jesus da Lapa, São Roque, Santa Luzia, Cosme e Damião, Santo Reis, geralmente era seis dias de festa (uma semana), passávamos nas casas e todos ajudavam. Aqui não havia médicos, os mais velhos cuidavam dos doentes, buscávamos remédios no mato como azeite de mamona, purgante, os filhos nasciam nas mãos de uma parteira (era minha mãe a parteira e eu aprendi com ela), quando uma mulher ia parir os homens vinham a cavalo, meu pai não gostava, mas ela sempre atendia o chamado na hora, então os homens traziam um outro cavalo arriado para ela montar, ela era considerada uma parteira boa, então todos a procuravam.
Aqui nossa comida era sebo com arruda e alho, eu trabalhava na roça e fazia beiju. A agua era de cacimba, fazíamos um buraco no chão e até hoje existe este lugar. Os tambores e as gaitas eram instrumentos que fazia parte da cultura desta gente. Quando os brancos falavam dos negros a gente rebatia com verso

Sai daqui porco pelado
lamia no teu terreiro
vou dar parte para o teu dono
pra te botar no chiqueiro

Havia por parte dos brancos discriminação, então respondíamos dentro da roda com versos para rebater a provocação, até hoje o pessoal vem para minha casa para lembrar versos
Minha mãe morreu com 80 anos e não teve aposentadoria, eu trabalhava com ela na roça, na enxada. Meu pai teve duas mulheres, a segunda foi minha mãe, na roça pagava 4 reis , aqui nós trabalhamos para os brancos na ursa (aqui próximo). O Boqueirão é dos negros (pretos) os pretos devem colocar os brancos para subir a ladeira.
Aqui não havia escola quando eu era pequena, fui estudar depois de 20 anos de casada, então aprendi assinar o meu nome, meus pais não sabiam ler nem escrever. Meu avó era como um carvão bem preto, ele chegou aqui no tempo da escravidão, pois sofria muito, então teve que fugir, encontrando esta mata ele foi abrindo e ficando, andava escondido correndo na escuridão, eu não sei de onde ele veio, morreu velho. Aqui nunca teve médico, hoje o médico não cura ninguém, Benzo cobra 70 reais para levar alguém na cidade quando está doente.
Aos 10 anos fui a Vitória da Conquista, - como?- caminhando e levando saco na cabeça de feijão, lenha e mamona para vender. Meu marido foi enterrado aqui próximo ao lado de nossa casa, lá também há três anjinhos (crianças enterradas). Benzo sempre os meninos porque eles têm quebrantes. Cuidei de muitas pessoas, então todos são meus filhos. Aqui hoje somos 300 pessoas no Boqueirão. As comunidades aqui perto/próximo de Boqueirão (Algodão, Ursa e Lagoa de Falcão)

4.1. A signature page of a quilombola petition. In their request to the FCP for cultural recognition the petitioners entered the name Associação e Comunidade Afro (Association and Afro Community). Photograph by the author.

4.2. Testimony of a quilombola elder. Photograph by the author.

process was a way of making sure everyone could communicate their own history or at least a historical narrative that fit within the official parameters of the "quilombo descendant" definition. Aline identified as a black-movement activist. She had worked very hard to clear the charges of fraud placed on Grande Paraguaçu by the *Jornal Nacional*. Aline made it clear that she was on the side of the community. Still, even with her good intentions, she placed the onus of authenticity and the blame for failure on the residents of the community.

Figures 4.1 and 4.2 illustrate parts of a petition for cultural recognition for a quilombola community in Vitória da Conquista, Bahia, a city more than two hundred miles south of Cachoeira. It is interesting to note in these documents the use of elders as primary petitioners, many of whom have signed with fingerprints due to their inability to write. Although this is not Grande Paraguaçu's petition, the resemblance is quite strong. These documents are required of all petitioning communities. Flipping through several petitions in large white folders in the FCP office, I noted the recurring similarities: declarations of African or slave ancestry, cultural traditions, artisan agricultural and fishing practices, and rights abuses inflicted by private landowners.

Figure 4.2 shows a page of a testimony given by a community elder in which she describes her family tree. She names her parents and declares that her mother had thirteen children. She states that she made dolls out of clay when she was young and that children were afraid of ghosts. She notes that there were never doctors to attend the community. People had to go into the forest to collect medicinal plants and women gave birth with a midwife. "My mother was a midwife and I learned with her," she recalls. She goes on to describe how when a woman was ready to give birth a man would pick her up by horse and take her to the midwife. In her oral history, this elder also remembers racial discrimination in her town. She writes,

> When the whites talked about the blacks, we retaliated with verse:
> Get out of here, naked pig
> *Lamia no teu terreiro*
> I will tell your master
> So he'll put you in the pigpen
> There was discrimination from whites, so we responded with verse
> in the *roda* [samba circle] to counter the provocations. Until this day
> people come to my home to remember these verses.

For the FCP and INCRA alike, elders are held as bearers of authentic truth. Their memories and experiences are a major part of re-creating the community's past. This particular elder emphasizes the familial history and unity of the community, exemplified in her mother being the midwife everyone sought (as Dona Pereira was in Grande Paraguaçu). She also emphasizes a history of suffering and discrimination inflicted by white racism but also by a difficult life of poverty and exclusion. While the search for elder experiences is a strategy for understanding how the land may have been used in years past, it also contradicts ABA's effort to expand and modernize the quilombo category to focus on present experiences. Throughout the quilombo bureaucratic process one finds ideological contradictions such as the tensions between an imagined past and a lived present. These contradictions are rooted in the unresolved and conflictive relations between the extant memory of the "colonial quilombo" and ABA's newer "ethnic quilombo." Thus it is very important that the historical report submitted by a community create a connection to an ethnic quilombo that has a collective history and communal relationship to the land.

A major part of the first step in cultural recognition is understanding, making sure communities understand the quilombola identity and how it is connected to the land and their everyday cultural practices. Communities often obtain a certificate of recognition from the FCP without much questioning. As long as all the required paperwork is submitted, theoretically any community can obtain cultural recognition as a quilombola community, even an urban neighborhood. However, before granting a cultural certificate, the FCP works to ensure that the people claiming quilombo ancestry understand the new identity and its social and cultural implications. Because it is quite a bit of documentation, communities can get help from universities, NGOs, and Social Assistance Offices (Secretarias de Assistência Social) from the municipal district.[2] It is the responsibility of the Palmares Cultural Foundation to make sure that these organizations do not coerce a community into identifying as quilombo descendants.

During one of our interviews, Aline introduced me to two quilombola leaders who were in her office discussing their petition. They were from a community along the Paraguaçu River that had just been certified the previous year. The community's petition was submitted to the foundation by the Secretaria de Assistência Social. All of the documents were stamped by the municipal government but did not have any sign of community involvement. Aline set the petition aside right away and got in touch with people from the community. She called them into her office to exchange information and make sure they understood what they were doing. With a cautionary tone, Aline explained to me why she was so careful:

We see a lot of NGOs that give support to traditional communities. When they are in the field, they identify these communities and then contact the necessary organizations to say that they have a community that fits the characteristics of a quilombo. I personally prefer that the community act first to represent itself. After a certification is secured, we come up against a lot of political conflicts that are aggravated if the community does not fully understand the process.

Although people have the right to self-identify, the conflict over land is a thorny issue. If the community is not able to demonstrate its understanding of quilombo history and identity, it will be penalized. The project analyst of the INCRA Quilombos office in Bahia,[3] Amélia Quiroz, emphasized the lack of community knowledge about "quilombo history" during our interview. She said it was the "hardest and most frustrating" aspect of her job. She often found herself in communities that had certificates of recognition from the FCP but did not know what the word *quilombo* meant:

> They ask me to define it for them, but I cannot define it for them, they have to know for themselves. That is why they are asking for recognition. Under the law they have to self-identify. If I tell them a definition I can be accused of coercion. I was accused of coercion in Grande Paraguaçu! Can you believe it? It is not true. I was naïve, and I explained to the residents what it meant to help them out. But now, I do not say anything any more. If a resident does not know, I write, "Não soube dizer" [Unable to answer].

Once a place is culturally certified as a quilombo-descendant community, it gets grouped into the category of Traditional Peoples and Communities (PCT, Povos e Comunidades Tradicionais). These are defined in Decree 6.040 of the constitution as "culturally differentiated groups that possess their own forms of social organization and occupy and use traditional territories and natural resources in order to maintain their social, cultural, religious, ancestral, and economic way of life."[4] This label solidifies the newly recognized quilombo as a unified and differentiated community. New quilombo-descendant communities are moved to the top of lists for more immediate social services and attention, alongside indigenous groups and others labeled traditional communities. No organization, whether federal, state, or private, will consider a quilombo-descendant community for special status in receiving aid unless it is first certified by the Palmares Cultural Foundation.

During interviews at the Ministries of Health and Education and at SEPROMI, the federal agency charged with promoting racial equality in Bahia, I asked if a community with serious social needs could be given priority without cultural certification from the FCP. All of the representatives of these organizations explained that because there were already so many certified quilombola communities that needed help (three thousand as of February 2015), it would be impossible to also meet the needs of the hundreds that had no formal recognition, regardless of the fact that many of the ineligible communities often shared identical sociocultural, racial, and economic characteristics with certified communities.

Each of these government organizations is part of the federal Brazil

Quilombola Program (Programa Brasil Quilombola), a government attempt to unify all of the agencies working with quilombolas under one umbrella that can distribute social services to these communities more quickly. These services include electricity, running water, *cesta básica* ("basic basket" of staple foods), Bolsa Família (supplemental income for poor families), medical services, and funding for local schools or cultural projects. In my interviews with the director of SEPROMI in Bahia, the Brazil Quilombola Program was hailed as a more efficient way of distributing social services to poor black quilombola communities. The downside was that many social development projects like fixing sewage problems, distributing running water, building much-needed health posts and new schools, could not be completed until the community was granted a land title.

During an interview at the Bahia Health Department, a representative of the quilombo health program explained the selectivity of public programs for certified quilombos as "unfortunate": "It is an unfortunate distinction we have to make, but logistically we have no choice. We just do not have the resources to help everyone." It is important to question the work of cultural recognition and certification and the ways ethnic groups and so-called traditional communities are politically separated and differentiated from society. Describing an issue of what I see as consequential exclusion, Hooker argues:

> Multicultural citizenship reforms in Latin America privilege certain kinds of subjects and certain modes of framing grievances that have potentially negative consequences. . . . The problem is that as a result Afro-Latinos who are unable to assert an "ethnic" identity lack a solid claim to collective rights even though they may also suffer from political exclusion and racial discrimination. (2005, 306)

The ethnic boundaries built around the new quilombo-descendant category confine and reduce participating communities to a specific representation of blackness that is somehow "traditional." For the government, being a traditional quilombola community means demonstrating a connection to ancestors, land practices, and interestingly, past forms of suffering. "Tradition" is rooted in the selective memory of the colonial quilombo as an isolated cultural enclave. Thus quilombo descendants who live in the middle of the Amazon forest may seem more authentically traditional than those who live an hour outside of the state capital such as Grande Paraguaçu.

Although quilombo-descendant communities are also rural black communities, the concept of tradition does not give primacy to race. What is most important to understand from the FCP certification process and the assignment of quilombo descendants as traditional communities is that they are built on a set of ideological assumptions about what it means to be "ethnic," "authentic," "traditional," and "black" in a multicultural Brazilian society. By defining quilombo descendants as traditional communities and organizing their legal recognition around an international convention written for "indigenous" groups and "tribal peoples," the state reaffirms a stereotypical image of a rural black community as a primitive, isolated, tribelike space. It is important to think critically about the adoption of ILO 169 and the inclusion of quilombolas as members of traditional communities. These create a foundation for self-identification and the right to difference; more importantly, they determine the political process and requirements for quilombo-descendant authenticity.

STEP TWO: THE LONG ROAD TO LANDOWNERSHIP WITH INCRA

FCP certification does not guarantee land rights. In addition to a certificate of cultural recognition, quilombo descendants must undergo a long and intensive period of field research conducted by the Quilombos Office of INCRA, the federal agency responsible for documenting a petitioning community's claims to the land. For hundreds of communities including Grande Paraguaçu, the road to becoming a rights-bearing quilombo-descendant community is often stalled for several years, if not permanently, in the INCRA investigation. Here now are the rights on a piece of paper buried at the bottom of a desk drawer that Dona Maria described in her public speech. It is also during the INCRA investigation that private landowners begin to retaliate against communities, intimidating them into rescinding their claims. Field research, anthropological and geographical investigations of the community and their knowledge and use of the land, is estimated by INCRA to take at least two years, with the actual time being five or more due to limited funding and resources.

INCRA's work is detailed in the federally sanctioned Statute 56 (N56). The INCRA process for determining quilombo lands is divided into six steps: identification, recognition, delimitation, demarcation, *des-intrusão* (deoccupation), and titling and registration of lands occupied by quilombo descendants.

The first three parts of the process are completed in a technical report of identification and delimitation. The report identifies in careful detail the limits of quilombo lands as claimed by members of the community. The INCRA regional administration appoints an interdisciplinary technical group composed of an anthropologist, agronomist, analyst, and land surveyor that is responsible for completing the research for the report. In addition to measuring and drawing out the limits of quilombo lands, the technical group reports on the demographics, history, work, economy, environment, and sociocultural life of the quilombola community. Because of the amount of work involved and the lack of appropriate funding for the research, the technical report can take several years to complete.

Anthropology for Hire and Culture Workshops

The most important researcher in the Quilombos Sector is the anthropologist. But who is she? The Brazilian Anthropological Association (ABA) recommended that the government hire trained anthropologists to conduct the research for quilombola land rights. Brazilian anthropologist, Elaine O'Dwyer, coordinator of an ABA collaborative project with the Ford Foundation, specifically identifies the importance of anthropologists having previous experience in rural black communities:

> To carry out the work of Mapping and Identification of areas indicated as quilombo descendant, we recommend anthropologists who have previously conducted research on this issue, based on discussions organized through the ABA/FORD project. In a meeting held at the Ministry of Culture in September, we put the Chair of the Palmares Cultural Foundation in direct contact with researchers at the state and/or regional level who we recommended for this work . . . a network of anthropologists with research experience in rural black communities. The high number of communities and the administrative timelines of government agencies made it imperative that [INCRA-hired] researchers who could convert their extant research towards the goals of the legal process, as well as update previously produced knowledge about various rural black communities mobilized for quilombola cultural recognition in accordance with the constitutional provision. (2008, 75)

In an interview with the regional director of the INCRA office in Bahia, I was told that there was little to no funding for hiring trained anthropologists to conduct the fieldwork required by Statute 56. Instead,

INCRA depended on temporary contract workers, usually recent college graduates willing to give two or three years of service. While some may have social science degrees, most do not. Anita graduated from film studies when she applied for the anthropologist position in the INCRA Quilombos Office. When I interviewed INCRA officials, there were nine contract researchers from different areas of study working in the Quilombos Office. These workers were contracted for two years. Although none of them had finished the technical reports for their assigned communities, their contracts ended at the end of the second year with no prospect for renewal. To make matters worse, beginning in 2009, INCRA was no longer allowed to subcontract researchers from universities or independent research organizations.

Most INCRA regional offices only have one anthropologist in the Quilombos Office to carry out research for an entire state. This one anthropologist is technically in charge of writing an almost two-hundred-page technical report for every quilombola community seeking land rights in Bahia. When Anita decided to leave her position at INCRA for an undetermined length of time, the Bahia office lost one of the most important professionals in the entire quilombo process. All of the full-time employees of INCRA, like any federal office, have to be hired through the normal federal hiring procedures. In Brazil, federal employees are hired through a national competitive process. This means that in order to work in a federal job, people have to wait for the government to open and announce a new position. At the time I was in the field, the federal government had not posted a new position for an INCRA anthropologist in more than four years, when Anita Souza was hired. In 2009, the regional directors of all the INCRA Quilombos Offices were informed that the hiring of anthropologists that was promised for 2010 was cancelled without any further provisions.

Deeply entrenched in the land process, the quilombolas of Grande Paraguaçu were left without an anthropologist in the middle of the their petition and struggle. The issue of contract workers and untrained anthropologists was a point of contention for the quilombolas of Grande Paraguaçu. Not only did they feel that INCRA did not have adequate resources to efficiently carry out its research, but they also did not trust contract workers who might bring personal agendas and biases that could jeopardize their land process.

The technical reporting is carried out in parts. The land surveyor is in charge of measuring the disputed lands, the analyst is responsible for cross-checking the validity of all land titles in the region, and the anthropologist is in charge of documenting the community's cultural connection to the land. The anthropologist begins her fieldwork with a series of workshops aimed at helping the community (re)member and reassemble stories about their ancestors. There are workshops on several topics, including land. Some workshops, called *oficinas de cultura* (culture workshops) are meant to help the community work out what it means for them to identify as the descendants of quilombos. Anita assured me that the purpose was not to teach a definition of *quilombola* but rather to gauge how the community imagined itself as quilombola and to help the petitioners understand the requirements of the state.

The workshops are an essential and systematic part of the land-acquisition process that government and civil-sector organizations use. In the past, INCRA depended on NGOs to help conduct these workshops. Usually the first workshop is the culture workshop. Here residents are asked to draw a map of their lands by marking significant geographical locations used for work, religious ceremonies, cultural education, and so forth. In my interview with Lorena Cardoso, one of the temporary anthropologists at INCRA, she showed me several community maps as examples of the many different ways that communities conceptualize their physical and cultural spaces. Interestingly, Grande Paraguaçu's INCRA report does not include a community map. This may have been due to the interruption of the research report by legal disputes against the community. One of the maps Lorena gave me was drawn during an INCRA workshop in the quilombo-descendant community of Jatobá. The quilombolas of Jatobá primarily wanted to highlight a flood region that had an impact on a large part of the community over the course of nearly a half century, from 1945 to 1992, forcing families to migrate north to a space called Serra Virote in a series of five main migrations. Jatobá's map shows homes submerged by water from the Lagoa Grande (Big Lagoon), where the map shows women collecting water and canoes carrying goats back to Virote. The 2005 technical report on Jatobá describes how life grew increasingly difficult for the quilombolas after all the floods: "Access to the forest, in this case, was prohibited by the owner of the fazenda. After the floods, state the residents, life becomes much more difficult given that their land plots, fruit trees, and homes have been totally devastated."[5]

It is during these workshops that a community begins to mobilize and learns how to disseminate the meaning of *quilombo* throughout their town. Drawing maps is only one part of a series of workshops that may last months. INCRA takes these workshops very seriously because they form the foundation for the process of developing a technical report. Moreover,

while the workshops represent an attempt to solicit a local or emic definition of *quilombo*, they also ensure that the community comes to understand the definition the government uses.

I did not attend any of Anita's workshops because by the time I started
my fieldwork, the technical report for Grande Paraguaçu was already finished. I did participate in a culture workshop conducted in Grande Paraguaçu by a research group called Projeto GeografAR from the Federal
University of Bahia (UFBA, Universidade Federal da Bahia). The GeografAR group was one of several that held workshops in Grande Paraguaçu
to help residents document their land use and cultural ancestry. The focus
of the GeografAR workshop was the social construction of space. Sandra,
the facilitator and a graduate student in geography, explained the concept
of space to a group of about fifty quilombolas. She said that everything
the residents did, planting, fishing, and samba de roda, was constructive
in that it created "quilombo lands." She handed out maps of a broad region of Iguape and asked the quilombolas to draw in important places in
their community using an assigned theme of history, culture, production,
and social conflicts. At first everyone complained that they did not understand the map and could not find their lands on it. Sandra urged them
to try and move on. After thirty minutes, Sandra called back the groups
and asked them to explain their maps and themes. None of the groups
had really been able to fulfill the task, and the discussion was taken over
by the "social conflicts" group. The group described landowner intimidations, destroyed crops, and threats. Rosinda Nascimento even pointed to
the discursive violence the community faced:

> Once they learned what we were doing, the landowners began to mobi-
> lize. They divided the community in half, putting one side against the
> other: those who were loyal workers and afraid to lose their jobs and
> homes against those who were determined to follow the quilombo cause.
> They held many meetings where they asked people, "Are you all by
> chance slaves? Because if you are saying you are a quilombo then that
> means you are saying you are a slave!" So here we are trying to teach
> people what it means to be a quilombola, and they tell people that to be
> quilombola is to be a slave.

Sandra explained to the group that it was important for them to map
their culture because it created proof that their everyday lives as quilombolas were real and active. A culture map would prove that they were
not slaves but living communities. "Active" was the key word, explained

Sandra, because INCRA was trying to prove to the justice system that Grande Paraguaçu was a quilombo community that deserved collective rights. The workshop ended in a song that only had four words: "Só os quilombolas sobreviveram" (Only the quilombolas survived). The workshop may not have gone according to Sandra's plan, but it was still important. More vocal quilombola leaders were able to express their opinions and experiences with conflict. Their reflections helped others understand what was happening. The idea that quilombolas needed to prove that their lives were real and active was a clear example of the discursive labor required of the cultural recognition process. It was not that communities did not have an active and living culture; however, it needed to be made visible in the criteria of the state and the eyes of the public. In other words, the habitus and embodied lives of Grande Paraguaçu needed to be explicitly grouped and defined to look and sound traditional and authentic even if in practice not much had changed.

Like the Palmares Cultural Foundation, INCRA also is invested in making sure that communities know how to explain their new quilombola identity and history to outsiders such as researchers and journalists who may be working to disprove the authenticity of their claims. Once INCRA begins the research process in a community, it is the agency's responsibility to protect the quilombolas of that community from landowner retaliation and violence. However, the researchers of INCRA complain that they are overworked and undercompensated. While they would like to protect communities, they explain that their hands are tied by the very bureaucracy that empowers them. Amélia explained this problem as an issue of equal rights: "Everyone has rights in this process, the quilombolas, the landowners, the merchants, and the state, and all of these different entities have to be heard, respected, and compensated."

Quilombolas feel hope and relief when INCRA begins research in their community. They feel that because INCRA has arrived they are very close to being landowners. INCRA representatives have to make it very clear that their arrival does not signify the end but rather the beginning of what will be a very long and difficult process. INCRA also uses the workshops to explain every aspect of the research process: the conflicts the community will face, the uncertain number of years for completion, the rights of private landowners to contest the process, and the fact that quilombola land titles are communal and cannot be divided or sold.[6] What INCRA officials do not reveal is that the rights of rural black quilombo communities are last on a long list of bureaucratic measures put in place to protect landowner rights.

Protecting Private Rights, Scrutinizing Black Rights

During our interview, I asked the INCRA regional director why it was so difficult to grant a land title to a quilombola community. His response focused on the financial aspect of transferring land rights; he explained that it was very expensive for the government because it had to financially compensate private landowners for the lands it transferred to quilombola communities. In addition to the issue of reimbursement, the land-distribution process privileged wealthy, private landowners over rural black communities at every stage.

Developing the technical report is the first and longest stage of the quilombo process in INCRA. If and when the report is finished, it has to be reviewed and approved by a special INCRA regional decision committee. If it is approved there, the report goes on to be published in the *Diário Oficial da União* (Official Daily Report of the Union). The *Diário Oficial* is one of the means through which the government communicates federal issues to the public. If the regional committee does not approve the technical report it is because the research did not fulfill all of the requirements outlined in Statute 56, and therefore it must be corrected before it can be published. After analyzing a quilombo technical report, the regional decision committee may decide that the area in question cannot be recognized as a quilombo. In this case, the committee would order that the case be filed away (at the bottom of a desk drawer) until INCRA has time to conduct more research and find new proof of the community's historical ties to the land. In this case, the community maintains cultural recognition but cannot be guaranteed land rights.

If a technical report is approved and published, it becomes open to contestation by any other entity with legal rights to the area. First, the report is sent to government agencies including the Institute of Historical and Artistic National Patrimony, the Brazilian Environmental and Renewable Resources Institute (IBAMA), the Office of Union Patrimony, the National Foundation for Indigenous peoples (Funai), and the Chico Mendes Institute for Biodiversity Conservation to assess whether the land in question overlaps areas overseen by these entities. If the land does overlap, then the agency involved has thirty days to make demands or contestations. Private landowners and any other occupants of the land who are not included in the quilombo community association are given three months from the date of publication to contest the technical report. If a private landowner contests—and most do—the quilombo's case will either be resolved by the INCRA regional committee or, in case of further discord, will be sent to civil court or the Advogacia Geral da União for mediation. If the case goes to court, it can remain paralyzed for years until the court and INCRA resolve all of the contestations.

Most quilombos have more than one private landowner in the territory they are claiming, and it is common for all landowners to file disputes against the technical report. Even if all contestations were to be resolved, INCRA would still have to conduct additional research, revise the report to include the new resolutions, and then republish it, at which point all of the entities have another three months to review and contest the revised report. Just this process of publication and contestation alone can stall land rights for an indefinite number of years. Because quilombolas usually have the least amount of formal, written documentation to contest their lands, their claims, which depend on oral histories, habitus, labor, community maps, and so forth, are always the ones in question, scrutinized over and over at every step of the process.

The length of time INCRA takes to move past the technical report and on to the next steps of the land-regularization process depends significantly on the number of private landowners in the territory, whether they live in the state where the property is being claimed, and how influential they are in the judicial sector. Often, every concession is made to first protect the rights of these wealthy landowners. Some landowners live out of state and even out of the country. Absentee landowners are not uncommon in Bahia and, according to Amélia, are the most difficult to deal with. She explained that with absentee landowners, INCRA is required to send a document announcing the initiation of the quilombo process before its people can set foot on the property. If a private landowner denies them access to the property, INCRA has to go to court to get official permission. "And of course," Amélia said, "none of these processes happen from one day to the next. It is the public sector, after all, and everything takes a very long time." More common, however, are highly influential landowners who have close relationships with judges and local police. Some judges are also private landowners involved in land disputes, and some simply have strong opinions against the quilombo process itself. All of these conditions determine how long a court will take to settle a dispute or whether it will settle it at all. Amélia further described the issue:

> We have cases where we have not even been able to close the [technical report], and it has been more than a year, just because of so many disputes. . . . We go into a territory knowing that it is being claimed by quilombolas, but then we discover that the land is also the ranch of a

federal deputy or the ranch of a businessman who does not want to give it up. And they both have rights. It is not just quilombolas who have rights. We have to see both sides of the coin. We can sit here and say that because *fulano* [so-and-so] is in quilombo territory he is wrong and should be moved out. Well, it is not that simple.

Although Amélia describes a complex yet equal playing field of democratic rights to landownership, a system in which poor rural black communities have the same rights as a federal deputy or wealthy businessman, that is simply not the case. In fact, it is clear from the very process as well as the words of the INCRA director and the issue of absentee landowners that bureaucratic complications take place due to the political focus on the careful protection of the rights of wealthy private landowners and not rural black communities, who are instead treated as "fraudulent" before being proven authentic. Thus, INCRA researchers can open an investigation in a community and agree to help its members obtain land rights, but they cannot say when it might actually happen or guarantee that it ever will happen. This was made very clear in my interviews with INCRA employees who said that when they first visit a community, they make sure the people there understand that they are entering a long and uncertain process that will require "patience and struggle." But patience and struggle are a vast understatement of what many communities face in their fight for land rights.

I asked Amélia if INCRA took the quilombolas' side during conflict or if it had to remain neutral. She responded that when conflicts took place, by law, INCRA had to protect the quilombo community. But, she said, the problem was that the government did not offer many resources to protect the community effectively. If a community was being threatened with expulsion, INCRA had an *interdito prohibitório* (interdiction) that would help at least keep the community on the land. However, the juridical resources that INCRA has are extremely limited. Amélia finally revealed her frustration with the lack of resources in the face of so many challenges in the Quilombos Office at INCRA:

> If a landowner submits a *reintegração de posse* [reintegration of possession], then it's all over for the quilombo because the judge obeys the private land title. It does not matter if the quilombola has a house and crops and was born there. We can respond and try to revert the situation. That is all I do here, try to revert these situations, but it is not easy.

Amélia was one of the most candid government officials I interviewed. She had been working in the Quilombo Office for several years when I met her, and she had encountered many frustrations, at one point even being accused by one of the private landowners of Grande Paraguaçu of coercing the community into identifying as quilombolas. Unlike many other officials, Amélia spoke from experience rather than script and revealed that even though INCRA was supposed to help quilombolas, it really had little to no legal power. A simple outline of INCRA's procedures, beginning with the technical report, reveals their length and tediousness. Amélia's responses in our interview illustrate the additional political difficulties the institution faces, mainly the complexity of challenging the rights of the rich and powerful:

> I would say that it is the government against itself. The right to land is sacred in the constitution, but how far can this sacredness extend? Corruption is endemic, and public archives are not exempt. Someone may have a legitimate right to register ten thousand hectares of land and pays for ten thousand, but, in fact, the registration is for fifteen thousand hectares because the landowner has a friend in the archives. But how do we prove this corruption? Sometimes we are able to because we have an analyst who actually goes to the field and looks at all the documents. She sees that on "X" day a landowner had two thousand hectares, and now he has twenty. Where did those eighteen come from? How did he pay? Who allowed it?

Land has been a symbol of racial status and wealth in Brazil since Pedro Álvares Cabral took his first step in the "new world." For nearly five hundred years, the Portuguese strategically colonized Brazil through a system of hereditary *capitanias*. During this time, the Lei de Sesmaria was the first attempt to regulate and register landownership. The law primarily required that land be used productively, but its enforcement was weak; lands were not surveyed and measured regularly, productivity was assumed but not examined, and land grabbing became a normal practice. During the time of sesmarias, *posse* (a form of squatting) also became very common, benefiting poor colonists who could not purchase land.

The sesmaria system had a profound impact on the distribution of land for many years because the practice of posse would remain a characteristic of the land situation in Brazil. When the Land Law of 1850 was enacted, it was supposed to change the system of sesmarias and regulate the largely uncontrolled land situation. Instead, the new law disenfranchised small-scale landowners and *posseiros* and gave more legal power to the wealthy by increasing the price and requirements of landownership (Viotti da Costa 2000). The Land Law of 1850 also made literacy a requirement of landownership, a change that instantly excluded many free blacks at the time and one that would continue to exclude large numbers from landownership even after abolition. Thus, the new land law not only maintained the hierarchy of landownership in place, but it actually widened the gap between the wealthy landowners and the landless.

Holston describes how nineteenth-century landed elites sent their sons to the University of Coimbra in Portugal to study law so they could return as "judges, legislators, politicians, administrators, and heads of state" and "enact laws to further their interests" (2008, 121). He shows how elites have manipulated and complicated the legal system to their advantage for centuries. The inability of blacks to own land during the colonial period left them in an inferior economic relation to landowning whites, and it meant that many of their descendants grew up landless. Most quilombo descendants do not consider themselves landless, though, because they believe that they are the rightful owners of the lands they and their ancestors have worked for years. Holston argues that land disputes are actually struggles over the definition of history, whether it should be defined through the lens of the colonizer or the colonized (2008); for disenfranchised groups, land conflicts are in great measure a fight to prove a history of exclusion and inequality.

Because they do not know how long it will take between certification by the Palmares Cultural Foundation and land rights, culturally recognized quilombo descendants are often left vulnerable to several forms of retaliation and abuse from private landowners who feel betrayed and threatened by the community's demand for land rights. The elite landowners who dispute quilombola rights are wealthy and well-connected businessmen, politicians, lawyers, and judges who know the law and its weaknesses;[7] they know the loopholes and the back doors to the law because they have written it in their favor throughout the history of the nation. The regional director of the Koinonia Quilombo Observatory in Bahia expressed as much in our interview:[8]

Landowners have connections to the mayor; they know the mayor personally; they are the mayor. They are friendly with the local police and even have police officers who work for them. They have a lot of connections, and that is why they can do whatever they want.

Once some landowners learn that there is a petition for quilombola land recognition on their properties, they initiate a campaign of retaliation against the community even before INCRA workers visit the territory. The retaliation is so common it almost seems to take place in an organized and predictable manner: first, landowners intimidate and threaten to expel residents involved in the quilombola process. Then, they send out henchmen (capachos) or even police officers to destroy quilombola crops, describing them as illegal planting. Next, the landowner works day and night to redo all of his fencing and fences off as much land as he can, including land that was previously uncultivated or used by quilombolas. These fences make it "illegal" for quilombolas to go anywhere near these lands without facing further threats and abuse.

In Grande Paraguaçu, the landowners fenced off one of the main mangroves in the community. Because mangroves are federal coastal lands, the act was illegal but was never addressed by the justice system. The fence was an outrage in the community, and quilombola leaders did everything in their power to denounce landowners for illegally fencing off public lands. While they were eventually able to take down the fence with help from INCRA, the Pastoral Commission of Fishermen and Women in Bahia, and the Palmares Cultural Foundation, it took the state more than a year to recognize the illegal act and rectify it. That the illegality of fencing off public lands was not reason enough to punish the landowners and have the fence removed immediately illustrates the effects of a justice system that is governed by the rights and privileges of the white elite. Many of the acts of retribution that quilombolas face from landowners are blatantly illegal but persist with impunity. Amélia's description of the illegal land practices she has witnessed shows how land is still controlled by elites who retain the ability to manipulate a system they helped create. Quilombolas decry the land grabbing, absentee landowners, and political privilege of the elite. But how can they obtain justice if even the organizations that are created by the government to secure their rights are tasked with first protecting the rights of the wealthy?

In my interviews with INCRA employees, they were quick to recognize the financial, legal, and bureaucratic roadblocks the organization faces, but not one of them mentioned racial inequality. Hooker has depicted this type of state behavior:

> The fact that many of the same Latin American states that have recognized cultural diversity have also consistently withheld the resources that would enable the implementation of collective rights suggests the possibility that the focus on cultural recognition in current multicultural

citizenship reforms might obviate questions of racial discrimination. (2005, 309)

While my conversations with people in the Palmares Cultural Foundation consistently highlighted the extant problem of institutional racism, INCRA representatives remained mute on the issue. Although INCRA workers regretted the situation of most quilombolas, they attributed it to the sad issue of land rights in Brazil and to their lack of resources, not to years of systemic racism and exclusion from landownership. Rural black communities are being thrown head first into an inegalitarian system that still does not fully recognize racial discrimination. Quilombos are forced to fight for cultural recognition within a system that cannot even protect their bodies from everyday police violence.

The three controlling documents of the Palmares Cultural Foundation and INCRA, Article 68, Decree 4.887, and Statute 56, outline procedures of authentication and proof. While these organizations are supposed to be facilitating the cultural recognition and rights acquisition of black communities with limited resources, they often end up stalled by the contradictions and bureaucracy of these very requirements. Moreover, the amount of consideration that is given to the rights of wealthy private landowners over the rights of quilombolas reflects a system where quilombo descendants are treated as fraudulent until proven authentic rather than bearers of their own cultural identity and their right to life as dictated by ILO Convention 169.

All of these bureaucratic issues place quilombolas in a complicated position of having to prove their authenticity with whatever documents they can find, such as the pamphlet on the Convento de Santo Antônio. Quilombolas are relegated to using the oral histories of their elders to supplement a paucity of documents in communities where quilombolismo and blackness as categories of racial exclusion and marginalization are embodied in everyday life, deep in the skin. With the onus of proving authenticity before land rights can even be pursued, quilombolas are made vulnerable to the violent retaliation of private landowners who have powerful political connections and legal resources. Quilombolas may find themselves in a vulnerable social and political position, but they are not defenseless. In response to landowner threats and intuitional racism, quilombolas have united in a national movement for quilombola rights. They are demanding that their rights to cultural identity, land, and a future livelihood be recognized and respected.

FIVE

Black Justice

GRANDE PARAGUAÇU AND THE GROWING
FIGHT FOR QUILOMBOLA JUSTICE

*Now, I will say one thing. We were born and raised on this territory
and we are quilombolas! We are! We are!* E de boca cheia! Tchau!

SUMIDO, GRANDE PARAGUAÇU, JULY 26, 2009

After the *Jornal Nacional* report aired, the quilombolas of Grande
Paraguaçu became consumed with regaining their credibility.
Not only had they been publicly painted as frauds, but they
also became an example of a problematic community, one that messed up,
was unprepared, and suffered the consequences. Their town was covered
in sparring signs that exposed their conflict and planted a seed of doubt
for anyone who visited. The anthropologist working with them was being
sued for libel, their land process was stalled, and it seemed like everyone
around them questioned their honesty. But what did this all mean for the
community? The quilombolas of Grande Paraguaçu did not blame themselves for the conflicts involved in their case. They did not feel that they
were unprepared; however, they did feel discriminated against. Throughout my fieldwork, I recorded several dialogues of the anger and reproach
that community members felt toward what they saw as an unjust, racist,
and classist system.

I describe here the experience of becoming a quilombola community and the emotional and individual effects of the political process of
cultural recognition on the people who identify as quilombolas. The quilombolas describe their legal process as beginning and stalling in conflict.
They highlight their experience not as a rare occurrence but rather as the
norm, the result of a legal process that is contradictory and does not pri-
oritize the lives and rights of black communities. I connect Grande Para-

5.1. *Quilombolas marching in protest. The occasion centers around a visit from the SEPPIR director, who was flying in from Brasília. Photograph by the author.*

5.2. *A gathering in the town square. Quilombolas are demanding their right to own land as they anticipate the arrival of SEPPIR officials. Photograph by the author.*

guaçu to the national struggle for quilombola justice through the National Coordination for the Articulation of Rural Black Quilombo Communities (CONAQ, Coordinação Nacional de Articulação das Comunidades Negras Rurais Quilombolas). I am particularly interested in how quilombolas have come to articulate a discourse of justice as quilombola justice—a call for racial justice and affirmative action and not just cultural recognition.

MEMORIES AND DENUNCIATIONS

With Antônio's help, I organized a series of community meetings focused on understanding the legal process of recognition and land distribution in Grande Paraguaçu. During one of these meetings, I asked a gathering of about twenty-five people to tell me how the quilombola process began in their community, what the process was like, and how it changed the way they lived. We sat in a crowded circle in a corner of the community meetinghouse. As always, I had my small recorder, and I began by asking if I could record the meeting. "Of course. You must record!" Sumido exclaimed. Quickly he took my recorder and placed it on a chair in the middle of the circle. "I am not afraid to speak," he affirmed. "Nobody here is afraid to denounce the injustices that we are living." Bending over to speak into the recorder, Sumido went on. "The person speaking here is Sumido, and I'm not afraid to speak." Seu Miguel, nodding his head in agreement, explained,

> Before the quilombo process began we were discriminated against and treated unjustly. We could not use the land to cultivate our own foods. We had to pay to build anything on the land, and if we did not pay it would be destroyed. I am Miguel, and you can tell anyone that we are here to say that we are not slaves. We are quilombolas!

Everyone in the room appeared to agree with Sumido and Miguel. They moved their chairs closer to the recorder, and some asked for quiet so that we could begin. I was surprised at first by Sumido's and Miguel's declarations of identity and felt nervous about what they might have expected from my recordings. I had already explained that the recording would be for my notes and that no one else would hear it. But hearing Sumido's and Miguel's eagerness to be heard reminded me of the community's focus. The quilombolas of Grande Paraguaçu were centered on regaining their credibility, and they needed as much documented proof as they could get.

Our meeting was essential for them to document their story through the recorder and notepad of an anthropologist. It did not matter that I was an outsider and had no connection with INCRA, something I had previously explained. For the quilombolas, I represented an authority that was on their side because I was there and ready to hear their perspective. Although my recorder was carefully placed on a chair in the middle of the circle, it would not remain there for long.

Returning the group's attention back to my initial questions about the quilombola process, Antônio started the conversation:

> We were at a community meeting being held in a town just a few miles away from here, still in the Iguape region. They were discussing how they could get land rights because their ancestors lived and worked on the same lands. They were talking about foresting piaçava, mariscagem, making azeite de dendê, capoeira, and maculelê, and I thought, that sounds like us. We do all of those things too, and we have also been living and working on our lands for generations. We are also a quilombo! I had first heard about quilombos from a book I have had for many years. The book describes the quilombos that existed back during slavery. That is how I heard about it. It's just that not a lot of people around here ever took any of that very seriously.

Rosinda, one of the youngest and most passionate of the quilombola leaders, spoke up next:

> We always knew about our culture and could explain the traditions of our ancestors; it is just that we never connected our culture to the word *quilombo*. We never knew to connect our lives and experiences to that word. For us it was a new word. We learned about quilombos in classes that were held in Salaminas, in the district of Maragogipe. A representative of SEPPIR visited the town many times and explained that the quilombos were blacks who fled from their captors and re-created their African culture in freedom and resistance. He said they were people who subsisted from agriculture and fishing and who fought against discrimination in order to survive. And that is how we discovered that this here [pointing to the space around her] is called a quilombo. We just did not know how to put all the parts together. That is when we asked for our certificate of recognition from the Fundação Palmares in 2005. We went there and told them that our community is a quilombo and that we wanted to get our certification so that we could fight together [*juntos*

e juntas] for our rights. We held several meetings in the community to teach as many people as we could what it meant to be a quilombola. At first there were few people who wanted to participate, but then it grew. We explained that all of our cultural traditions, dances, capoeira, and our labor in the fields, river, and mangroves have the name of *quilombo*. We told people that our resistance as black Brazilians and our fight to survive is what it means to be quilombolas.

Antônio's and Rosinda's narratives provide an ideal reference point for thinking about how the quilombolas of Grande Paraguaçu understood the application of the quilombo-descendant identity in their community. The first and most important step in the quilombo process is understanding. For the people of Grande Paraguaçu, understanding came first from seeing their neighbors obtain cultural recognition. In the framework of Paulo Freire (1970), the quilombolas of Grande Paraguaçu developed a critical awareness of quilombo-descendent identity through their friends in a nearby community and the social groups that worked with them, a process of conscientization in its most exemplary form.

Two ideas come together in Rosinda's and Antônio's statements. Antônio connected his first exposure to quilombos to a book. He explained that it was an elementary school book that discussed slavery in Brazil. But he cautioned me not to expect everyone to have his same experience. Many of the people identified as quilombolas did not have the opportunity to go to school—even elementary school—as they had to help their parents in the forest and mangroves. Even Antônio was not able to continue his studies because he worked with his father in the forest, which was one of the reasons he forbade his own children to work the land. Antônio wanted his children to learn the medicinal traditions of the forest and how to collect mariscos, but he also wanted to make sure they went to school and had other opportunities. The representative of SEPPIR who visited Salaminas helped Antônio, Rosinda, and others connect their lives to African cultural traditions and blacks who resisted slavery. According to Antônio most people in the community had not read about colonial quilombos, and still this narrative of African cultural resistance made sense to them as a framework for understanding their own quilombola identity.

On the other hand, Antônio and Rosinda described the immediate connection that they made between their labor and the new quilombo-descendant identity. They had never used that term to describe their everyday practices, but they recognized that it represented a certain way of living with which they identified. Thus, the quilombolas of Grande Paraguaçu were primarily responding to the descriptions of labor, land, and culture modeled and described by their friends and neighbors of the Iguape region.

Agreeing with Rosinda's recollection of the story, Antônio added more:

> Yes, we learned in Caonde and Salaminas, which are two fishing communities just a few miles away. We noticed that they have engenhos and are surrounded by the sugarcane where their enslaved ancestors once worked. If we have three engenhos here and we are also surrounded by sugarcane where our ancestors also worked, why wouldn't we also be quilombolas? We are in between Caonde and Salaminas. When the slave ship came through this area to drop off slaves and collect cargo, they would stop here on the shores of Grande Paraguaçu before going to Cachoeira. It was during those stops that slaves fled into the quilombos of Boqueirão, Engenho Velho, and Caibongo. If all of these communities that surround us are quilombos, why wouldn't we also be a quilombo? Today we have the knowledge to declare that we are a quilombo.

Here Antônio reminds us that Grande Paraguaçu is as much a part of the history of the Recôncavo as any other town in the region. He argues that there were several sugar mills in the region where their ancestors were forced to work. Furthermore, Antônio brings up a more interesting and perhaps more controversial point. If nearby communities are quilombos,[1] then why wouldn't Grande Paraguaçu also be a quilombo? Antônio pinpoints one of the main problems that paralyzes the quilombo clause in Brazil: the problem of who is and is not a quilombo descendant and the politics of ethnic differentiation that cultural recognition wedges between communities. Antônio's statement could be made even broader. With its deep history of slavery and black resistance, shouldn't all of the Recôncavo Baiano be a quilombo-descendant community? According to the terms of quilombola recognition and rights, the entire Recôncavo legally qualifies as one massive quilombo. For some communities in the Recôncavo to enjoy rights and recognition while others with the same identifying characteristics do not is not just a problem of the politics of cultural recognition—it seems to be part of the design.

Luis Claudio Dias "Cacau" do Nascimento, a local anthropologist, historian, and research coordinator of the Center for the Studies, Research, and Sociocultural Action of Cachoeira, referred to the Recôncavo as the "Recôncavo Açucareiro Baiano." In decades of independent

research, Cacau had found that this enormous region, especially the city
of Cachoeira and its surrounding districts, was greatly distinguished by
the presence of people from various African nations, particularly Nigeria,
Togo, and Ghana, who in Bahia became known as Jejes e Nagôs. In our
conversations and in a presentation I later invited him to give in the United
States, he described the conflict and grief that would have been spared
if the entire Iguape region had been recognized as one single quilombo-
descendant community.

In 2007, Cacau wrote a project proposal that did just that. He argued that given the history and cultural traditions of the entire region,
Article 68 of the constitution should recognize the entire Iguape region as
a quilombo-descendant community, a move that would benefit nearly ten
thousand Afro-descendants living in the area. Unfortunately, the project
was derailed, and individual towns were forced to seek cultural recognition independently, spiraling them each into their own land conflicts and
political struggles. Cacau attributed the death of his project ambiguously
to "powerful political interests." He explained that the division of Iguape
into separate communities, some culturally recognized as quilombo descendants and others not, weakened the social and political strength of
the quilombola movement in the region by creating legal impasses with
private landowners. A key example was the conflict generated in Grande
Paraguaçu.

While some of the residents of Grande Paraguaçu were soon convinced that their town was a quilombo-descendant community, not everyone was persuaded so quickly. The initial supporters became the quilombola leaders of the community, and they had to work to encourage a larger
majority of residents to join the cause and support the process. These early
quilombola leaders organized workshops together with research groups,
NGOs, and INCRA to help disseminate information about the changes
that would come about as a result of the new identity such as the process
of identification and land delimitation that INCRA would initiate in the
upcoming years.

During our community meeting, Antônio went on to describe the details of the mobilization effort in Grande Paraguaçu:

> I only remember a little bit about how the quilombo process here began
> because we have been in this struggle for many years. We spent a long
> time having meetings and more meetings and still more meetings. Then
> we began to mobilize. We spent more than eight months just organizing
> meetings. We held meetings all over the community. And when we felt

that everything was just about ready, we contacted the Palmares Foundation and asked for the certificate. We already had dozens of signatures declaring agreement with the recognition process. Our coordinators, Anselmo, Dona Maria, and Seu Altino, were the ones who went to [the Fundação] Palmares to make the request. Dona Maria and Seu Altino passed away last year because of pressure from the police that they could not withstand. The doctors say they died of heart attacks, but we know that they really died of broken hearts.

It didn't take very long for us to obtain our certificate from [Fundação Cultural] Palmares, and that is when our problems began. That is when people started to mobilize against us, when the *Jornal Nacional* came into our community, and when the landowners turned our own people against us by handing out cestas básicas and making threats. [Antônio listed the names of landowners and politicians in the region whom he accused of bribing residents.] [They] began to spread rumors that we were all frauds. How can something that was given to us by the Fundação Palmares be fraudulent?

INCRA has been here for about three years. They did all of the fieldwork. They called on laborers and landowners to go out together to see the fieldwork as it was conducted. We would go out to the forest to map the territory and do anthropological research about the community. INCRA held meetings in the main square asking people if they were quilombolas and whether they wanted to register their names as quilombolas or not. They explained to us what it meant and what made us quilombolas or not. And even after all of that, the landowners sued INCRA, saying that they were forcing people to identify as quilombolas.

These meetings were public. They were held out there in the square for everyone to see and hear. The problem is that a lot of people who work for the landowners were actually calling the landowners to ask for permission to register. [Here Antônio and others in the meeting gave the names of dozens of people who called to ask the landowners for permission to identify as quilombolas.] They said, "Doctor, should I register as a quilombola?" And the landowner said, "Yes, you can. Do it." So the young lady from INCRA set up a table for people to sign the petition, and everyone signed it. [The landowner] told them to sign and they obeyed. And then he turned around and said they were forced. Coerced! With that accusation of coercion, the court suspended our political process for over a year. Now we are attempting to reinitiate our process with INCRA.

Antônio's story coincides with some of what the INCRA analyst, Amélia, told me about her experience in Grande Paraguaçu, particularly how she was accused of coercion for telling people what *quilombo* meant. Here we also see that conflict began immediately following the community's cultural recognition from the Palmares Cultural Foundation. Antônio and all of the quilombolas angrily blamed a few private landowners in the area for maliciously stalling their progress in obtaining rights. The meeting grew heated after Antônio's story, as he reminded everyone of the abuses they had experienced. My recorder no longer remained lazily on a chair in the middle of the circle. It was picked up and used as a microphone and passed around to everyone who wanted to speak. As men and women shouted into the recorder, declaring that they were not afraid to speak or to denounce publicly the people who were intimidating them and trying to throw them out of their homes, I began to understand many of my own misperceptions about the quilombola process such as a persistent question I asked myself: "If this process causes so much conflict, then why do people continue to do it?"

I saw in the enraged and fed-up faces of those who spoke and in the quiet though deliberate nods of those who did not that becoming a quilombola was not so much about claiming a new ethnic identity. While the quilombola process began as one that was about obtaining visibility and long-overdue rights from the government, it had, perhaps more urgently, become about exposing and ending persistent racial injustice. I understood the strong connection these quilombolas felt to a history of suffering and their rage at the reality that not much had changed for them. The quilombola struggle made many of them realize that they were still treated like slaves, a feeling of repression that they could share with communities across the nation and world by identifying as quilombolas. Quilombo descendants entered the recognition process mobilized by the knowledge of their civil rights. Over time, they were fueled by the backlash of those who wanted to take away those rights.

"JUSTICE OF THE LAND": VIOLENCE, FEAR,
AND ANGER IN GRANDE PARAGUAÇU

A new way of life came about for the people of Grande Paraguaçu in 2005. The certificate of cultural recognition from the Palmares Cultural Foundation spiraled the community into internal conflict; landowners and nonquilombolas united against quilombolas in an effort to disrupt the recognition process. If the certificate brought them the attention they needed from government organizations focused on public health, education, and racial equality, it also subjected them to various forms of violence. Quilombolas accuse local landowners of retaliation and of working with public servants such as the police to intimidate them into dropping their claims to the land.

In 2006, the worst-case scenario happened. One of the landowner families disputing land rights with the quilombolas of Grande Paraguaçu submitted a petition for the reintegration of possession to the state court in Cachoeira, supported by a property title from 1904. Any landowner who has his or her rights to land disputed has the right to a reintegration of possession (reintegração de posse). If conceded by the court, this petition forces the disputing party, in this case the quilombolas and INCRA, to stop their investigation and leave the property. The court in Cachoeira approved the landowner's petition and sent the military police to remove the quilombolas from their lands.

Before the police were able to remove every quilombola family, the Palmares Cultural Foundation, the Ministério Público Federal (Federal Public Ministry), and INCRA spoke out in defense of the quilombolas. They argued that because quilombo rights were written into federal law and were not part of state law, or even the state's constitution, state courts would not be competent in deciding such rights, and thus the case should be sent to a federal court. With a change in judges, the quilombolas and their supporters believed that the court would reverse the state's decision and respect the quilombo rights outlined in the federal constitution. But the federal court upheld the state's decision without a proper investigation or a hearing from the quilombola defense. The decision was a major blow to the community, and it only affirmed their belief that the justice system did not include them. Without support from the courts, quilombola lives in Grande Paraguaçu were further exposed to landowner threats and aggressions.

In her 2007 INCRA report,[2] Anita quotes several quilombola leaders describing the police invasions that took place during and after the petition for reintegration of possession. It was this police harassment that took a toll on the hearts and nerves of Seu Altino and Dona Maria, as described earlier by Antônio. Sumido recalled how the police arrived in seven cars and a van, in plain clothes, and armed with shotguns. "They were destroying everything in sight and demanding to see Seu Altino." Dona Maria described how she stood up for her right to cultivate the land, even if it put her life at risk:

> One morning while I was planting manioc, an [officer] was following me and pulling out everything I planted. I planted it and he was behind me throwing it out. People were screaming at me: Maria, Maria, leave that manioc for God's sake, do not plant anything else or this man might hurt you. And I was *tranquilinha* [very calm] planting my manioc; I planted and he threw it out. I planted and he threw it out. And people screamed: Maria, Maria, for God's sake, leave that manioc before that man kills you. At that moment I said: I will not stop. If he kills me, he will be killing an honest working woman! That's the deal here.

Thanks to support from the Palmares Foundation, the Federal Public Ministry, and INCRA, the quilombolas were not removed from their homes; however, legal pressures against them only increased after the first petition for reintegration of possession. In her report, Anita lists four petitions filed against the quilombolas of Grand Paraguaçu in 2006 and 2007, one by each of the four private landowners in the town—all members of the same family. As if this mounting legal pressure weren't enough, in 2007 *Jornal Nacional* aired their report accusing the quilombolas of fraud.

During another community meeting, I asked the quilombolas to discuss how they felt about the legal progress of the their land process. I asked them to tell me specifically about the emotions they were experiencing. Brought to tears by frustration, Nildo asked for the floor.

> Is it that the justice system will never hear our side? Will we always be the ones who are *justiçados* [judged]? We don't want conflict. We don't! But it is so much injustice. . . . The justice system never considers our side. We are indignant about this! There are never summons for [the landowners]. Why is it that there are never any complaints against them? We are the only ones who get summoned all the time. What kind of justice is this? If the law is for one, it is for all. We want equality for everyone. So if you have money and file a complaint against us, then we get our summons right away. But since we are poor, just honest workers, when we go to file a complaint we just get ignored. What kind of country is this? Lula says that this is a country of equality for all. I do not think that is right because justice still does not pay attention to the side of the less wealthy worker. I personally do not believe in the justice of the land.

I only believe in God's justice because man's justice cannot be trusted. I do not believe in it.

After several other people also shared their stories, Antônio took the recorder. Antônio's story was emotional, and his voice trembled as he told it.

Everyone in this room knows my situation. There are men constantly banging on my door, frightening my wife and children, demanding to see me. They come when I'm not home and threaten my wife! [Antônio held the recorder tightly as everyone in the room nodded, responding, *Pois é* [That's right]. My wife is sick. Her condition is always made worse by stress. The doctor even ordered her to stop working in the mangroves because of her condition. And when these men come to my house they terrify her—she doesn't know if I am going to come home alive or if the men will do something to our home. I have filed a report against them, I've told INCRA and the lawyers of the AATR, but to this day nothing has happened. It just angers them and they keep threatening us.

After a special delegation from the Palmares Foundation came to the community to conduct an investigation and officially reported to Brasilia that we were not frauds, that is when the landowners really protested and came out in force. They accused us of everything and anything they could. One of the landowners even accused me of beating his wife in the public plaza! I ask you, how is that possible, if this man was with his wife the entire time? ["And filming everything!" a woman shouted from the circle.] Yes! He was recording every single step his wife took. I don't hit women, and there is proof that this could never have happened. [Antônio pointed to four other male quilombola leaders and said they had all been summoned to court for some far-fetched allegation and were all being summoned again to appear that month.] We never get out of this situation. I received a confirmation that my report against the landowners was received, but so far they have not been summoned.

Rosinda followed Antônio's story:

I don't know if you all have already mentioned Altino's lands here. [People mumbled.] Well, I'm going to tell this story anyway. Altino had already planted for forty years on that land, and last year he got a subpoena demanding that he leave the land because he was accused of invading it! After forty years, they accused him of invasion. Well, he couldn't stand that accusation, and he died from a sudden heart attack in the middle of his field. Twelve days after Altino died, [his wife] Maria das Dores also passed away in her home from what doctors called a sudden heart attack. But we knew what it was. We knew that her heart was also broken. Ever since we got the certificate of cultural recognition, these landowners have come at our community in the most violent form. After Altino and Maria died, we tried to strengthen the spirit of the community by holding public protests in the plaza and organizing meetings with the community to talk about our rights. We worked hard to strengthen ourselves again.

As if the loss of another community leader was not painful enough, Dona Maria was summoned to appear in court for illegal planting one year after she passed away. Outraged, the community held Maria and Altino as examples of the unending violence they had endured from landowners. Since the court's decision, the quilombolas have been fighting to stay on their lands. Joined by the AATR, and the Pastoral Commission of Fishermen and Women in Bahia, the quilombolas protested in Brasília and staged sit-ins at the local INCRA office.

The quilombolas of Grande Paraguaçu name the people who have destroyed their crops, fenced off their access to public mangroves, and threatened their family members. Jumping in after Rosinda's narrative, Antônio exclaimed, "For the past five years, there has been so much misery in our lives. Never before have we lived so much misery." Rosinda continued,

At this moment what we feel is disrespect. Because after making it this far, with a lot of difficulty and struggle, INCRA moves so slowly. That to us is disrespect toward the rights of rural black communities in this country. It's a situation of disrespect, and we are indignant about it. But we will not let things remain this way because we have made it this far and this cannot end. Yes, our struggle continues, but the disrespect is there, very explicitly, for all to see, for all of society to feel.

The quilombolas of Grande Paraguaçu expressed their rage at injustice as a fundamental feeling of exclusion and disrespect. The disregard for their basic civil and human rights by people in powerful positions and the public sector led them to feel desperation, an intense but uncertain longing to force the system to change. It is clear that there is a disconnect between a legal process that allows black communities the right to self-identify as quilombo descendants, thus setting them up for inclusion in a constitutional provision that grants them land rights, and the authentication and misrecognition that happens at the level of application. This rupture between theory and application takes place between the legal right to self-identify as a quilombo descendant and the ability to successfully obtain constitutionally sanctioned rights based on that category.

While it is important to contemplate identity from a conceptual standpoint of social and cultural construction and even performance (French 2009; Pinho 2010), it is also important to study the instances when identities (and all of their complexities) are fixed by political structures of representation for the purpose of creating public policies. In the case of the politics of cultural recognition, cultural and racial identification can either become a straightjacket or a mechanism for resistance, depending on the reaction and mobilization of the community. In the case of quilombo recognition, quilombolas have aligned themselves with the racial discrimination and misrecognition that black Brazilians, especially poor, rural black communities, live on a daily basis; quilombolas are calling cultural recognition into question, demanding that the justice system also respect their rights to life and land.

Grande Paraguaçu represents a constant back-and-forth between the community's ability to demonstrate its ethnic identity and the social and legal legitimation of that identity. Although the conflict is about landownership, the subtext is about race and power. As the Brazilian government has moved toward the promotion of cultural recognition, important structural issues have remained the same, particularly the hierarchical and patron-client relations of landownership. In the twentieth century, Florestan Fernandes tried to call attention to the unequal social and economic integration of blacks into society. He wrote that blacks were being assimilated culturally but still marginalized politically and economically: "every decisive phase of differentiation and progress has occurred between relatively prolonged phases of commitment to the past and even selective resistance to urgent sociocultural innovations" (1969, 131).

Although Fernandes was speaking of the economic changes taking place in the 1920s and 1930s, his analysis seems to be a warning about the continuation of economic development without social development. Fernandes argued that serious and direct attention needed to be given to the racial discrimination that blacks suffered before and after abolition if their position in the power structure were ever to be reverted. Indeed, although the quilombola fight is largely about land, it is undeniably rooted in a historically unequal distribution of land and power along racial lines, with black Brazilians being excluded from de facto landownership for more than a hundred years.

The quilombolas of Grande Paraguaçu have come to understand the power struggle in which they are involved. After Anita Souza was indicted, Maria and Altino died of broken hearts, and the court stalled the legal process, the quilombolas of Grande Paraguaçu have come to understand that their fight is about more than just an identity. Their fight is about racial, political, and socioeconomic injustice. Rosinda illustrates this realization in some of her comments:

> You know that when these landowners come to these small towns they like to "baptize" a bunch of people in the community by giving them other names like *menino* [boy] and *afiliado* [relative, godchild]. Because of that, people grow close to the landowner and begin to develop a certain respect for him, for their new *padrinho* [godfather]. So the landowner begins to hire several people from the same family to work on his lands, and when these people pass away their sons and daughters also go to work for the landowner, and so on and so on for generations. These people think, "I cannot risk getting my father fired from his job because he supports our whole family. INCRA will not resolve the land dispute soon, and then how would we live? It is better that I mind my own business. I hope that the quilombolas win, but I better just mind my own life." Then another person says, "Oh but that is my godfather. I cannot be against my godfather!"
>
> Then there is the capacho. That is what we call him, a capacho. He is the one who goes out at night and puts up signs on all the houses that say, "We are not quilombolas." I'm sure you have seen them. Even when we take them down, he puts them back up so that when outsiders come they will take pictures of them and think that there are no quilombolas here.

Wanting to make sure I understood what Rosinda was saying and what the community was feeling, Antônio made a more literal connection:

> We are living through so many threats here, so many threats. You remember in history that there were blacks in the senzala that helped capture slaves? They helped the capitães do mato. That's what is happening here. These men that threaten us on behalf of the landowner are the landowner's afiliados. People resisted slavery, but I am still a slave. All of us here are still enslaved because we don't have freedom.

Like Antônio, many other quilombolas referred to slavery to speak of a system of racial inequality that kept them in a violent position of disenfranchisement, a system that taunted them with cultural recognition but without granting them actual rights or protecting them from everyday violence. It took courage and trust for these men and women to speak out to me as they did. But it took rage at injustice as well. Seu Miguel's and Dona Maria's statements on suffering carried deep within the skin can be combined with Antônio's reflection on slavery and Rosinda's feeling of being disrespected to illustrate a collective sense of racial injustice that connects the quilombolas of Grande Paraguaçu to other black communities. Although Grande Paraguaçu is just one community, violence, threats, intimidations, and accusations of fraud are not confined to it alone. Sadly, many communities face the same issues. In the case of quilombolas throughout Brazil, conflict and not rights seems to be the norm.

"YOU'VE GOT TO FIGHT FOR YOUR RIGHTS": THE QUILOMBOLA FIGHT FOR BLACK JUSTICE

In 2009, I was invited to the 2nd State Conference on Politics for the Promotion of Racial Justice (CONEPIR) held in Salvador, Bahia. Quilombolas from all over Brazil were invited to a session led by the Pastoral Commission for Fisherman and Women. The director of the INCRA office in Bahia, Luiz Eduardo Barreto, was invited to answer questions and hear complaints from the quilombolas. Luiz spoke about the many bureaucratic challenges, including the shortage of federal funding and of employees that inhibited INCRA's work. He argued that the INCRA office in Bahia only had the funding to hire one anthropologist to carry out the fieldwork on hundreds of communities. Jokingly he said, "This woman would have to live hundreds of years to finish all of these [technical reports]." At the end of his talk, Luiz, in a spirited tone, told the quilombola leaders to "keep fighting." In a tone that called on the spirit of quilombolismo and the black civil rights movement all in one, the director told quilombolas to march, organize sit-ins, and "give [their] lives to the movement." Astonished by his call to action, I was unsure if anyone else in the room felt the irony of the INCRA director's words.

A woman named Graciela, from the quilombola community of the island of Maré, stood up and angrily asked for the microphone. "Why should we have to give our lives, and why do we have to fight?" she asked, frustrated by the suggestion.

The reason we have all come here is because we are trying to go through the system to obtain what is rightfully ours. Your job is to fight for us, to get us what the constitution says belongs to us. We come here to hear solutions from you, to get answers about our [land rights], and you tell us that you have no money! You tell us to fight because the system is broken!

Graciela went on for several minutes as others in the room nodded and raised their fists in agreement. Some people in the room had traveled more than five hours by bus and boat to be there. They were all there to get answers and wanted to hear that there were legal solutions to the conflicts taking place in their communities. Several communities were facing landowner violence. The community on the island of Maré was in desperate need of a title so the people there could improve their living conditions, including repairing sewage systems and installing access to running water, on parts of the island. Quilombolas from the Bahian mining region of Seabra were fighting with landowners who refused to follow the law and keep their cattle corraled. The cattle were eating and destroying quilombola crops. Graciela's comments highlighted the underlying issue of quilombola struggles in Brazil.

On one hand, the "quilombola" is a new category of black identity that was resuscitated by black-movement activists to mobilize rural black communities around their racial history and right to land. On the other hand, it is a political process fragmented by a weakly supported bureaucracy and a long history of racial exclusion. Quilombo descendants have learned that even though their land rights are guaranteed by the constitution, that does not mean the government will simply hand them those rights.

Although thousands of black communities are obtaining cultural recognition and quilombolismo is even thriving as a new ethnic representation of blackness in Brazil, quilombolas are also facing real and violent barriers to the acquisition of their constitutional land rights. The quilombola struggle for land rights has exposed the ugly inequality that poor black communities face every day in the justice system and the violence with impunity that they have to endure as a result of demanding justice. Understanding that their only option was to fight or risk losing everything, quilombola leaders formed the National Coordination of Rural Black Quilombola Communities (CONAQ) to represent quilombola struggles throughout the nation.

CONAQ was founded in 1996 in Bom Jesus da Lapa, Bahia. The organization has gained more ground and become more vocal with the implementation of affirmative action policies in Brazil since 2001. CONAQ's political and media discourse uses primarily campaign posters and a "Manifesto pelos direitos quilombolas" (Manifesto for quilombola rights) that the organizers wrote to the Brazilian Supreme Court. I focus on CONAQ's public discourse because it represents the ideological labor that the organization is conducting to strengthen and in some cases change the social and political understanding of the everyday lives of quilombolas and their fight for rights. With the rapidly increasing number of rural black communities seeking rights as the descendants of quilombos, a slew of dominant narratives, questions of authenticity, and preconceived notions about blackness have grown out of control, diverting social and juridical attention away from what is a clear issue of racial injustice within land-reform policies.

Through publicly distributed posters, CONAQ speaks directly to the Brazilian Supreme Court and society in general in a language that fundamentally describes quilombola land rights as a matter of racial equality. The posters necessarily connect quilombolas to other "Afro-rural" communities across the Americas, highlighting the Quilombo das Américas (Quilombo of the Americas) project that was launched in 2010 as a collective effort of various Brazilian government entities including SEPPIR, IPEA, and agencies of the United Nations (Melo et al. 2012). By speaking to quilombola rights in Brazil through an international discourse of Afro-rural rights, CONAQ physically and discursively pulls quilombolas out of a narrative of isolation, an ideological prison created both by the historical construction of the colonial quilombo and an ethnic discourse of differentiation demanded by the politics of cultural recognition. Here CONAQ also taps into Brazil's 2001 international commitment to combat racial inequality.

Just a year after Lula signed Decree 4.887, in 2004, the Banca Ruralista, a conservative, political action group made up of wealthy private landowners, filed a direct action of unconstitutionality in the Brazilian Supreme Court threatening to terminate the decree. The court was set to decide on the fate of quilombola rights in 2012, but the decision was postponed by one judge who asked for more time to review the case (Souza 2012). With the dispute over the authenticity of quilombola identity comes the legal questioning of rights, both juridically and socially. Juridically, there is a real accusation of unconstitutionality placed on quilombolas before the Supreme Court. And socially, quilombolas face accusations of fraud by a society that cannot understand the validity of their right to land based on a black identity (I. Leite 2000, 334).

CONAQ's "Manifesto pelos direitos quilombolas" speaks directly to this accusation of unconstitutionality. CONAQ declares that the quilombola rights written into the 1988 constitution and subsequently reinforced by Decree 4.887 were meant to overturn "colonial legislation" that classified the quilombo as a "crime" instead turning *quilombo* into a category of "self-identification" meant to "repair colonial damages and grant rights." To call these rights unconstitutional is, according to CONAQ, to express the discourse of "the same people who fought tirelessly to maintain the institution of slavery." In sixteen pages, the manifesto brings together historical and legal data to make a case for the constitutionality of quilombola self-identification and land rights more broadly. Most interesting in this document is the specific reference to slavery to describe an extant experience of racial exclusion. CONAQ asks the court to understand that denying constitutionally sanctioned rights to black Brazilians is the equivalent of denying blacks the right to live in freedom and a reproduction of the discourse of slavery and the physical enslavement of the black population.

Quilombolas describe the challenges they face in obtaining land rights as an example of a system of slavery that has not ended for them. This is a discourse that I also heard repeatedly in Grande Paraguaçu. For quilombolas, the ability to become legal landowners signifies a break with a historical exclusion that has lasted into the twenty-first century and has kept blacks from exercising their full rights as citizens of the nation. Although there was not a single law that specifically excluded blacks from owning land, there were political processes in place that allowed for the concentration of property and wealth in the hands of specific sectors of society; it is a system of racial hierarchy in disguise, especially when it comes to land-ownership (I. Leite 2000, 335). For instance, the Land Law of 1850 classified Africans and their descendants in the category of *libertos* (freedmen) while excluding them from the category of *brasileiros* and thus full citizenship (ibid.). Liberto men were considered citizens if they were born in Brazil, but women were excluded from that right; however, even liberto men could not exercise full citizenship rights, as they had to meet certain literacy and income requirements in many cases (Chalhoub 2006).

Libertos born in Africa could not be citizens; they acquired certain civil rights but could not vote or enjoy other rights. Brazilian historian Sidney Chalhoub has found that "the epithet *liberto*—freedman—carried with it considerable burden" (77). It was a category that exposed many Africans and Afro-Brazilians to racial exclusion throughout many years. Because *liberto* was not a racial category but rather a legal status, it was not recorded as a way of legally segregating and excluding blacks, even though it was experienced in that way by thousands of people. Ilka Leite notes, "All of this history is revealed when the quilombo comes into center stage as a form of organization, a fight, of a space maintained and conquered throughout generations" (2000, 335).

CONAQ's manifesto opens with a quote by one of the founders of CONAQ, Givânia Maria da Silva, the director of the Office of Policies for Traditional Communities (Subcom, Secretaria de Políticas para Comunidades Tradicionais, a division of SEPPIR). Da Silva makes a direct connection between the history of slavery and the legacy of racial discrimination that continues in Brazil:

> The challenges of today are the challenges of yesterday. Why yesterday? Because those were challenges of overcoming the slave ships, slavery, anonymity, abandon, etc. The challenges of today are different but they have the same finality, which is to cancel any possibility that the *preto* [black person] in this country will be treated like the rest of the population. When the mainstream media, the *latifúndio* [wealthy, private landowning class], and conservative sectors of society react against this policy, we understand that what is really happening today is the same as what took place yesterday, except through different mechanisms. What is certain is that every day we have to be more united. This is a difficult fight, and above all, it is a collective fight, as only in that way will we have the strength to fight for a right that is denied to us, that is, the right to our lands.

I was introduced to CONAQ's manifesto by Carlos Marinho of the AATR, the Association of Lawyers for Rural Workers, who gave me a copy during one of our interviews. It was actually written as a petition for the purpose of obtaining enough signatures to convince the Brazilian Supreme Court to vote on the side of quilombolas. In her opening quote, Da Silva describes a historical exclusion that has changed its discourse but not its goal: the denial of full participation for blacks in social and economic life. The manifesto further points out that while there are more than 3,000 quilombola communities all over Brazil, only 185 of them have land titles; it illustrates how a great majority are left without constitutional rights and in a "fragile" and "difficult" situation. Da Silva speaks to this contemporary position of blacks in Brazil as only partial citizens when she states that black Brazilians are not treated "like the rest of the population." In this sense, land rights, as a historical marker of status and political power in Brazil, signify the ability of blacks to participate fully as citizens of the nation. This became the mantra of the quilombola movement as it defined its place in affirmative action discussions.

In 2011, CONAQ initiated a two-year campaign in defense of quilombola rights called "Brasil tambem é quilombola: Nossa identidade, nossa riqueza, nossa história" (Brazil Is Also Quilombola: Our Identity, Our Richness, Our History). The purpose of the campaign was to make visible the everyday lives and political struggles of quilombo descendants in a series of nationwide protests and marches. The campaign poster includes an image of Brazil in the shape of a thumbprint, a powerful visual symbol for connecting the body, race, culture, citizenship, and labor into one compact banner. The campaign set out to deal with the political and social issues of the quilombola as a contested identity and claims to land by emphasizing an image of quilombolas as a living group of rural, fishing, and foresting communities throughout Brazil. In the poster, CONAQ defines quilombolas as members of

> communities that fight a day-to-day battle for the right to land and specific public policies. They face a context of exclusion that has taken place over the past five centuries, due to racial and ethnic discrimination and historical practices of concentration of landownership in Brazil. This context is reinforced by the enslavement of black men and women in various parts of the world.

CONAQ's definition of *quilombola* is notably different from those of the Palmares Cultural Foundation and the Brazilian Anthropological Association, primarily in the way it speaks specifically to the embodied black experience as a "day-to-day" battle. What is more, CONAQ connects the quilombola issue to a fight against an everyday reality of racial inequality; it again points to slavery and the concentration of land in Brazil as a context for the continued discrimination and exclusion of blacks in contemporary society. Here the leaders of CONAQ provide an answer to Graciela's unanswered question "Why should we have to fight?" According to CONAQ, quilombolas have to fight for their constitutionally granted rights because they are still living in a system that is fundamentally rooted in racial inequality. CONAQ demonstrates that quilombolas understand that when INCRA claims to not have the funding to fulfill its duties to quilombola communities and when the Supreme Court entertains an act of unconstitutionality, these issues really represent a historical negation and devaluation of black rights and black lives. In the final paragraph of the poster, CONAQ makes a final appeal to the Supreme Court:

The Supreme Court had the greatness to validate and guarantee education for the black populace by voting on the side of equality and a racial quota system in public universities. Now the court has the opportunity to add one more fundamental dimension to the full consolidation of the legitimate patrimony of black Brazilians—the right to land and the right to life of quilombola communities. Brazil is also quilombola!! And the federal Supreme Court can preserve this recognition, in the same way that it did with university quotas for blacks, so that the equality indicated in the Constitution will not be just a formality but a fact. What is more, [the court] will recognize that the Brazilian state used enslaved black labor in order to construct its wealth, and today, the minimum that it should do is lessen the damages caused to those populations by validating their real right to land.

Here we recognize in CONAQ's statements a discourse not only of affirmative action but also of reparations for enslavement and the centuries of exclusion from all aspects of social life that it caused blacks. However, it is important to recognize that CONAQ is not demanding reparations, which were given in the Brazilian Constitution when it granted land rights to the descendants of quilombos. What makes CONAQ's campaign and the collective quilombola frustration at the 2009 CONEPIR meeting important to this conversation on affirmative action is that they are demanding rights that are already given in theory (or rather, constitutional law) but still denied and contested in practice. This is the way racism functions in Brazil, according to CONAQ—not through legal exclusion and segregation but, despite legal inclusion and integration, through the delegitimation of black rights as unconstitutional and therefore in opposition to the racially democratic values of the constitution.

Quilombolas understand that they are part of a larger fight of racial justice for blacks, but does the government? On the same poster, CONAQ declares that the right to land for quilombolas is "a public policy with eyes to the future": "It is the guarantee of a property that has been occupied for centuries and centuries by black families who were expropriated with the expansion of agribusiness, mineral exploitation, and monoculture. These lands are fundamental to the survival of these identities." Although the Brazilian government has invested in the quilombola issue by restructuring the political process of cultural recognition as a way of enacting Article 68, the process of granting actual rights has been slow and riddled with problems.

Carlos Marinho explains that one of the main problems inhibiting quilombo land rights is that there is not a federal law in place that mandates these rights, such as the new Law of Quotas that mandates the increased admittance of black and brown students in all universities. Quilombo land rights are written in a transitory or temporary article of the constitution, a reality that has made them vulnerable to every form of contestation. Lula granted quilombolas the right to self-identification, and with that the government reformed the political process for cultural recognition and rights distribution. But without a federal law mandating land rights for quilombolas and obligating all states to recognize these rights,[3] the rights are politically weak and open to institutional inequality. I do not critique political efforts in order to discredit them but rather as a way to invite a more critical discussion on the politics of cultural recognition and land distribution for black Brazilians, a process that demands ethnic authenticity without a system in place for guaranteeing and protecting rights.

For the national quilombola effort, justice means political visibility and legally sanctioned rights, especially the rights to land and life. Quilombola justice became a way of talking about the rights violations and racial exclusion engrained in the politics of landownership. While I was in Grande Paraguaçu, I had the opportunity to witness the visit of several government representatives from SEPPIR. The quilombolas of Grande Paraguaçu had prepared for the visit by organizing a community meeting and inviting quilombolas from all of the surrounding regions to participate in a large-scale march through the town. The visit was a huge ordeal, even causing the people who did not identify as quilombolas to organize their own counterdemonstration as an interruption to the visit. As the meeting with SEPPIR started, Antônio and Rosinda began by giving the representatives an overview of all of the conflicts they had endured, stating that they were being denied their own history and identity by people who did not want to see them obtain land rights. The community meeting-house, which always felt spacious during our meetings, felt small and tight with so many people there to see the representatives from SEPPIR. As he wrapped up his speech, Antônio raised his fist in the air and yelled, "Justiça!" Energetically, the crowd responded, "Quilombola!" The chant went on for a few seconds with loud cheers and yells of emotional support.

"Quilombo justice" is a response to the problems black Brazilians face in obtaining collective rights in a system that recognizes them as culturally integrated, even when they are economically and politically excluded (Gomes da Cunha and Gomes 2007). The quilombola recognition process reflects the contradictions and conflicts that arise when ethnic authenticity and historical memory, especially a history that is primarily constructed by colonialists, become the only criteria for collective rights in a nation where racism and classism still permeate everyday life. The fact of blackness and quilombola identity in Brazil is that while they can seem socially fluid as self-ascribed ethnic identities, they are also politically and socially rigid as lived and manifested in the body. Although black identities can be reimagined and self-defined in the process of identity formation, when it comes to demanding rights, black bodies and black lives become the direct targets of a discursive and physical violence of misrecognition. For quilombolas, blackness is both a "visible identity" (Hooker 2009, 13), one they embody as an everyday form of marginalization and political invisibility, and an oral narrative of black resistance to historical oppression.

Quilombolas are historically racialized subjects; the colonial quilombo may now be a memory of African resistance, but during the eighteenth century it was a criminal organization; black bodies (whether real or imagined) were feared and policed by the Portuguese crown. It makes sense that a history of racial persecution has become the discourse of choice for the quilombola movement. What is more, for CONAQ there is no division between racial and ethnic identity; these are inseparable as part of the multiple narratives of blackness in Brazil that speak to cultural stories of ancestry and sociohistorical belonging but that also speak to the "visible markers of difference " (Hooker 2009, 6), that is, the markers of race that are laden with social valuations and preconceptions of morality, intelligence, belonging, and more. A quilombola politics of solidarity is thus forged out of a shared feeling of racial injustice that is painfully described as slavery. While race-based policies have been introduced in the twenty-first century, forcing intellectual and political leaders to reckon with the place of race within public policy, racial democracy as a uniquely Brazilian attribute has not lost its voice, even, and especially, among anthropologists. The politics of cultural recognition thus renders CONAQ's discursive and political labor vital to the attainment of land rights by questioning the nation's real commitment to affirmative action for all black Brazilians in the present and future.

Conclusion

T he body was found dismembered with its intestines strewn all over the ground; with over a hundred cuts, everything indicated that parts of the body had been eaten." It was a weeknight, and like every other evening, we were all having coffee and bread and watching the *Jornal da Record*. The report was about three indigenous men in a town in the state of Amazonas who were accused of murdering and eating a twenty-one-year-old fazendeiro. The nonindigenous residents of the town were accusing indigenous residents of cannibalism. The reporter emphasized that the conditions in which the victim was found indicated that parts of his body had been eaten. Fearing violent repercussions from society, many of the indigenous families in the area fled their homes and went into hiding. Only a few families stayed behind. The reporter spoke with members of these families, who insisted that it was a mistake, that cannibalism was not involved, and that the body was most likely eaten by dogs. The report then flashed to a conversation with a historian who affirmed that cannibalism did not exist any more in any part of Brazil. "It is a practice that has been extinct for decades," he said. The reporter explained that the indigenous men accused had not been found and that the case was being overseen by Funai in order to "ensure that the customs and culture of the indigenous offenders are understood and respected." When the report ended, Antônio turned to me and said, "What a shame. Our brothers are being accused of cannibalism. I don't believe it. I think it's just another example of the racism in this country."

I felt that Antônio identified with the fear of misunderstanding that drove the indigenous families to flee rather than face the wrath of people who imagined them as cannibals. While cannibalism strikes a nerve in the national moral code, that collective "sense of decency" to which the ethnic "other" must ascribe (Povinelli 2002, 5), the accusation of quilombo fraud struck a collective nerve in liberal-democratic values in Brazil, where blackness is still disregarded as a legitimate collective experience. Once they were accused of fraud, the quilombolas of Grande Paraguaçu be-came characterized as land thieves, violent, conflictive, and problematic. Stripped of their right to self-identification and their embodied forms of knowing, the quilombolas of Grande Paraguaçu have been forced to fight for their constitutional right to a self-defined identity and a historical con-nection to their land.

I have worked to illustrate, both recursively and analytically, the mul-tiple layers of knowledge production that have impacts on the rights and lives of black Brazilians throughout the history of the nation. In order to understand how black lives become delegitimated in the demands for jus-tice within a multicultural, democratic society, it is essential to understand the calculated ways in which black identities have been historically, intel-lectually, politically, and legally conceptualized: physiologically excluded as black bodies while culturally included as relics of African ancestry and tradition. The quilombo-descendant identity, like other forms of black identity, has been molded within the formation and interests of the Bra-zilian liberal-democratic nation.

As a way of understanding this constructive process, I divided my ethnographic data within different analytical frameworks to demon-strate the multiple forms of thinking and conceptual constructions that take place around the quilombo-descendent identity—historical, politi-cal and legal, intellectual, and embodied. Here the purpose was to create what Jackson (2005) calls "productive juxtapositions" between theory and practice—between concepts and everyday life—to highlight the ruptures, contradictions, and exclusions that occur when theoretical imaginations (such as those of cultural recognition) orient public policies (tangible and urgent needs) for racially and economically marginalized black Brazilians.

Government organizations do not create multicultural policies in a vacuum free of historical imaginations. In the same way, quilombolas do not define their own identities outside of political structures of representa-tion, nor do they determine their own conditions of authenticity and access within the political processes of cultural recognition and rights distribu-tion. In this regard, Jackson writes that "the connection between institu-tional mandates and the interiorized, intentional bodies they assume— and upon which they seek to act—foregrounds a debate about 'the body as a site of knowing'" (66). The institutional mandates in this case are the po-litical boundaries that designate the appropriate representation of a modern quilombola subject. Thus, I argue, at the moment of cultural recognition, black bodies are "partially co-constructed" and "constrained" by the political process itself. I critically dig into the constructive political process of the quilombola identity; however, I also take seriously the body as a site of knowing, understanding, and embodied narratives of life in practice.

I began my research in Brazil by interviewing representatives of government agencies and NGOs before approaching quilombolas or moving into the quilombo. In almost every interview, including those with representatives of INCRA and the Palmares Cultural Foundation, the interviewee consistently asked why I was interviewing him or her about the quilombo identity when I should have been interviewing quilombolas themselves. "They are the ones who define their own identity; they are the ones who have to self-identify," the director of the Palmares Cultural Foundation proclaimed in our first interview. Although I always responded vaguely yet respectfully that I would be interviewing quilombolas soon, so as not to disregard their suggestion, I was very clear about the order of my fieldwork.

I needed to first understand how government agencies legally defined the terms of recognition for quilombo descendants. These were the agencies and people who ultimately decided which communities would obtain land rights and why or why not; thus, their definitions and bureaucratic processes, whether they understood them as such or not, were essential to understanding quilombola narratives of identity formation and struggle. The quilombolas of Grande Paraguaçu had been working hand in hand with INCRA, the Palmares Cultural Foundation, and several NGOs for years, learning to reconnect and reframe their everyday lives within historical and political narratives of cultural tradition and African resistance. Learning these frameworks did not negate nor erase the community's own embodied forms of knowing and remembering. However, it was important in learning the process of cultural recognition to understand how these two frameworks, one legal and one embodied, were at times intertwined and at others in complete contradiction. For quilombolas, the primary rupture in the cultural recognition process happens at the moment ideological promises are supposed to be put into practice, when actual rights are not granted and won but rather promised and then withheld indefinitely.

I reflect here a way of thinking about ethnic and racial identities as predetermined categories as well as embodied narratives of self and belonging, as complex and constantly evolving narratives in practice and conflict. The politics of cultural recognition depend on predetermined definitions of ethnicity, culture, and tradition as a way of establishing boundaries and parameters for the collective rights of specific, ethnically differentiated communities. The problem of cultural recognition as a means of rights distribution within the liberal multicultural nation-state is that it turns ethnic specificity and cultural preservation into legal parameters for the ostensibly democratic distribution of rights. These legal parameters create the illusion that collective rights for historically excluded and marginalized ethnic and racial groups can be restored and protected simply through a democratic process; in this case, rules for cultural recognition are established through legal processes and procedures that are apparently open to all through self-identification. As Amélia protested in frustration, "Everyone has rights in this process, the quilombolas, the landowners, the merchants, and the state, and all of these different entities have to be heard, respected, and compensated."

The idea is that any community that adequately meets the legal terms and conditions established through the democratic processes of cultural recognition is eligible for rights. Here again, the rupture takes place when, after all of the work and effort of going through the democratic process, the end result is not rights; in fact, it is a shameless denial of rights defended by bureaucratic excuses and dismissals and supported by a racialized power structure. It was this devastating understanding of an unjust political process that motivated Graciela's angry protest to the director of INCRA at the CONEPIR conference in 2009 that highlighted just how patient and cooperative the quilombolas had been. Graciela reminded the director that the reason they were all there that day was precisely because they were "trying to go through the system." She told him, "Your job is to fight for us, to get us what the constitution says belongs to us." At that time, Graciela's community desperately needed a land title to fix several development issues, including sewage problems that were growing worse each day. Wastewater flowed freely between homes and under children's bare feet, threatening the health and safety of the community.

Like every leader in Grande Paraguaçu, Graciela had also been threatened by landowners and seen her family members intimidated by henchmen in her own community. Without blinking, Graciela stood up that day and made it clear to everyone in the room that what the INCRA director was saying was that they were on their own, that just because the constitution says quilombolas deserve land rights does not mean that the government—and much less the private landowners—would actually grant them those rights, at least not without a fight.

Many quilombolas referred to their frustration of trying to go through the system. The quilombolas of Grande Paraguaçu no longer believed that the government was working in their favor. Having been called to court numerous times to respond to unfounded accusations by landowners and yet never seeing the justice system punish the visible and documented violations committed against the community, the quilombolas of Grande Paraguaçu felt that their only option was to unite with a larger fight for racial justice. For quilombolas throughout Brazil, the rupture between the legal promise of rights through cultural recognition and the systemic refusal to grant those rights boils down to racial injustice and historical black exclusion. As the quilombola identity solidifies and gains more support among rural black communities, it is important and even urgent to study the conflicts and retaliations that these communities experience as a result of seeking rights. Grande Paraguaçu represents the difficult experience of one community that has been stalled in the quilombo process for over seven years, but Grande Paraguaçu is not alone. The majority of certified quilombola communities are in the same situation: while they have obtained cultural recognition from the Palmares Cultural Foundation, they have not obtained land rights.

The cultural recognition of quilombo descendants rallies black communities to civic action but then leaves them without the political resources they need to obtain comprehensive rights. Rather than blaming rural black communities for the conflicts they encounter and castigating them for "unpreparedness" or "not knowing," narratives of conflict and the resulting community anger at racial injustice should be documented and recorded as fundamental rifts in the politics of cultural recognition that cannot by itself address historical structures of racial inequality imbedded within institutional practices and extant power relations. These narratives vividly illustrate the physical and emotional ways quilombolas connect their everyday lives of labor and struggle to a history of oppression in the form of slavery and to a collective experience of blackness, or of being black, and thus being systematically devalued and marginalized in Brazil. Quilombola rights are not just about the performance of cultural identity; they are essentially about the legitimation of racial justice as a valid focus of public policy.

Everyday lived experiences of struggle and conflict, particularly the complexities and contradictions of racial and ethnic identities in struggle within a liberal multicultural system, are fundamental to thinking about the formation and application of public policies aimed at these groups. In the case of quilombolas, these experiences demonstrate the embodiment of blackness, an experience of blackness that is lived through the body often in a state of conflict and conciliation, or as Seu Altino and Dona Maria expressed it, an experience of being black that is felt deep in the skin as both "sorrow" and "great pride." The body here, as Caldwell argues, is a "site and reference point for gendered and racialized constructions of social meaning" (2007, 105). The black body for the quilombola is a reference point for decades of racial discrimination as well as a site for resistance and opposition.

Using the case of Grande Paraguaçu, I have illustrated the ways in which the lives of an entire community were shaken by the quilombo process, the pain and frustration that emerge when the benefits of becoming a quilombola never materialize, and the hope that drives quilombolas to "give their lives" to the process. In addition to their everyday lives in the forest and mangroves, the quilombolas of Grande Paraguaçu have also come to embody quilombolismo as a new, lifelong struggle for black justice. The quilombolas of Grande Paraguaçu have joined with national struggles for quilombola justice as a way of showing that the conflict that has descended upon them is not their fault and is not due to their own unpreparedness or inability to understand the definition of *quilombo*. But rather, the violent conflict they face is the result of a system of inequality in which the lives and rights of poor black communities are devalued and consistently disempowered. Hanchard describes the Brazilian black movement in the twentieth century: "The ever-present challenge for the movement is the unification of culture and politics and, more importantly, the differentiation between culture as folklore from culture as a valuative basis for ethno-political activity" (1994a, 100). Decades later, the quilombola movement has taken this challenge head on by demanding that the nation acknowledge that within narratives of cultural ancestry and tradition there is also a history of politically sanctioned and intellectually approved racial discrimination.

Antônio's empathy toward an indigenous community's fight against a racist image of cannibalism illustrates how quilombolas have come to define the lines of their solidarity within a larger discourse of racial justice. Although the quilombola fight for land rights may be, immediately, about the urgent need for land titles within rural black communities, the quilombola movement for rights and recognition is about something greater; it is about racial justice in the twenty-first century and for generations to come. It is about spotlighting the persistent devaluation of black life in Brazil, a life still on the margins of justice that cannot simply be imagined or conceptualized away but that must be reckoned with.

Epilogue

I returned to Grande Paraguaçu in the summer of 2013 and then again in 2014. The dirt road that had so poignantly marked my difficult access to the community in 2009 had been paved by the state. The new asphalt road made life easier for quilombolas who were constantly going into Cachoeira and Salvador for a variety of reasons, including college classes, doctor and hospital visits, grocery shopping, and applying for ID cards and social services. But the most important change I hoped to see was a land title; sadly, that was not the case.

As I walked up to Antônio's home, I was greeted by his eldest daughter—"Elizabete! It's you! We were just talking about you the other day," she said as she hugged me. The house was the same as I remembered except that the words "We are quilombolas with a lot of pride" and "I know what it is: that is why I AM a quilombola" had been repainted and now looked bolder and brighter than I recalled. Antônio arrived shortly afterward and told me that most of the quilombola leaders were at a meeting in a nearby town discussing funding for cultural projects in their communities.

The meeting was with representatives of SEPPIR. There were about twenty-five quilombolas present, a surprising turnout since it was the beginning of São João, and everyone in Bahia was busy preparing for the festivities. When I arrived at the meeting, Sumido was speaking. Sumido had always been one of the most passionate leaders of the movement in Grande Paraguaçu, so I was not surprised that he was upset:

> I'm so tired of these meetings! I don't want any more meetings about culture, about projects, about anything. No more conversations! We need our land title! That is what we need. We don't need any more of

E.1. *Quilombola meeting with SEPPIR officials, 2013. Photograph by Márcio Soares.*

this. This is just a waste of time. What good are these conversations if we will never see our land title?

As Sumido spoke, quilombolas around the room nodded in agreement. When he was finished, a lot of people raised their hands to speak. Before giving the word to anyone else, one of the representatives of SEPPIR took the microphone and asked to respond to Sumido's statement.

> I understand that you are upset about your land title, but we are here to provide resources for cultural projects and ways of earning an income from the artisan activities that everyone here practices. You are focused on the land title but there is more than just that. Just because you don't have a land title doesn't mean you have to just sit and wait and do nothing. In the meantime, until your community gets a title, we can work on cultural projects.

Not at all satisfied with her answer, Sumido turned his gaze down toward his feet in silence. He stayed quiet through the rest of the meeting, and then he got up and walked out without speaking to anyone. I followed Sumido out of the meetinghouse. He was so upset he hardly noticed me. "Tudo bom, Sumido?" I asked. "No. I'm not fine," he replied. "All of this is wrong. We don't need any more of this." Not saying anything else, Sumido angrily paced back and forth as he waited for his ride home. I remained silent, knowing that anything I said at that moment would be woefully insufficient. A land title—the land title promised by the constitution—was all Sumido and every quilombola in Grande Paraguaçu wanted. No more meetings about culture, just the legal right to their land.

For Sumido, sitting through another meeting about cultural projects after nearly a decade of "waiting" for a land title—a decade of violent division, conflict, and threats in his community and within his own family— was not only frustrating, it was disrespectful to the real and urgent concerns that occupied his life. After all, how can the quilombolas of Grande Paraguaçu be excited about securing support for their basket making, capoeira, forestry, fishing, and mariscagem if their future and lives on the very land that allows them those cultural activities is still under threat? What the SEPPIR representative didn't understand in Sumido's emotional statement is that for him and the quilombolas, conversations about culture have to be connected to conversations about security and the real prospect of a future livelihood. The quilombolas of Grande Paraguaçu were not yet in a state of security, and thus meetings about cultural projects were difficult to conceive. Quilombola leaders were inundated with court summons and threats, and worst of all, it seemed that everyone around them still saw them as "frauds." This was made clear by the freshly painted declaration of quilombola identity on the wall of Antônio's home.

Today one of the major issues of concern for Grande Paraguaçu is the territorial overlap of lands identified as environmental reserves. After a technical report is published in the *Diario Oficial da Uniao*, it becomes open to contestation by any other entity that may have legal rights to the area—that includes federal agencies such as the Chico Mendes Institute for Biodiversity Conservation (ICMBio), among others—in case the land in question overlaps with territories overseen by these agencies. If the jurisdiction does overlap with quilombola lands, the entity involved has thirty days to make demands or contestations. Grande Paraguaçu had two technical reports published; one in 2007 that was called into question by the *Jornal Nacional*'s accusation of fraud, and the second was a revised version in 2009. In a comment posted on March 19, 2013, on his website, *Étnico: Etnicidade e direitos: Índios, quilombos e populações tradicionais*, anthropologist Maurício Arruti documented that during those two years of revision and publication of the technical report, the ICMBio never contested any territorial rights in Grande Paraguaçu. Still, in 2013 it carried out plans to expand its extractive reserve (*reserva extravista*) in the Iguape

Bay, thus encroaching on quilombola territories recognized and outlined in INCRA's 2009 report. In chapter 3 I described a manguezal that had been closed off as an environmental preservation area in Grande Paraguaçu. The fact that marisqueiras could no longer work in the manguezal on a regular basis actually made the area more vulnerable to pollution. As a result, quilombolas spent their weekends organizing cleanup crews to collect the garbage that got caught in the mangroves throughout the week. Quilombolas have a personal interest in protecting and preserving the land on which they depend; however, their protection of the environment is grounded in a symbiotic relationship between their labor and the land. The quilombola community organization was even named Amantes da Terra (Lovers of the Land). If this relationship between a sustainable, traditional life and environmental preservation is broken and lands are closed off, both the community and the environment will suffer. Without the legal right to their land, quilombolas have limited protection over the encroachment of any entity, be it federal or private.

The fight for quilombo land rights has only grown since my field research in 2009. As of April 29, 2015, the Comissão Pro-Índio of São Paulo (CPI-SP) reported on its website that the distribution of land titles for quilombolas remained slow and limited, even as the number of culturally recognized territories increased by the hundreds. The organization estimates that out of the nearly three thousand quilombola communities in Brazil, only about 8 percent have obtained land titles. During my fieldwork, interviews with government officials and activists revealed a great deal of hope and expectation for change given the new policies implemented by the Lula administration in 2003, especially Decree 4.887. However, as I have shown throughout this book, these polices are highly detailed and bureaucratic and thus have not led to the large-scale social change that supporters hoped to see. The CPI-SP documented that in eight years, the Lula administration only granted twelve land titles; and up until December 2014, the Dilma administration had only granted twelve partial land titles.

Although Grande Paraguaçu still does not have land rights and other conflicts have emerged since I left the field, there has been one significant change in the community. Quilombola leaders describe a much more solidified, collective quilombola consciousness among the residents of Grande Paraguaçu and in solidarity with hundreds of quilombola communities statewide. Sumido, Antônio, Rosinda, and other quilombola leaders continue to demand the rights of their community and to expand their advocacy for the support of rural, black territories in their region. Corresponding with Rosinda, I learned that she completed bachelor's and master's degrees in social sciences at the new Universidade Federal do Recôn-cavo da Bahia (UFRB) in the heart of Cachoeira. Rosinda proudly explains how women are participating more in the political decision making of the community. A central leader of the quilombola movement and recently a self-identified anthropologist, Rosinda has become the force behind the mobilization of female activists in Grande Paraguaçu.

Quilombolas throughout Brazil are putting their lives on the line to fight, without fear, for their land rights. Securing the right to land, al-though not the end of a larger battle, symbolizes more than just a property title; it signifies the recognition of a life that is intimately, emotionally, and physically intertwined with the land, without which quilombolas would be left without a home but, more importantly, without a sense of life security and belonging. During my interviews in Grande Paraguaçu, quilombo-las described their fear of being displaced and thrown into urban centers, where without the security of the forest they might starve and be forced to "live under the freeways." In its appeal to the Brazilian Supreme Court, CONAQ asked the court "to add one more fundamental dimension to the full consolidation of the legitimate patrimony of black Brazilians—the right to land and the right to life of quilombola communities" (CONAQ 2013). While the quilombola movement is, on the surface, demanding certain concrete citizen rights—in this case, land rights—its activists are doing so within a larger plea for the legitimation and valuation of black life in Brazil. The movement is seeking more than just the recognition of qui-lombola communities as cultural entities, and consequently it is speaking to a much larger issue of how black lives and black bodies are conceived and treated on an everyday basis within the present social systems, a black mode of existence that centers on the lived experience of blackness *na pele*. By placing the black body at the center of the struggle, the quilombolas in this movement fight against a moral structure that constitutes black bodies as less deserving, a racialized moral measure that still makes up the lens of "justice" in the twenty-first century. Within this moral frame, black lives are systemically delegitimized and all too easily dismissed in their collec-tive demand for rights even as the state creates broad policies for cultural recognition and affirmative action.

In my role as an anthropologist in the quilombola fight for land and racial justice, I am motivated by the quilombola response to policies of cultural recognition that still do not take into account the everyday lived experiences of blackness in Brazil. I argue in this book that applied anthro-pologists, who seek political engagement and social change through their research and scholarship, can begin by aligning themselves with communities in their fight for a reversal of hegemonic discourses. Anthropologists are particularly positioned to bring large-scale visibility to the lives and struggles of those who experience racial marginalization and violence every day. However, we must resist the urge to neutralize and package within formulaic knowledge structures the complex stories and emotional narratives of everyday life that are entrusted to us, especially narratives of racialization and racial exclusion. Dismissing the need to understand and document the urgency of identity politics and racialized experiences for the promotion of a universal humanity (or post-humanity) or multicultural fluidity is not productive if communities of color are marching and yelling in the streets, just outside our ivory towers, "Justiça Quilombola!"

Anthropological fieldwork but more importantly, aligned anthropology that does not pretend to be neutral when neutrality does not exist and that does not apologize for its own subjective and political positioning is imperative in capturing and documenting the struggles and discursive revolutions of everyday people in their fight for legitimacy. Here I align myself with public scholars, cited and engaged throughout this book, who understand anthropology as deeply politicized and socially accountable, a position that is messy and vulnerable and always exposed. In their inspiring edited volume, *When People Come First*, João Biehl and Adriana Petryna write,

> For anthropologists, . . . peopled accounts — stories that are so often hidden from view, obscured by more abstract and bureaucratic considerations of public policy — are the very fabric of alternative social theorizing. By looking closely at . . . the ups and downs of individuals and communities as they grapple with inequality . . . we are able to see them in the making or in the process of dissolution, and we understand the local realities, so often unspoken, that result when people are seen or governed in a particular way, or not at all. (2013, 3)

Whether these "peopled accounts" and "alternative forms of social theorizing" will be allowed to survive within anthropological writing in a way that has the potential to drive political and social change depends on the methodological and discursive choices that the anthropologist makes in the production of her research. More critical ethnographies that take seriously the complicated ways in which individuals and communities experience, both physically and emotionally, everyday forms of racial marginalization and violence are necessary in order to dismantle the discourses that delegitimate their demands and struggles for justice.

My choice to write "from the gut," in solidarity with the quilombola fight for racial justice, meant coming to terms with an inherent pull of identification that I felt toward the pain of misrecognition that quilombolas were experiencing and a fear of having my research dismissed as "activist" or "unscholarly" in my field, an issue with which many women of color in the social sciences have had to grapple (Perry 2013). In the end, the choice was simple. I would write from the perspective of the quilombolas. I would document their words of anger and protest and allow their pleas to guide my discourse. The result is a book in which I attempt to bring legitimacy and urgency to everyday lives in struggle and conflict. The quilombolas featured in this text are not the authentic representations of "real" African culture or the quilombos of the nineteenth century; their lives, like many of ours, are chaotic, unresolved, and sometimes contradictory, but their pursuits and demands for justice are real and pressing, not fraudulent, and no longer patient.

Notes

INTRODUCTION

1. Grande Paraguaçu and all personal names are pseudonyms used to meet institutional review board requirements for the protection of human subjects.

2. Translations are mine unless otherwise attributed. Article 68 states: "Aos remanescentes das comunidades dos quilombos que estejam ocupando suas terras é reconhecida a propriedade definitiva, devendo o Estado emitir-lhes os títulos."

3. Cultural recognition has also presented problems for indigenous communities that are also held to certain standards of authenticity. See Alcida R. Ramos 1992, *The Hyperreal Indian*.

4. The Comissão Pro-Indio de São Paulo is an NGO that publishes documentation of rights violations against quilombola and indigenous communities throughout Brazil on its website, http://www.cpisp.org.br, which can also be viewed in English.

5. Unlike in the United States, Brazil's suburbs, or subúrbios, are poor neighborhoods on the outskirts of major cities.

6. Ibraim only accompanied me for this initial meeting in the quilombo. I conducted the rest of my fieldwork in Grande Paraguaçu and Salvador on my own. I am very cautious about having people with me during my fieldwork for all of the different ways their presence can change the dynamics of my interactions with others.

7. I will use the term "nonquilombola" to describe the residents of Grande Paraguaçu who oppose the quilombo title. While they do not call themselves nonquilombolas, they have devoted their time and energy to protesting the quilombola movement in their town and define themselves in opposition to the quilombolas. The term is also used by INCRA. The agency's Statute 56 of 2009 requires that "não-quilombolas" be interviewed and registered by the INCRA anthropologist completing the report for any community seeking quilombo rights.

8. A list of acronyms is included at the front of the book.

CHAPTER 1

1. Maculelê is an Afro-Brazilian dance and martial art performed using sticks made out of biriba wood.

2. The term *sertão* is used to describe the arid Northeast. It has also been translated as "backlands" to denote remoteness and wilderness, an imaginary painted by twentieth-century historians such as Euclides da Cunha in *Os sertões*, first published in 1902.

3. In Portuguese, *recôncavo* means "back bay." In Brazil the term has become attached to the Baía de Todos os Santos; Barickman 1998, 9.

4. I am not the first one to think critically about the resistance narrative of quilombos. Reis and Gomes edited a volume called *Liberdade por um fio* (1996) that brings together critical reflections on quilombo history. The text seeks to find a balance in resistance history between the heroic and isolated stories of major slave revolts and the everyday forms of resistance that Africans demonstrated.

5. The Conselho Ultramarino was the Portuguese Overseas Council created in 1642 to administer all business matters dealing with Portuguese colonies. It was an effort to maintain order and avoid conflicts of jurisdiction overseas; Fragoso et al. 2001.

6. *Branqueamento* was a pseudoscientific idea that racial mixing would eventually lead to a whiter population, eliminating Brazil's dominant black and brown (*pardo*) population; Schwarcz 1999.

7. Brazil was under military rule from a 1964 coup until a return to civilian government in 1985 and gradual democratization.

CHAPTER 2

1. On the critique of "Mama Africa" see Patricia de Santana Pinho, 2010, *Mama Africa: Inventing Blackness in Bahia*, Duke University Press.

2. In the early and mid-twentieth century, American anthropology was still a heavily empiricist field dedicated to studying and cataloguing "primitive" cultures before they disappeared; Ortner 1984.

3. In 1947, North American anthropologist Ruth Landes wrote about being sent by Columbia University to Brazil to study "the culture of blacks": "We had heard that the Negro population lived with ease and freedom among the general population, and we wanted to know more" (1). Prior to her departure to Brazil, Landes was bombarded with terrifying stories of the danger the blacks in Brazil posed and of the black magic and backwardness that she would encounter among those "forest people." Landes was even sent to Tennessee, to Fisk University, so she might live among, and become "used to the Negroes" (2–4) before traveling to Brazil.

Shortly after Landes' work was published, the UN Educational, Scientific, and Cultural Organization (UNESCO) sponsored a series of studies on race relations in Brazil. The studies were headed by Arthur Ramos, who was also selected as the director of the UNESCO Department of Social Sciences. The UNESCO studies presented a conflicted image between the confirmation that Brazil was in fact a racial democracy, at least when compared to racially torn nations like the United States, and the revelation that there were "mild" racial tensions in Brazil; Maio 2001; Wagley 1963.

4. Some scholars have pointed earlier, to the 1930s as the birth of the black movement in Brazil in the sense that black organizations like the Frente Negra Brasileira (Brazilian Black Front) and the Teatro Experimental do Negro emerged and already "mobilized around the idea of a 'black race'"; Pinho 2010, 73.

5. See Luiza Bairros' 1996 response to Hanchard, "Orfeu e poder: Uma perspectiva afro-americana sobre a política racial no Brasil." Luiza Bairros served as chief minister of Brazil's Special Office for the Promotion of Policies for Racial Equality (SEPPIR).

6. World Conference against Racism, Racial Discrimination, Xenophobia, and Related Intolerance Report, 2002; Durban Declaration and Programme of Action, United Nations, http://www.un.org/WCAR/durban.pdf.

7. This international recognition represents a major shift in national ideology, from a twentieth-century political focus on promoting racial democracy and Brazil's peaceful race relations in comparison to places such as the U.S. and South Africa. Most famous is the 1950 UNESCO study that declared to the world, using case studies, the uniqueness of Brazilian race relations. In the introduction to the study, Charles Wagley declares that in Brazil "race prejudice and discrimination [were] subdued as compared to the situation in many countries," emphasizing that class is a more important issue of inequality than race; 1952, 7.

8. "O que você precisa saber sobre a Lei de Cotas," SEPPIR, 2012.

9. Fry, Maggie, Maio, and Monteiro, in the volume *Divisões perigosas*, represent the most publicly vocal Brazilian historians and anthropologists against racial quotas.

10. See Edward Telles, *Race in Another America* (2004), for an extensive list of color categories in Brazil.

11. See Fry et al. 2007.

12. Here Brazilian anthropology reflects a similar problem as North American anthropology, that is, a systemic exclusion of research studies that take seriously the social and political constructions of racialized subjects and racism as a lived experience. The emergence of new anthropologists of color, however, is changing this pattern as we produce anthropological knowledge through our own racialized subjectivities and experiences with racial exclusion. See Hale 2006; Rosa-Ribeiro 2000; Visweswaran 1998.

13. Not all rural black communities are necessarily quilombos. A community must first self-identify and formally seek cultural recognition before becoming a quilombo. Urban black communities also can obtain cultural recognition as quilombos but not necessarily land rights. Communities and activists are fighting the urban/rural distinction because it likewise reflects a dominant history of quilombos as isolated spaces.

14. In 2009, when I did my fieldwork, several homes in Grande Paraguaçu had only recently obtained electricity and some were still waiting for running water.

15. Pontos de Cultura is part of the Cultura Viva (Living Culture) initiative created by ex-president Lula to financially support projects that contribute to the cultural life within their communities, including art, dance, and artisan crafts. See the Ministry of Culture's website on the initiative, http://www2.cultura.gov.br/culturaviva /ponto-de-cultura/.

16. The law includes all public and private schools at all levels, primary through higher education.

CHAPTER 3

1. *Piaçava* is a Tupí name for a palm tree native to Bahia and other parts of the Brazilian Northeast. A fibrous tree, its trunk is peeled and stripped manually to make artisan brooms, baskets, and brushes that are still commonly used throughout Brazil.

2. All of the labor in Grande Paraguaçu is divided among men and women. Although I spent much of my time with groups of women, the community does not consider any form of labor gender-specific. Men also worked in the mangroves, and women also went into the forest with machetes to cut piaçava. The domestic labor of cleaning the home and watching over the children was probably the only form of labor that I observed women doing more exclusively. Although men often cooked meals and helped carry water to the home, they were rarely surrounded by children while they worked.

3. Because of the times of year when I did my fieldwork in Grande Paraguaçu, primarily during the winter season, I was not able to observe the production of *azeite de dendê* (palm oil) from the seeds of the palm trees. Dendê is an important staple for the community because it is used in most of the local cuisine, such as *muqueca* (a type of stew with dendê, fish or other seafood, and spices), catado (crabmeat cooked in dendê and spices but with less stew), fried fish, and *caruru* (okra, spices, and seafood). Dendê is primarily made in the summer.

4. "Brasil sem miséria: Foco será 16,267 milhões de brasileiros que vivem na extrema pobreza," Blog do Planalto, May 3, 2011, (Brasília: Presidência da República), http://blog.planalto.gov.br/brasil-sem-miseria-foco-sera-16267-milhoes-de-brasileiros -que-vivem-na-extrema-pobreza/.

CHAPTER 4

1. Convention Concerning Indigenous and Tribal Peoples in Independent Countries: C169, International Labor Organization (ILO), 1991, http://www.ilo.org/dyn /normlex/en/f?p=NORMLEXPUB:12100:0::NO::P12100_ILO_CODE:C169.

2. The social assistance sectors are part of the Sistema Único de Assistência Social a program of the Ministério do Desenvolvimento Social e Combate a Fome (Ministry

of Social Development and Battle against Hunger). It offers various resources, services, and protection for vulnerable populations.

3. The INCRA analyst is in charge of verifying that all land titles to a contested property are real and authentic. Fabricated land titles, often made by *grileiros*, are very common throughout Brazil, most often in territories that are rich in environmental resources that can be heftily exploited. The analyst also verifies that a private landowner has not taken more land than he or she actually owns and pays for, a situation that is also common.

4. Ministério de Desenvolvimento Social e Combate a Fome, Decree no. 6.040, http://www.mds.gov.br/.

5. "Relatório técnico de identificação, delimitação e demarcação da comunidade quilombola Jatobá: Muquém do Grande Paraguaçu-Bahia," INCRA and UFBA, 2005.

6. Disagreements over the obligation to live communally and share land have led to violent divisions among residents and even between family members. Some communities have desisted from the quilombo process after learning that their land would become communal. This was not the case in Grande Paraguaçu.

7. Not all landowners in quilombola disputed lands are large, private landowners. However, smaller-scale landowners rarely dispute with quilombolas, as they are usually allowed to maintain autonomy on their land.

8. Koinonia Observatório Quilombola is a watchdog program and holds a series of civic empowerment workshops for quilombos. It is working in more than fifty quilombos throughout Rio de Janeiro and Bahia to teach residents about the bureaucratic steps to becoming a quilombo, such as learning the quilombo's history, how to obtain certification and a land title, and how to teach others about quilombo culture.

CHAPTER 5

1. Antônio and others in the community often used the word *quilombo* to talk about their community and other quilombo-descendant communities. Throughout the book, I have mostly tried to use the terms *quilombo descendant* or *quilombola* when referring to modern quilombo-descendant communities and *quilombo* when describing colonial-era quilombos.

2. "Relatório antropológico quilombola [Grande Paraguaçu]," INCRA, 2007, Ministério do Desenvolvimento Agrário, Superintendência Regional da Bahia.

3. In my fieldwork I learned that one of the major roadblocks to quilombo land rights in Bahia was that quilombo rights were not written in the state constitution, a situation that further complicated the land process.

References

Albuquerque, Wlamyra Ribeiro de, and Walter Fraga Filho. 2006. *Uma história do negro no Brasil*. Salvador: Centro de Estudos Afro-Orientais e Fundação Cultural Palmares.

Alcoff, Linda Martín. 2006. *Visible Identities: Race, Gender, and the Self*. New York: Oxford University Press.

Anderson, Mark. 2007. "When Afro Becomes (Like) Indigenous: Garifuna and Afro-Indigenous Politics in Honduras." *Journal of Latin American and Caribbean Anthropology* 12 (2): 384–413.

———. 2009. *Black and Indigenous: Garifuna Activism and Consumer Culture in Honduras*. Minneapolis: University of Minnesota Press.

Anderson, Robert Nelson. 1996. "The Quilombo of Palmares: A New Overview of a Maroon State in Seventeenth-Century Brazil." *Journal of Latin American Studies* 28 (3): 545–566.

Andrews, George Reid. 1991. *Blacks and Whites in São Paulo, Brazil, 1888–1988*. Madison: University of Wisconsin Press.

Anzaldúa, Gloria. 1999. *Borderlands = La frontera*. San Francisco: Aunt Lute Books.

Arias, Arturo, ed. 2001. *The Rigoberta Menchú Controversy*. Minneapolis: University of Minnesota Press.

Appelbaum, Nancy P., Anne S. Macpherson, and Karin Alejandra Rosemblatt. 2003. *Race and Nation in Modern Latin America*. Chapel Hill: University of North Carolina Press.

Appiah, Kwame Anthony. 1994. "Identity, Authenticity, Survival: Multicultural Societies and Social Reproduction." In *Multiculturalism: Examining the Politics of Recognition*. Edited by Amy Gutmann, 149–163. Princeton, NJ: Princeton University Press.

Araujo, Evaldo. 2007. "Portaría N98 de 26 de novembro 2007." Fundação Cultural Palmares. http://www.palmares.gov.br/legislacao/.

Arruti, José Maurício A. 2005. *Mocambo: Antropologia e história do processo de formação quilombola*. São Paulo: EDUSC; ANPOCS.

———. 2008. "Quilombos." In *Raça: Novas perspectivas antropológicas*. Edited by Osmundo Araújo Pinho and Livio Sansone, 315–350. Salvador: ABA.

———. 2013. "Situações de sobreposição na Bahia." *Étnico. Etnicidade e direitos: Índios, quilombos e populações tradicionais*. May 19. https://etnico.wordpress.com /2013/05/19/situacoes-de-sobreposicao-na-bahia/.

Associação Brasileira de Antropologia (ABA). 2007. "Histórico. Associação Brasileira de Antropologia." http://www.abant.org.br/?code=1.0.

Bailey, Stanley R., and Michelle Peria. 2010. "Racial Quotas and the Culture War in Brazilian Academia." *Sociology Compass* 4 (8): 592–604.

Bairros, Luiza. 1996. "Orfeu e poder: Uma perspectiva afro-americana sobre a política racial no Brasil." *Afro-Asia* 17: 173–186.

Barickman, B. J. 1998. *A Bahian Counterpoint: Sugar, Tobacco, Cassava, and Slavery in the Recôncavo, 1780–1860*. Stanford, CA: Stanford University Press.

Barth, Fredrik. 1969. *Ethnic Groups and Boundaries*. London: Universitets Forlaget.

Bastos, Elide Rugai. 2006. *As criaturas de prometeu: Gilberto Freyre e a formação da sociedade brasileira*. São Paulo: Global Editora.

Benedict, Ruth. 1934. *Patterns of Culture*. Boston: Houghton Mifflin.

Bennett, Marcus. 2008. "Terra a quem de direito." *Palmares: Cultura afro-brasileira*, 23–33.

Biehl, João, and Adriana Petryna. 2013. *When People Come First: Critical Studies in Global Health*. Princeton, NJ: Princeton University Press.

Boas, Franz. 1921. *The Mind of Primitive Man*. New York: Macmillan.

———. 1928. Foreword to *Coming of Age in Samoa: A Psychological Study of Primitive Youth for Western Civilisation*. New York: W. Morrow.

Bourdieu, Pierre. 1977. *Outline of a Theory of Practice*. Cambridge, England: Cambridge University Press.

———. 1990. *The Logic of Practice*. Stanford, CA: Stanford University Press.

Briggs, Charles L., and Clara Mantini-Briggs. 2003. *Stories in the Time of Cholera: Racial Profiling during a Medical Nightmare*. Berkeley: University of California Press.

Butler, Kim D. 1998. *Freedoms Given, Freedoms Won: Afro-Brazilians in Post-Abolition São Paulo and Salvador*. New Brunswick, NJ: Rutgers University Press.

Caldwell, Kia L. 2007. *Negras in Brazil: Re-Envisioning Black Women, Citizenship, and the Politics of Identity*. New Brunswick, NJ: Rutgers University Press.

Cardoso, Fernando Henrique. 1997. *Reforma agrária: Compromisso de todos*. Brasília: Presidência da República/Secretaría de Comunicação Social.

Carneiro, Edison de Souza. 1951. "Arthur Ramos: Brazilian Anthropologist (1903–1949)." Translated by James W. Ivy. *Phylon* 12 (1): 73–81.

———. 1966. *O quilombo dos Palmares*. Rio de Janeiro: Civilização Brasileira.

———. 1991. *Religiões negras: Notas de etnografia religiosa*. Rio de Janeiro: Civilização Brasileira.

Caulfield, Sueann. 2003. "Interracial Courtship in the Rio De Janeiro Courts, 1918–1940." In *Race and Nation in Latin America*. Edited by Nancy P. Appelbaum, Anne S.

Macpherson, and Karin Alejandra Rosemblatt, 163–186. Chapel Hill: University of North Carolina Press.

Cavalcante, José Luiz. 2005. "A Lei de Terras de 1850 e a reafirmação do poder básico do estado sobre a terra." *Histórica* 2:1–7.

Chalhoub, Sidney. 2006. "The Politics of Silence: Race and Citizenship in Nineteenth-Century Brazil." *Slavery and Abolition* 27 (1): 73–87.

Clifford, James. 1988. *The Predicament of Culture: Twentieth-Century Ethnography, Literature, and Art*. Cambridge: Harvard University Press.

Clifford, James, and George E. Marcus, eds. 1986. *Writing Culture: The Poetics and Politics of Ethnography*. Berkeley: University of California Press.

Cole, Jennifer. 2003. "Narratives and Moral Projects: Generational Memories of the Malagasy 1947 Rebellion." *Ethos: Society for Psychological Anthropology* 31 (1): 95–126.

Cole, Sally Cooper. 2003. *Ruth Landes: A Life in Anthropology*. Lincoln: University of Nebraska Press.

Comissão Pró-Índio São Paulo (CPI-SP). 2011. "Comunidades quilombolas do estado de Minas Gerais: Quilombos urbanos." Accessed June 30. http://www.cpisp.org.br/comunidades/html/i_brasil_mg.html.

Coordinação Nacional de Articulação das Comunidades Negras Rurais Quilombolas (CONAQ). 2013. "O Brasil também é quilombola: Campanha em defesa dos direitos do povo quilombola." March 5. http://quilombosconaq.blogspot.com/2013/03/obrasil-tambem-e-quilombola.html.

———. N.d. "Manifesto pelos direitos quilombolas." In author's possession.

Costa, Alexandre Emboaba da. 2010. "Anti-Racism in Movement: Afro-Brazilian Afoxé and Contemporary Black Brazilian Struggles for Equality." *Journal of Historical Sociology* 23 (3): 372–397.

Covin, David. 2006. *Unified Black Movement in Brazil, 1978–2002*. Jefferson, NC: McFarland.

Csordas, Thomas J. 1990. "Embodiment as a Paradigm for Anthropology." *Ethos: Society for Psychological Anthropology* 18 (1): 5–47.

Cunha, Euclides da. 1902/1970. *Rebellion in the Backlands*. Translated by Samuel Putnam. Chicago: University of Chicago Press.

DaMatta, Roberto A. 1991. *Carnivals, Rogues, and Heroes: An Interpretation of the Brazilian Dilemma*. Notre Dame, IN: University of Notre Dame Press.

———. 1995. "For an Anthropology of the Brazilian Tradition; or, 'A Virtude está no meio.'" In *The Brazilian Puzzle: Culture on the Borderlands of the Western World*. Edited by David J. Hess and Roberto A. DaMatta, 270–291. New York: Columbia University Press.

Eltis, David, and David Richardson. 2010. *Atlas of the Transatlantic Slave Trade*. New Haven, CT: Yale University Press.

Fanon, Frantz. 1967. *Black Skin, White Masks*. New York: Grove Press.

Fernandes, Florestan. 1969. *The Negro in Brazilian Society*. New York: Columbia University Press.

Ferreira da Silva, Denise. 2009. "No-Bodies." *Griffith Law Review* 18 (2): 212–236.

Fragoso, João, Luis Ribeiro, Maria Fernanda Bicalho, and Maria de Fatima Gouvea. 2001. *O Antigo Regime nos trópicos: A dinámica imperial portuguesa, séculos XVI–XVIII.* Rio de Janeiro: Civilização Brasileira.

Frazier, E. Franklin. 1942. "The Negro Family in Bahia, Brazil." *American Sociological Review* 7 (4): 465–478.

Freire, Paulo. 1970. *Pedagogy of the Oppressed.* New York: Herder and Herder.

Freitas, Décio. 1973. *Palmares: A guerra dos escravos.* Porto Alegre, Brazil: Editora Movimento.

French, Jan Hoffman. 2009. *Legalizing Identities: Becoming Black or Indian in Brazil's Northeast.* Chapel Hill: University of North Carolina Press.

Freyre, Gilberto. 1956. *The Masters and the Slaves: A Study in the Development of Brazilian Civilization.* 2nd edition. New York: Knopf.

Fry, Peter, Yvonne Maggie, Marcos Chor Maio, Simone Monteiro, and Ricardo Ventura Santos. 2007. *Divisões perigosas: Políticas raciais no Brasil contemporâneo.* Rio de Janeiro: Civilização Brasileira.

Frye, Northrop. 1957. *Anatomy of Criticism: Four Essays.* Princeton, NJ: Princeton University Press.

Funari, Pedro Paulo de A. 1996. "A arqueologia de Palmares: Sua contribuição para o conhecimento da história da cultural afro-americana." In *Liberdade por um fio.* Edited by Reis and Gomes, 26–51.

———. 2003. "Conflict and the Interpretation of Palmares, a Brazilian Runaway Polity." *Historical Archaeology* 37 (3): 81–92.

Funes, Euripedes. 1996. "'Nasci nas matas, nunca tive senhor': História e memória dos mocambos do baixo Amazonas." In *Liberdade por um fio.* Edited by Reis and Gomes, 467–497.

Gilroy, Paul. 1993. *The Black Atlantic: Modernity and Double Consciousness.* Cambridge: Harvard University Press.

Golash-Boza, Tanya Maria. 2011. *Yo Soy Negro: Blackness in Peru.* Gainesville: University Press of Florida.

Goldstein, Donna M. 2003. *Laughter out of Place: Race, Class, Violence, and Sexuality in a Rio Shantytown.* Berkeley: University of California Press.

Gomes, Flávio dos Santos. 2005. *Palmares: Escravidão e liberadade no Atlântico Sul.* São Paulo: Contexto.

Gomes da Cunha, Olívia Maria, and Flávio dos Santos Gomes. 2007. *Quase-cidadão: Histórias e antropologias da pós-emancipação no Brasil.* Rio de Janeiro: Ed. FGV.

Gonzalez, Anita. 2011. *Afro-Mexico: Dancing between Myth and Reality.* Austin: University of Texas Press.

Goulart, José Alípio, Israel Cysneiros, and Arthur Cézar Ferreira Reis. 1972. *Da fuga ao suicídio: Aspectos de rebeldia do escravo no Brasil.* Rio de Janeiro: Conquista.

Graham, Richard, Thomas E. Skidmore, Aline Helg, and Alan Knight. 1990. *The Idea of Race in Latin America, 1870–1940.* Austin: University of Texas Press.

Guimarães, Antônio Sérgio Alfredo. 1995. "'Raça,' racismo e grupos de cor no Brasil." *Revista Estudos Afro-Asiáticos* 27: 45–63.

———. 2001. "A questão racial na política Brasileira." *Revista Tempo Social* 13 (2): 121–142.

———. 2004. "Intelectuais negros e formas de integração nacional." *Estudos Avançados* 18 (50): 271–284.

Guimarães, Ruth. 1968. *Lendas e fábulas do Brasil*. São Paulo: Editora Cultrix.

Gupta, Akhil, and James Ferguson. 1992. "Beyond "Culture": Space, Identity, and the Politics of Difference." *Cultural Anthropology* 7 (1): 6–23.

Hale, Charles R. 1994. *Resistance and Contradiction: Miskitu Indians and the Nicaraguan State, 1894–1987*. Stanford, CA: Stanford University Press.

———. 2002. "Does Multiculturalism Menace? Governance, Cultural Rights, and the Politics of Identity in Guatemala." *Journal of Latin American Studies* 34 (3): 485–524.

———. 2005. "Neoliberal Multiculturalism: The Remaking of Cultural Rights and Racial Dominance in Central America." *Political and Legal Anthropology Review* 28 (1): 10–28.

———. 2006. "Activist Research v. Cultural Critique: Indigenous Land Rights and the Contradictions of Politically Engaged Anthropology." *Cultural Anthropology* 12 (1): 96–120.

Hanchard, Michael George. 1994a. *Orpheus and Power: The Movimento Negro of Rio de Janeiro and São Paulo, Brazil, 1945–1988*. Princeton, NJ: Princeton University Press.

———. 1994b. "Black Cinderella? Race and the Public Sphere in Brazil." *Public Culture* 7 (1): 165–185.

Henriques, Ricardo. 2001. *Desigualdade racial no Brasil: Evolução das condições de vida na década de 90*. Rio de Janeiro: Instituto de Pesquisa Econômica Aplicada.

Herskovits, Melville J. 1943. "The Negro in Bahia, Brazil: A Problem in Method." *American Sociological Review* 8 (4): 394–404.

Hess, David J., and Roberto DaMatta. 1995. *The Brazilian Puzzle: Culture on the Borderlands of the Western World*. New York: Columbia University Press.

Holston, James. 2008. *Insurgent Citizenship: Disjunctions of Democracy and Modernity in Brazil*. Princeton, NJ: Princeton University Press.

Hooker, Juliet. 2005. "Indigenous Inclusion/Black Exclusion: Race, Ethnicity, and Multicultural Citizenship in Latin America." *Journal of Latin American Studies* 37 (2): 285–310.

———. 2009. *Race and the Politics of Solidarity*. Oxford, England: Oxford University Press.

Htun, Mala. 2004. "From 'Racial Democracy' to Affirmative Action: Changing State Policy on Race in Brazil." *Latin American Research Review* 39 (1): 60–89.

Jackson, John L. 2005. *Real Black: Adventures in Racial Sincerity*. Chicago: University of Chicago Press.

Kent, R. 1996. "Palmares: An African State in Brazil." In *Maroon Societies: Rebel Slave Communities in the Americas*. Edited by Richard Price, 170–201. Baltimore, MD: Johns Hopkins University Press.

Landes, Ruth. 1947/1994. *The City of Women*. Albuquerque: University of New Mexico Press.

Lara, Silvia Hunold. 1996. "Do singular ao plural: Palmares, capitães-do-mato e o governo dos escravos." In *Liberdade por um fio*. Edited by Reis and Gomes, 81–109.

———. 2010. "Palmares and Cucaú: Political Dimensions of a Maroon Community in Late Seventeenth-Century Brazil." Conference paper presented at the 12th Annual Gilder Lehrman Center International Conference, "American Counterpoint: New Approaches to Slavery and Abolition in Brazil." Yale University, New Haven, CT, October.

Leite, Ilka Boaventura. 2000. "Os quilombos no Brasil: Questões conceituais e normativas." *Etnográfica* 4 (2): 333–354.

———. 2008. "O projeto político quilombola: Desafios, conquistas e impasses atuais." *Estudos Feministas* 16 (3): 965–977.

———. 2012. "The Transhistorical, Juridical-Formal, and Post-Utopian Quilombo." In *New Approaches to Resistance in Brazil and Mexico*. Edited by John Gledhill and Patience A. Shell, 250–268. Durham, NC: Duke University Press.

Lessa, Carlos. 2007. "O Brasil não é bicolor." In *Divisões perigosas: Políticas raciais no Brasil contemporâneo*. Edited by Peter Fry, Yvonne Maggie, Marcos Chor Maio, Simone Monteiro, and Ricardo Ventura Santos, 121–126. Rio de Janeiro: Civilização Brasileira.

Lima, Ari. 2006. "Blacks as Study Objects and Intellectuals in Brazilian Academia." *Latin American Perspectives* 33 (4): 82–105.

Lorde, Audre. 1997. "The Uses of Anger." *Women's Studies Quarterly* 25 (1/2): 278–285.

Maggie, Yvonne. 2005. "Políticas de cotas e o vestibular da UnB ou a marca que cria sociedades divididas." *Horizontes Antropológicos* 11 (23): 286–291.

Maio, Marcos Chor. 2001. "UNESCO and the Study of Race Relations in Brazil: Regional or National Issue?" *Latin American Research Review* 36 (2): 118–136.

Marcus, George E., and Dick Cushman. 1982. "Ethnographies as Texts." *Annual Review of Anthropology* 11: 25–69.

Marske, Charles E. 1987. "Durkheim's 'Cult of the Individual' and the Moral Reconstitution of Society." *Sociological Theory* 5 (1): 1–14.

Marx, Anthony W. 1998. *Making Race and Nation: A Comparison of South Africa, the United States, and Brazil*. Cambridge, England: Cambridge University Press.

Mauss, Marcel. 1973. "Techniques of the Body." *Economy and Society* 2 (1): 70–88.

Mead, Margaret. 1928. *Coming of Age in Samoa: A Psychological Study of Primitive Youth for Western Civilisation*. New York: W. Morrow.

Melo, Paula Balduíno de, Priscila Prado, Carlos Alberto Santos de Paulo, and Raimundo Marques, eds. 2012. *Quilombo das Américas: Articulação de comunidades afrorurais: Documento síntese*. Brasília: Instituto de Pesquisa Econômica Aplicada (IPEA), Secretaria Especial de Políticas de Promoção da Igualdade Racial (SEPPIR).

Menchú, Rigoberta, and Elisabeth Burgos-Debray. 1984. *I, Rigoberta Menchú: An Indian Woman in Guatemala*. London: Verso.

Merleau-Ponty, Maurice. 1965. *Phenomenology of Perception*. London: Routledge and K. Paul.

Meskell, Lynn, and Rosemary A. Joyce. 2003. *Embodied Lives: Figuring Ancient Maya and Egyptian Experience*. London: Routledge.

Metcalf, Alida C. 2005. *Go-Betweens and the Colonization of Brazil, 1500–1600*. Austin: University of Texas Press.

Mintz, Sidney, and Richard Price. 1976. *The Birth of African American Culture: An Anthropological Perspective*. Boston: Beacon Press.

Mott, Luiz. 1996. "Santo Antônio, o divino capitão-do –mato." In *Liberdade por um fio*. Edited by Reis and Gomes, 110–138.

Moura, Clóvis. 1959. *Rebeliões da senzala: Quilombos, insurreições, guerrilhas*. São Paulo: Edições Zumbi.

———. 1981. *Os quilombos e a rebelião negra*. São Paulo: Brasiliense.

Munanga, Kabengele. 1990. "Negritude afro-brasileira: Perspectivas e dificuldades." *Revista de Antropologia* 33: 109–117.

———. 1996. *Estratégias e políticas de combate à discriminação racial*. São Paulo: Estação Ciência, Universidade de São Paulo.

———. 2001. "Políticas de ação afirmativa em benefício da população negra no Brasil: Um ponto de vista em defesa de cotas." *Sociedade e Cultura* 4 (2): 31–43.

———. 2004. "A difícil tarefa de definir quem é negro no Brasil." Interview. *Estudos Avançados* 18 (50): 51–56.

Nascimento, Abdias do. 1980. "Quilombismo: An Afro-Brazilian Political Alternative." *Journal of Black Studies* 11 (2): 141–178.

———. 1989. *Brazil, Mixture or Massacre? Essays in the Genocide of a Black People*. Dover, MA: Majority Press.

Nascimento, Elisa Larkin. 2007. *The Sorcery of Color: Identity, Race, and Gender in Brazil*. Philadelphia: Temple University Press.

Nina Rodrigues, Raimundo, and Homero Pires. 1932. *Os africanos no Brasil*. São Paulo: Companhia Editora Nacional.

O'Dwyer, Eliane C. 2002. "Quilombos: Identidade étnica e territorialidade." Rio de Janeiro: FGV.

———. 2005. "Os quilombos e as fronteiras da antropologia." *Antropolítica* 19: 91–111.

———. 2008. "O caso dos laudos: Pesquisa aplicada ou exercício profissional da antropologia?" In *Antropologia extramuros: Novas responsabilidades sociais e políticas dos antropólogos*. Edited by Gláucia Silva, 75–85. Brasília: Paralelo 15.

———. 2010. *O papel social do antropólogo: Aplicação do fazer antropológica e do conhecimento disciplinar nos debates públicos do Brasil contemporâneo*. Antropologias 6. Rio de Janeiro: E-Papers.

Oliven, Rubem George, and Ilka Boaventura Leite. 1996. *Negros no sul do Brasil: Invisibilidade e territorialidade*. Florianopolis, Brazil: Letras Contemporâneas.

Pacheco de Oliveira, João. 1994. "Associação Brasileira de Antropologia: Documento do Grupo de Trabalho sobre Comunidades Negras Rurais." Associação Brasileira de Antropologia. http://www.abant.org.br/?code=2.39.

Pedreira, Pedro Tomás. 1973. *Os quilombos brasileiros*. Salvador: Prefeitura Municipal do Salvador, Departamento de Cultura da Secretaria Municipal de Educação, Cultura, Esporte e Lazer.

Pereira, A. 1997. *The End of the Peasantry: The Rural Labor Movement in Northeast Brazil, 1961–1988*. Pittsburgh: University of Pittsburgh Press.

———. 2003. "Brazil's Agrarian Reform: Democratic Innovation or Oligarchic Exclusion Redux?" *Latin American Politics and Society* 45 (2): 41–66.

Peirano, Mariza G. S. 1981. *The Anthropology of Anthropology: The Brazilian Case*. Brasília: Universidade de Brasília, Instituto de Ciências Humanas, Departamento de Antropologia.

Perry, Kiesha-Kahn Y. 2013. *Black Women against the Land Grab: The Fight for Racial Justice in Brazil*. Minneapolis: University of Minnesota Press.

Pierson, Donald. 1942. *Negroes in Brazil: A Study of Race Contact at Bahia*. Chicago: University of Chicago Press.

Pinho, Osmundo Araújo, and Livio Sansone, eds. 2008. *Raça: Novas perspectivas antropológicas*. Salvador: Associação Brasileira de Antropologia.

Pinho, Patrícia de Santana. 2010. *Mama Africa: Reinventing Blackness in Bahia*. Durham, NC: Duke University Press.

Pinto, Ana Flávia Magalhães. 2010. *Imprensa negra no Brasil do século XIX*. São Paulo: Selo Negro.

Povinelli, Elizabeth A. 2002. *The Cunning of Recognition*. Durham, NC: Duke University Press.

Price, Richard. 1996. "Palmares como poderia ter sido." In *Liberdade por um fio*. Edited by Reis and Gomes, 52–59.

———. 2002. *First-Time: The Historical Vision of an African American People*. Chicago: University of Chicago Press.

———. 2003. "Refiguring Palmares." *Tipití* 1 (2): 211–219.

Ramos, Alcida Rita. 1991. "A Hall of Mirrors: The Rhetoric of Indigenism in Brazil." *Critique of Anthropology* 11 (2): 155–169.

———. 1992. *The Hyperreal Indian*. Brasília: Universidade de Brasília, Instituto de Ciências Humanas, Departamento de Antropologia.

———. 1998. *Indigenismo: Ethnic Politics in Brazil*. Madison: University of Wisconsin Press.

Ramos, Arthur. 1939/1980. *The Negro in Brazil*. Philadelphia: Porcupine Press.

Reis, João José. 1988. "Um balanço dos estudos sobre as revoltas escravas da Bahia." In *Escravidão e invenção da liberdade*. Edited by João José Reis. São Pauo: Editôra Brasiliense.

Reis, João José, and Flávio dos Santos Gomes. 1996. *Liberdade por um fio: História dos quilombos no Brasil*. São Paulo: Companhia das Letras.

Ribeiro, Darcy. 1982. *Os índios e a civilização: a integração das populações indígenas no Brasil moderno*. Petrópolis, Brasil: Vozes.

Ribeiro, Gustavo Lins. 2004. "Practicing Anthropology in Brazil: A Retrospective Look at two Time Periods." *Practicing Anthropology* 26 (3): 6–10.

Rosa-Ribeiro, Fernando. 2000. "Racism, Mimesis, and Anthropology in Brazil." *Critique of Anthropology* 20 (3): 221–241.

Sahlins, Marshall. 1983. "Other Times, Other Customs: The Anthropology of History." *American Anthropologist* 85 (3): 517–544.

———. 1985. *Islands of History*. Chicago: University of Chicago Press.

Said, Edward W. 1979. *Orientalism*. New York: Vintage Books.

Sansone, Lívio. 2003. *Blackness without Ethnicity: Constructing Race in Brazil*. New York: Palgrave Macmillan.

Scheper-Hughes, Nancy. 1990. "Three Propositions for a Critically Applied Medical Anthropology." *Social Science and Medicine* 30 (2): 189–197.

———. 1992. *Death without Weeping: The Violence of Everyday Life in Brazil*. Berkeley: University of California Press.

Schmitt, Alessandra, Maria Turatti, Cecília Manzoli, and Maria Celina Pereira de Carvalho. 2002. "A atualização do conceito de quilombo: Identidade e território nas definições teóricas." *Ambiente e Sociedade* 5 (10): 1–6.

Schwarcz, Lilia Moritz. 1999. *The Spectacle of the Races: Scientists, Institutions, and the Race Question in Brazil, 1870–1930*. New York: Hill and Wang.

———. 2006. "A Mestizo and Tropical Country: The Creation of the Official Image of Independent Brazil." *European Review of Latin American and Caribbean Studies* 80:25–42.

Schwartz, Stuart B. 1985. *Sugar Plantations in the Formation of Brazilian Society: Bahia, 1550–1835*. Cambridge, England: Cambridge University Press.

———. 1996a. "Cantos e quilombos numa conspiração de escravos haussás: Bahia, 1814." In *Liberdade por um fio*. Edited by Reis and Gomes, 373–406.

———. 1996b. "The Mocambo: Slave Resistance in Colonial Bahia." In *Maroon Societies: Rebel Slave Communities in the Americas*. Edited by Richard Price, 202–226. Baltimore, MD: Johns Hopkins University Press.

Sheriff, Robin E. 1999. "The Theft of Carnaval: National Spectacle and Racial Politics in Rio de Janeiro." *Cultural Anthropology* 14 (1): 3–28.

Skidmore, Thomas E. 1972. *Toward a Comparative Analysis of Race Relations since Abolition in Brazil and the United States*. Cambridge, England: Cambridge University Press.

Slenes, Robert W. 2010. "Brazil." In *The Oxford Handbook of Slavery in the Americas*. Edited by Robert L. Paquette and Mark M. Smith, 111–133. Oxford, England: Oxford University Press.

———. 2012. "The 'Great Arch' Descending." In *New Approaches to Resistance in Brazil and Mexico*. Edited by John Gledhill and Patience A. Shell, 100–118. Durham, NC: Duke University Press.

Sousa, Leone Campos de, and Paulo Nascimento. 2008. "Brazilian National Identity at a Crossroads: The Myth of Racial Democracy and the Development of Black Identity." *International Journal of Politics, Culture, and Society* 19 (3–4): 129–143.

Souza, Diane. 2012. "STF adia julgamento do Decreto 4887/2003." April 18. Brasília: Fundação Cultural Palmares. http://www.palmares.gov.br/?p=19216.

Spivak, Gayatri Chakravorty. 2010. "Can the Subaltern Speak?" In *Can the Subaltern Speak? Reflections on the History of an Idea*. Edited by Gayatri Chakravorty Spivak and Rosalind C. Morris, 21–78. New York: Columbia University Press.

Stepan, Nancy. 1991. *"The Hour of Eugenics": Race, Gender, and Nation in Latin America*. Ithaca, NY: Cornell University Press.

Stocking, George W. 1966. "Franz Boas and the Culture Concept in Historical Perspective." *American Anthropologist* 68 (4): 867–882.

Stoll, David. 1998. *Rigoberta Menchú and the Story of All Poor Guatemalans*. Boulder, CO: Westview Press.

Sue, Christina A. 2013. *Land of the Cosmic Race: Race Mixture, Racism, and Blackness in Mexico*. Oxford, England: Oxford University Press.

Sweet, James H. 2003. *Recreating Africa: Culture, Kinship, and Religion in the African-Portuguese World*. Chapel Hill: University of North Carolina Press.

Tavares, Luís Henrique Dias. 2001. *História Da Bahia*. Salvador: Editora da UFBA.

Taylor, Charles. 1994. "The Politics of Recognition." In *Multiculturalism: Examining the Politics of Recognition*. Edited by Amy Gutmann, 25–73, Princeton, NJ: Princeton University Press.

———. 2004. *Modern Social Imaginaries*. Durham, NC: Duke University Press.

Teles dos Santos, Jocélio. 1998. "A Mixed-Race Nation: Afro-Brazilians and Cultural Policy in Bahia, 1970–1990." In *Afro-Brazilian Culture and Politics: Bahia, 1790s to 1990s*. Edited by Hendrik Kraay, 117–133. New York: M. E. Sharpe.

———. 1999. "Dilemas nada atuais das políticas para os afro-brasileiros: Ação afirmativa no Brasil dos anos 60." In *Brasil: Um país de negros?* Edited by Jeferson A. Bacelar and Carlos Caroso, 221–233. Rio de Janeiro: Pallas.

Telles, Edward Eric. 2004. *Race in Another America: The Significance of Skin Color in Brazil*. Princeton, NJ: Princeton University Press.

Torres, Arlene, and Norman E. Whitten. 1998. *Blackness in Latin America and the Caribbean: Social Dynamics and Cultural Transformations*. Bloomington: Indiana University Press.

The Trans-Atlantic Slave Trade Database: Voyages. 2013. Introductory maps. Accessed July 12. http://slavevoyages.org/tast/assessment/intro-maps.faces.

Trilling, Lionel. 1972. *Sincerity and Authenticity*. Cambridge: Harvard University Press.

Twine, France Winddance. 1998. *Racism in a Racial Democracy: The Maintenance of White Supremacy in Brazil*. New Brunswick, NJ: Rutgers University Press.

Van Cott, Donna Lee. 2000. *The Friendly Liquidation of the Past: The Politics of Diversity in Latin America*. Pittsburgh, PA: University of Pittsburgh Press.

Vargas, João H. Costa. 2011. "The Black Diaspora as Genocide: Brazil and the United States—A Supranational Geography of Death and Its Alternatives." In *State of White Supremacy: Racism, Governance, and the United States*. Edited by Moon-Kie Jung, João H. Costa Vargas, and Eduardo Bonilla-Silva, 243–270. Stanford, CA: Stanford University Press.

Vasconcelos, José. 1925/1997. *La Raza Cósmica: The Cosmic Race*. Baltimore, MD: Johns Hopkins University Press.

Viotti da Costa, Emília. 2000. *The Brazilian Empire: Myths and Histories*. Chapel Hill: University of North Carolina Press.

Visweswaran, Kamala. 1998. "Race and the Culture of Anthropology." *American Anthropologist* 100 (1): 70–83.

Wade, Peter. 1995. *Blackness and Race Mixture: The Dynamics of Racial Identity in Colombia*. Baltimore, MD: Johns Hopkins University Press.

———. 1997. *Race and Ethnicity in Latin America*. London: Pluto Press.

Wagley, Charles. 1952. *Race and Class in Rural Brazil*. Paris: UNESCO.

———. 1963. *An Introduction to Brazil*. New York: Columbia University Press.

Weinstein, Barbara. 2003. "Racializing Regional Difference: São Paulo versus Brazil, 1932." In *Race and Nation in Latin America*. Edited by Nancy P. Appelbaum, Anne S. Macpherson, and Karin Alejandra Rosemblatt, 237–262. Chapel Hill: University of North Carolina Press.

Wimberly, Fayette. 1998. "The Expansion of Afro-Bahian Religious Practices in Nineteenth-Century Cachoeira." In *Afro-Brazilian Culture and Politics: Bahia, 1790s to 1990s*. Edited by Hendrik Kraay, 74–89. New York: M. E. Sharpe.

Wolf, Eric R. 1982. *Europe and the People without History*. Berkeley: University of California Press.

Index

Page numbers in italics refer to photographs.